Edwin Hall

The ancient historical records of Norwalk, Conn.;

With a plan of the ancient settlement, and of the town in 1847 - Vol. 1

Edwin Hall

The ancient historical records of Norwalk, Conn.;
With a plan of the ancient settlement, and of the town in 1847 - Vol. 1

ISBN/EAN: 9783337724078

Printed in Europe, USA, Canada, Australia, Japan

Cover: Foto ©ninafisch / pixelio.de

More available books at **www.hansebooks.com**

THE

ANCIENT

HISTORICAL RECORDS

OF

NORWALK, CONN.;

WITH A

PLAN OF THE ANCIENT SETTLEMENT,

AND OF

THE TOWN IN 1847.

COMPILED BY

EDWIN HALL,

PASTOR OF THE FIRST CONGREGATIONAL CHURCH.

ANDREW SELLECK, NORWALK. CONN.;

Ivison, Phinney, Blakeman & Co.,

48 AND 50 WALKER STREET,

NEW YORK.

1865.

ADVERTISEMENT TO THE READER.

THE design of the compiler of this work has not been to write a History of Norwalk; but to copy from the Records whatever matters appeared to be of any historical interest; and in all cases to let the Records speak for themselves.

The genealogical registers are very imperfect; and if any families are omitted, it is because they were not put upon the public records; and because the compiler, after repeatedly advertising, and after some months' delay, has failed to obtain them.

It was the compiler's design, strictly to limit these registers to the familes of such as were married before the year 1800; but during his absence some names were forwarded directly to the printer; and among them a very few families of later date, which were inserted and printed before the compiler had an opportunity to correct the error.

The compiler is aware that much more might have been accomplished, by searching through the numerous volumes of records of later years; by copying the monuments in the burying grounds; and by researches after the old records and registers of private families. But he has had no time for such an extended research; he did not consider the patronage sufficient to warrant the additional expense; and if he had not failed in his efforts, for several years, to enlist some one else in a labor which he deemed so desirable, he would himself never have undertaken it at all He therefore trusts that all concerned, instead of complaining that no more is given them, will be thankful that so much is rescued from the oblivion to which it was hastening; and will use whatever efforts they deem proper, to secure what is yet left behind.

NORWALK, Nov. 5, 1847.

INDEX

HISTORICAL RECORDS.

A

Abbott, George. 17 ; notice of. 18. estate in 1617. 61 ; his children. 62 ; estate in 1687, 84.

Abbott, Jonathan. a soldier in the French and Indian war. 87.

Abbott, John. estate in 1687, 84.

Arms and ammunition, 98 ; brought from Stamford, 99.

Ash-house, 55.

Association of ministers. called in case of Rev. S. Buckingham. 115 ; for advice, 147 ; their answer, 147 ; advice for procuring a minister, 148 ; advice in case of Mr. Buckingham, 150.

Austin. Thomas. 105.

Authority pew, 150.

B

Baptist church, 171.

Barnam. Thomas. 20 ; estate in 1671, 61; in 1687. 84; keeps young people still in meeting. 76.

Beacham, Robert, 17 ; gate-keeper, 45, 47.

Beard. Captain. 82.

Beckwith, Stephen, 17, 18 ; estate, 61. 84.

Belden (or Belding). John, 18 ; estate, 61 ; a soldier in the Indian war, 84 ; ensign. 87.

Belden, Thomas. 127.

Belden, Samuel. 21 ; estate, 61, 84.

Benedict. Thomas, 18, 19, 24, 27 ; town clerk, 58 ; selectman, 58 ; estate. 61 ; his children, 62 ; estate. in 1687, 83.

Benedict. Thomas, Jr., 18, 28 ; children. 62 : estate. 83.

Benedict. N ithaniel. 127.

Benedict. Samuel, 28, 61, 84 ; estate in 1687, 81.

Benedict. Thomas. 132 ; John, 28, 83 ; John, Jr., 61 ; James, 61, 84 ; Nehemiah. 132 ; Daniel, 61, a soldier in the Indian war, 63.

Betts, Thomas, 18. 19, 22. 25, 27 , estate in 1671. 61 ; children, 62 ; estate in 1687, 83.

Betts, Thomas, Jr.. 21. 61. 83 ; Thomas. 127 ; Daniel. Jr., 127 ; Dr Thaddeus. 127. 133 ; James, sends a man to the wars, 64 ; estate, 63 ; Daniel, 83.

Birchard. Joseph, 103.

Blacksmith. 45.

Bouton. John, 17, 23 ; estate. 61 ; children, 62 ; estate in 1687, 83 : sergeant. 87 ; John, Jr., 83, 84.

Brooks, Lemuel. 127.

Bridge. over river. 59 ; at the great rock, 75 ; repaired, 88.

Brown. James, 84.

Bryant. 18.

Buckingham. Rev. Stephen, 28 ; settlement. 91 ; ordination, 93 ; firewood. 100 ; difficulties. 114 ; salary stopped. 115 ; letter to the town, 116 ; town dissatisfied with, 118 ; proposals to the town. 119 ; town treats with him. 119 ; his visits at Mr. Line's, 120 ; further difficulty, 155.

Burnet. Rev. Dr., 165.

Burning the woods. 98.

Burying-ground, over river, 102 ; Mill Hill. 126.

Bushnell, Francis, 61, 84 ; Richard. 18.

Butler, John, 87.

C

Campfield, Matthew. 17, 19 ; removes to Newark. N. J., 20 ; Samuel, 18, 21, 24 ; estate, 61 ; children, 62 ; Ebenezer, 87 ; Nathaniel, 24.

Carter. Samuel. 105 ; John, 127.

Cannon. John. 127.

Cannon and cannon-ball, 131.

Caner. Rev. Mr., 156.

Chesnut Hill, 62.

Children, estate for, 61 ; of the town, 62.

Church, Edward, 18.

Church, call the minister ; the town concur. 92.
Church of England.* sundry persons draw off to in the difficulties with Mr. Buckingham, 146 ; grant of land to Professors, 122 ; deed to, 123 ; land on Strawberry Hill. 124 ; also, 124 ; its professors exonerated from taxes to Congregational societies, 156 ; to pay their rates to their own minister. 156 ; meeting of its professors with the Prime Ancient Society, 157.
Clothing for soldiers, 141, 137.
Clappum, Peter. 84.
Colts. marked. 74.
Cockenoes Island, 58, 62.
Commonage. 110.
Comstock. Christopher, 18. 25 ; estate in 1671. 61 ; tavern keeper, 61 ; estate in 1687. 84 ; serjeant. 87 ; Samuel. ensign, 108 ; Daniel, 84 ; Moses. 120.
Committee of Inspection, 127, 128, 130.
Confederation, 124.
Consociation. 118. 163.
Continental Battalions, 131 ; currency. 137 ; Congress, 127.
Copp, John. 96.
Cornish, Mr., 69.
Cosiar. Richard. 83.
Council for advice, 117 ; advice accepted. 117.
County Congress, 128.
Cowherd. 48. 53.
Crampton. John, 18, 26. 61 ; a soldier in the Indian war, 65 ; estate, 83.

D

Deacon's Seat. 98.
Deed of Indians to Roger Ludlowe. 30 ; to Mr. Hanford, 93.
Dickinson, Rev. Moses, his manuscripts, 13 ; sent for, 149 ; settled. 160.
Drains. 43.
Drum beaten by Walter Haite, 52, 58. 71, 76 ; town drum, 76 ; drum-cord. 93.
Dry Hill, 79.

E

Eells, Captain, 82.
Elders and messengers at ordination, 93.
Eli, Nathaniel. 17 19, 22.
Estates. list of, 46, 61, 83 ; for children, 61.

F

Fairfield. difficulty with, 50 ; line, 61· Fasting. 146.

Fences, 52.
Fenn, Joseph. 18, 27.
Fines. upon majority, 77.
Firewood, price of in 1699, 94.
Fillio, John, 105.
Fitch. Thomas. 17, 19. 22, 43, 48, 52, 58, 61, 83 ; Thomas. Jr., 18, 27, 61 ; children. 62 ; estate. 84 ; Colonel Thomas. 127, 141 ; John, 84, 105 ; Timothy. 128 ; Joseph, 18.
Fort Point. 21.
French war. soldiers quartered in Norwalk, 125.

G

Gallery in Meeting-house. 92.
Governor Fitch, 158 ; adorning his pew, 158.
Gregory. John, 17. 19. 21. 24. 61, 62, 83 ; John, Jr., 61. 62, 83 ; Jachin, 18, 26, 61. 62, 84 ; Thomas. 61 ; a soldier in the Indian war. 63 ; estate, 84 ; Joseph. 61, 83 ; Jabez, 128.
Gregory's Point, 104.
Gruman. Samuel. 109. 127.
Guard. 58, 131. 141, 142.
Guard-house, 125.
Gunpowder, be saving of, 128.

H

Hales, Thomas. 17 ; Samuel. 17, 20, 22, Hanford. Rev. Thomas, 14, 17. 24, 29. 41, 49. 59, 61, 62, 81. 83, 93 ; his death. 85 ; Mrs. 112 ; Elnathan, 85 ; Eliezer, 86 ; Phineas, 127 ; Theophilus. 83 ; Thomas. Jr., 85.
Haies (or Hayes), Nathaniel, 17, 61, 62, 83 ; Samuel, 18, 24, 61, 62, 78, 84.
Haite (or Hoyt), Walter, 17, 19, 23, 47. 61. 84 ; Asa, 127 ; Goold, 127 ; Zerubabell. 84. 96 ; John, 62.
Haynes. William, 86.
Herdsmen. 54.
Home Lots. table of. 22.
Homes, Richard, 17, 20. 61, 62, 69, 83.
Horseneck. the enemy there, 136.
Horses. stray. 73 ; unmarked. 74.
Horsesheds. 98.
Hubbell. Thaddeus, 132.
Hungry Spring, 94.
Hyatt. Thomas. 21. 61 ; a soldier in King Philip's war, 64, 83.

I

Indian Deed. to Roger Ludlowe, 30 ; to Captain Patrick, 31 ; to first settlers, 35.
Indians. 49. 56. 57.
Indian war, 62.
Islands recorded to the town, 98.
Isaacs, Captain Benjamin, 127.

J

Jades, stray, 112.

* On p. 170, l. 17 from top, the date 1726 should read, " Feb. 27, 1726-7."

Jesup, Blackleach, 127.
Judson, Mr., 82.
Jupp. James, 65, 83.
Justices, how seated in the meeting-house, 158.

K

Keeler. Ralph, 17, 19. 24, 26, 41, 61, 83 ; Walter, 17 ; John, 18. 61, 83 ; Samuel, 61 ; a soldier in the direful swamp fight, 64. 84.
Kellogg. Daniel, 17, 25, 58, 61, 62, 83 ; Samuel. 86.
Ketchum, Joseph, 18, 27, 84, 96.
King's Commissioner, 80.

L

Labor, price regulated, 125.
Ladders. 46.
Land, allotments of, 44, 56. 79 ; of the Indians, 57, 82 ; division of, 66 ; division of, over river. 82.
Law for toleration, 156.*
Leaming. Rev. Mr., 130 ; his rate, 159 ; collectors of his rates, 161.
Lees, William. 61, 84.
Lines. Mr., 120.
Lockwood, Ephraim, 18, 25, 61, 62, 83; John, 83 ; Daniel, 86 ; Eliphalet, 127 ; Ebenezer, 130.
Lots drawn for land, 79, 83.
Ludlowe. Richard, Indian deed to. 30 ; agreement with the first settlers, 32 ; assignment to first settlers, 34.
Lupton, Thomas, 17, 23, 53, 61, 62, 83 ; Peter. 61.
Lyon, Andrew, 87.

M

McAuley. Donald. his salt, 130.
Magazine, town, 111. 130 ; Mamachimon. coats to. 56. 59.
Marvin. Matthew, Sen., 17, 19, 23, 61, 83 ; Matthew, Jr., 17, 25, 56, 61, 62 ; Samuel, 98.
Marsh. Jonathan, 17, 23. 47.
Meeting-house, nails for, 40 ; the first, 49 ; clap-boarded, 50 ; addition to, 50 ; a new one. 69 ; committee. 70, 72 ; building, 70, 71 ; site of old one, 78 ; new seats, 78 ; seating. 80 ; fortifying, 84 ; gallery. 92 ; bell. 98, 99 ; seating. 99. 100 ; the great pew. 102 ; belfry. 104 ; seating. 105 ; ringing bell at 9 o'clock. 105 ; new house. 106 ; whether to repair. 107 ; beginning new one. 109 ; seats taken from the old one, 111 ; seating. 111 ; no town meetings to be held there. 112 ; selling

the old one, 112 ; the old bell hung on the new house, 113 ; seating, 113 ; stone steps. 114 ; old pulpit, 115 ; windows. 158 ; Justices' seat, 158 ; repairing, 162 ; the present one built, 160.
Merwin, Thomas. 84 ; Ozias, 127.
Messenger, Andrew, 21, 61. 84.
Methodist church, 171.
Mill, 44, 51 ; Henry Whitney's, tide, 103.
Miller, James, 61.
Minister, 14 ; procuring one, 87, 89 ; his lot, 89 ; firewood. 90 ; salary, 90, 91 ; house. 91 ; one allowed to Saugatuck, 116 ; one sent for, 149.
Ministers of the 1st Congregational church, 165 ; of the Episcopal church, 168 ; Methodist, 170 ; 2d Congregational church, 168 ; Baptist, 171.
Monopolies and oppressions, 131.
Monroe. David, 87.
More. Isaac, 17, 22, 43 ; builds a wolf pit, 47.
Morgan, widow, 17.

N

Name of the town of Norwalk ; its origin. 14.
Nash, Edward. 18 ; builds a wolf-pit, 47, 61. 84 ; John. 28, 61, 62, 84.
New Canaan, parish, 122 ; grant to, 122.
Non-importation, 127.
Norfield. nullifiers, 128.

O

Officers of the town in 1654, 43 ; in 1658, 48 ; in 1670. 58.
Olmstead. Richard, 17, 19, 22, 48, 58, 61 ; John, 61, 84 ; James, 61.
Oysters. gathering, 110.

P

Patent from the General Court, 30.
Patrick. Captain, 31, 33.
Parsonage, 121.
Perkins. Jonathan, 21, 61.
Pew for the Authority, 158.
Pickett, James. 18, 28, 61.
Planting field. 41.
Platt. Joseph, 18. 28 ; a soldier in the French and Indian war, 64 ; captain. 105 ; John, 22, 26, 61, 62, 83 ; John. Jr.. 86.
Poplar Plain. nullifiers, 128.
Pound. 42. 74.
Powder and lead, 95.
Presbytery of New Brunswick ; its attempted interference resented, 159.
Prime Ancient Society organized,146.
Provisions for the army, 139.
Pulpit, supplying, 117, 146, 164.

Q

Quakers exempted from ministers' rates, &c., by law of 1727, 156.

R

Raymond. Richard, 21, 26 ; John, 21, 61. 62. 84 ; John, Jr., 84. 96, 105 ; Eliakim, 127 ; Gershom. 127 ; Clap, 128 , Samuel, 87 ; Jesse, 128.
Rail Hill, 179.
Records, town, 15 ; church, 15, 16 ; of the Prime Ancient Society, 146.
Reminiscences of aged inhabitants— Mrs. Philips, 172; Phebe Comstock, 173. 174; Onesimus, 173 ; Thomas Benedict, 174 ; Mrs. Benedict, 176 ; Daniel Nash, 177 ; Nathaniel Raymond. 178 ; Mrs. St. John. 179.
Reede, John. 21, 48, 84 ; John, Jr., 87.
Ridgefield. 101, 105, 106.
Riotous proceedings, 126.
Richards, Nathaniel, 17, 19, 51, 58, 61; James, 127 ; Samuel, 127.
Rogers, Uriah, 128.
Roach. John, 63.
Rockwell, Jonathan, 83 ; Thomas, 87 ; Joseph, 87.
Ruscoe, John, 17, 27, 61, 62, 83 ; Thomas, 85.

S

Sabbath-day house, 106.
Salt brought from Boston, 133 ; distributed, 136.
Saybrook platform, 135.
Sawmill. 69.
Saltpetre works. 129.
Saugatuck, school dame, 112.
Scrivener, Benjamin. 87.
School, 69. 79, 110, 112.
School-house, 95.
School society, 157.
Seamer (or Seymour), Thomas, 17, 20. 23, 61, 62, 84 ; Richard. 20, 45 ; Seth, 123 ; Lieut. Matthew, 103.
Sention (or St. John), Matthew, 17, 47 ; Matthias, 17, 20, 23, 61, 62, 70, 84 ; Matthias, Jr., 17, 84 ; Mark, 18. 47, 61, 84 ; Samuel, 29, 61, 62 ; Captain Stephen, 127 ; Stephen, 2d. 127 ; James, 61 ; Ebenezer. 83 ; Elizabeth, 83 ; Joseph, 86.
Settlement, time of, 13 ; plan of the ancient, 16.
Settlers, first. 17, 18 ; notices of. 18 ; agreement for the planting of Norwalk. 32.
Sedge, 101.
Silliman, Samuel, 128.
Sherwood, Isaac, 87.
Small-pox, 138.

Smith, Samuel, 18, 20, 27, 29, 61, 83 ; Joseph, 20 ; Thomas. 20.
Soldiers, in the Revolution, clothing, 58. 124 ; their families supplied, 124, 136 ; to be raised, 139 ; classes for raising, 191 ; hired, 143.
Soldiers in the Indian war, 62.
Stamford, difficulty with, 54, 57.
St. Paul's parish. 123.
Strawberry Hill, 79.
Stewart. Robert, 18, 22, 27, 61, 71, 84 ; John, 103 ; James, 84. 105.
Stevenson, Jonathan, a soldier in the swamp fight, 65.
Stone, Mr., 88.
Swamp fight, 63, 66.
Swaine, Lieut., must leave off building the mill, 44.

T

Taylor, Thomas, 18, 27, 61, 62 ; John, 106, 107.
Tarrytown, the enemy there, 136.
Tavern-keeper, 61. 70.
Tennent. Rev. William, 159, 160, 162, 164.
Tide mill, 103.
Timber, felling of, 42.
Toleration, law of 1727, 156.
Town burnt, 143.
Town charges, 95. 96.
Town herd, 45.
Town house. 120, 125, 137.
Town meetings, 48, 73, 77, 101, 102
Town rate, 97.
Townsmen, 43, 45.
Tories, 140, 144.
Training, 53.

V

Volunteers in the Revolutionary war, 133.

W

Ward. Thomas, 18, 25.
Watch, 68, 73, 131.
Webb, Richard, 20, 25 ; Elizabeth, 20, 61 ; Ebenezer, 86.
Wilton parish, 113, 121.
Winter Wheatfield, 54.
Whitney, John. 68, 84 ; Henry, 51, 52.
Whitlock. Oliver, 132.
Wolf-pits, 47, 49.
Wolves, 53, 85, 95.
Wood, Richard, 87 ; Jonathan, 106.
Woods, burning of, 42, 59.

Y

Young people to be kept still in meeting, 63, 76.

INDEX

TO THE

GENEALOGICAL REGISTER.

The name of the male head of each family is here given. His marriage, and the names of his wife and children will be found at the place.

[In reading these registers, it should be borne in mind that the Old Style year began in March. This will explain several cases, which might otherwise appear very singular.]

Abbott. Jonathan. 190, Jonathan, 196; Ebenezer, 213 ; John. 219 ; John, Jr., 276 ; Stephen, 291 ; Ebenezer, 292.

Adams, Isaac, 263; Aaron, 272 ; Peter, 290.

Arnold. James. 264 ; Isaac, 2d, 289.

Ayres, Benjamin, 262 ; Ebenezer, 268.

Barnam. Thomas, 191, 192.

Bartlett. John, 199.

Bartrum. Job. 223.

Batterson Stephen, 271 ; Powell, 294.

Bebee, James, 192.

Beers, Nathan. 200.

Belden. Lieut. John, 205 ; John, 217 ; Samuel, 262 ; Thomas, 262.

Belknap. Abel. 238.

Benedict. Thomas, 184 ; John, Jr., 185, 188, 196 ; James. 188 ; Samuel. 190, 191 ; James, 196 ; Thomas, 205 ; Samuel. 211 ; Nehemiah. 212 ; Thomas, Jr.. 214 ; William. 240 ; William, 260 ; Nathan, 260 ; Thomas. Jr., 264 ; John, Jr.. 253 ; William, Jr., 261 ; Aaron, 265 ; Nehemiah. 268 ; Nathaniel, Jr., 270 ; Jesse. 271 ; James, 289 ; Isaac, 290 ; William. 239 ; Nathan, 301.

Betts, Samuel, 204 ; John. son of John, 207 ; Thomas. 212 ; Nathan, 220 ; John, 222 ; Thaddeus, 223 ; Matthew, 227 ; Stephen. 231 ; Seth. 232; Isaac, 251 ; Enoch. 255 ; Stephen 2d. 259 ; William M., 260 ; Reuben. 273 ; Thomas, 274 ; Thomas, 274 ; John, 274 ; Matthew, 274; Thomas, 275 ; John, 275 ; Lewis, 277 ; Philo, 277 ; Daniel. Jr., 282 ; Thadeus, Jr., 283; Silas, 287; Hezekiah. 235 ; Peter. 299

Blackly. Joseph. 198.

Bolt. John. 203 ; William. 231 ; David, 238 ; David. 260 ; John, 266

Bouton (Bowten), John. 182, 183 ; Joseph, 222 ; Esaias. 232 ; William, 244 ; Samuel, 257 ; Isaac, 256 ; Joshua, 260 ; Aaron, 271 ; Stephen, 280.

Brooks, Lemuel. 258 : Henry, 295.

Brown. James. 197 ; James. 208; John, 214 ; Avery. 241 ; Jedidiah. 249.

Buckingham. Stephen, Jr., 209.

Burgess. Joseph. 233.

Burnet. Rev. Matthias, 248.

Burrall. Jonathan. 235 ; Samuel, 239.

Burwell. Samuel, 273.

Bushnell. Francis. 188.

Butler. Daniel, 236.

Byxbee. Moses, 250 : Hopkins, 256 ; Joseph. 256 ; John, 260, John, 290.

Cameron. John, 208.

Camp. Abraham, 221 ; Jonathan. 229; Jonathan, Jr., 220 ; Stephen, 229 ; Isaac. 262 ; Richard, 267 ; Samuel Jervis. 231.

Canfield. Samuel, 202.

Cannon. John. 227; John, 258; James, 272 ; Samuel. 286.

Carter, John, 234 ; Samuel, 234; Ebenezer. 235 ; John, 235 ; Ebenezer, 275 ; Samuel. 275.

Carver. Melzer, 238.

Chapman, John. 251 ; Joseph, 283.

Chichester, Abraham, 279; Henry, 293.

Church. Ebenezer. 230 ; Daniel, 256.
Clinton. Joseph. 231 ; Joseph. 297
Cole. Thomas, 276 , Asa. 277.
Comstock. Christopher, 185, 189. 190, 195 ; Daniel. 190 ; Samuel. 195 : Moses, 196 ; Caleb. 239; David, 246 ; Strong. 276 ; Thomas, 230 ; Aaron, 237.
Copp. John. 296.
Crampton. John, 188, 190, 191.
Crofoot, Ebenezer. 277.
Curtis, Ephraim. 243.
Day. Absalom, 257.
Durrow, John. 219.
Dean. Jonathan. 212.
De Forest. Eliud. 302.
Dickinson, Rev. Moses, 225.
Dickson. John, 202, Hugh, 301.
Dikeman, Levi, 207 ; Wolcott, 275 ; Stephen. 279.
Downs, William, 252 ; Wolcott, 275.
Edwards. William. 209.
Eells. Jeremiah B . 225 ; Moses C., 295.
Everett. Joseph. 267.
Eversley. John. 283 ; John. 283.
Fairchild. Thomas, 222 ; Samuel, 226, Gilbert. 230.
Fairweather, Hanford, 247 ; Jacob, 291.
Finch. Nathaniel, 207 ; Billy, 269 ; Seth. 281 : John. 286.
Fitch. Thomas. 189, 287 ; John. 191 ; Nathaniel. 191 ; Thomas, Gov.. 206 . Ebenezer. 213 ; Matthew. 221 ; John, 223 ; James. 230 ; Samuel. 233 ; Elijah. 233 ; Theophilus. 241 ; Nathaniel. 244 ; James, Jr., 247 ; Haynes. 252 ; Elijah, Jr.. 273 ; William. 273; Zachariah Whitman, 290: John. 294 ; Timothy, 295 ; Henry, 298 ; Jonathan. 302.
Fountain. Moses. 210.
Gaylord, Rev. William, 282
Green. Jacob, 216.
Gregory. Jakin, 186, 191 ; John. Jr., 186 ; Judah, 187. 190, 192, 193 ; Thomas. 191 ; Ebenezer. 199 : Samuel. 222 ; Nathan, 234 , Thomas. 236; Aaron. 240; Elias. 246, Isaiah. 246 ; Moses. 260 ; Jabez. 265 , Ebenezer. 266 ; Thomas. 267 : Moses, 284 ; Jehiel. 289 ; Elijah. 302.
Gruman. Samuel. 206 ; John, 244 ; Jeremiah, 254 ; Isaac, 272 ; Thomas. 296.
Haite. (Hoyt). John, 183. 185. 187. 190; Zerubabell. 193 ; Caleb. 198 ; Caleb, Jr., 199 ; Ezra, 215 ; David. 215 ; Daniel. 218 ; Nathan, 224 ; Asa, 239 ; Thomas, 239 ; Job. 241 ; Ebenezer. 247 ; Goold, 248 ; John. 250 ; Walter. 250 ; Jonathan. 251 ; Samuel, 257 ; Justus, 272 ; Goold. 272 ; Stephen, 272 ; Isaac, 276 ;

Thomas, 283 ; Isaac, 284 ; Elijah, 292 : Jonathan. 294 ; Matthew. 296; **Matthew,** Jr.. 301 ; David, his children, 302 ; Timothy, 302 ; Walter, 302
Hanford. Rev. Thomas. 183. 187 ; Elnathan. 225 ; Samuel. 228 : Levi, 235 ; Daniel, 243 ; Theophilus. B., 250 ; Levi. 253 : Ebenezer 253 ; John, Jr.. 265 Hezekiah. 276 ; Phinchas, 278 ; John. 280 ; Stephen, 296 ; Abijah. 296 : Bartlet, 301 ; Moses. 301 ; Thaddeus. 301.
Hartshorn. Jonathan. 204.
Hawkins Jos.. 271.
Hayes. Samuel. 191, 207 ; Isaac, 198 ; James. 202; James. 219 ; Silas, 254; John. 288.
Hendrick, Nathan, 268 ; Nathaniel, 272.
Hickox (Hickok). Carter. 228 ; John, 229 ; John, 231 ; Noah. 271 ; Seth, 277 ; Jesse, 290.
Hull. William, 247.
Hubbell, Zadock. 277.
Hull. Josiah. 216.
Hur.butt. Joseph, 243 ; Daniel, 281 ; John. 284.
Husted, Jonathan. 235; Theodore. 243.
Hyatt. Thomas, 183 : Ebenezer, 223 ; Gilbert. 255 ; John. 261 : Alvin, 290.
Isaacs, Ralph. 212 : Isaac Scudder, 240.
James. Peter, 240 ; Daniel, 255 ; Jemmy. 265.
Jarvis. William. 211 ; Nathan, 234 ; Melancthon B., 257; Hezekiah, 269; Nathan. 270.
Jelliff. William. 285.
Jennings. Jacob. 266 : Hezekiah, 294; Isaac. 301 : Isaac, 302.
Jesup. Joseph. 254 ; Blackleach, 278.
Johnson, Chauncey. 293.
Jupp. James. 191.
Keeler. John (son of Ralph). 189, 190, 191 ; Samuel, 191 ; John. Jr.. 197 ; Samuel. Jr , 201 ; Samuel. 201 ; Timothy. 227; Samuel. 238; Aaron, 248 ; Seth. 251 ; William. 258 ; Stephen. 262 ; Jeremiah. 252; Isaac, 267 ; Thomas. 268 ; Phinehas, 302 ; Luke. 302 ; Timothy, 301 ; Isaac, 298 ; Isaac, 303.
Kellogg. Daniel. 187. 192 ; Samuel, 199 ; Joseph. 204 ; Eliasaph, 211 ; John, 214 ; David. 218 ; John. 249 ; Epenetus. 265; Stephen, 273 ; Enos, 293 ; Samuel, 296.
Ketchum, Joseph. 190; Nathaniel. 198.
Knapp. Alick. 247 , Epenetus, 254.
Knight. Doct Jonathan, 258.
Knox, Dr. Hugh, 250.
Lambert, David, 207 ; David, Jr., 248.
Little, John, 217.
Lockwood, Ephraim, 184, 189, 192 ;

alet, 201; James.
  Ephraim, 215;
  222; John. 236;
  246; Ebenezer.
  Ephraim 234;
ephen, 201; Fili-
lliam S., 301;

ccount of. 181:
John, 194; John.
.
imes, 266; John.
.
Marvin), Seth.
  Barnabas, 242;
  iew, 222; Ste
  as, 285; Samuel.

l, 278; Nathan,

. 233.
5; Noah, 297.
0, 271; James,

n, Jr.. 193; John,
1; Noah, 234;
than, 268: Na-
:70; Daniel, 273.
John, 193, John.
  Joseph, 266;
amuel, 21. 279;
Reuben, 291.

nry, 301.

7.
12; James, 208;

188, 192; John,
h. 197: Samuel,
muel, 251.

John, 184, 186;
n, Jr,. 195; Tho
0; Samuel. Jr.,
  Eliakim, 223;
Benjamin, 225;
im, 230; Asahel.
Nathaniel, 240:
,252; Gershom.
  Naphtali, 257;
siah, 264: Tho-
31; Moses, 257;
; John, 3d, 294.

Reed. Thomas. 200; Thomas, Jr.. 207;
  William. 211; Nathan, 221; Daniel,
  221; Benjamin, P., 257; John, 259;
  Benjamin. 261; Daniel, 261.
Resseguie. Alexander, 186.
Richards. Samuel 210; Gershom, 242;
  Daniel, 246; Isaac, 252; Samuel,
  249.
Riggs. Jonathan. 259.
Rockwell. Thomas. 233; John, 215.
Rogers. Uriah. 213; Hezekiah, 292.
Sanford. Nathan. 302.
Saunders, Jabez, 226; John. 236;
  Holmes. 243; Thomas, Jr., 251.
Scott. William, 263.
Scrivener (Scribner). Benjamin, 189;
  John. 200: Abraham. 233; Mat-
  thew. 233; Enoch. 301.
Seamer (Seymour), Thomas, 182, 193;
  William. 261; James. 271; Seth,
  293; Ezra, 293; Jonathan. 296;
  Lewis. 298; Samuel, 298; Samuel,
  303; Lewis, 303.
Selleck. Nathaniel, 249; James. Jr.,
  265; Charles, 280: Jacob, 281;
  Uriah. 301.
Sention. (St. John), James. 185; Sam-
  uel, 190; Mark. 192. 195; Samuel,
  192; Joseph. 196; James, Jr., 204;
  Nehemiah, 223; Caleb, 231; Abijah. 245; Peter, 245; Cook, 245;
  Stephen. 245; Phinehas, 246; Jesse,
  247; Adonijah, 251; William. 256;
  Josiah, 257; Abraham, 259; Isaac,
  263; Ezra, 263; Silas, 253; Matthias. 259; Enoch, 260; Stephen,
  273; Eliphalet, 236; Joseph, 291;
  Benjamin, 2 15; Matthias, 300; John,
  300; John, 300; Bela. 300; Samuel,
  301; Aaron, 302; Isaac, 249; Buck-
  ingham. 300: George. 300; Isaac,
  303; Isaac, sen., 303; Bula, 304;
  Matthew. 304; John. 304.
Sherman. Roger M.. 239; Richard,
  249.
Silliman. Samuel C., 247; Joseph,
  294.
Smith, Ebenezer 208; Robert, 220;
  Eliakim, 250; Eliakim, Jr., 250;
  Asa, 253; Daniel. 270; Phinehas,
  272; David. 275; Charles. 278;
  James, 285; Noah, 239; Peter, 301.
Stewart (Stuart). Robert, 186; John,
  211; Simeon, 279; Isaac, 291.
Stone. Olney. 248.
Street, Nathaniel, 219.
Sturdivant, William. 190.
Sturges, Ezekiel, 255.
Taylor, Thomas, 184, 195; Lt. John,
  220: Josiah, 217; John, Jr., 220;
  Noah, 223; Seth. 277.
Thacher, Josiah, 214; Thomas Fitch,
  243; Josiah. 251.
Treadwell, John P., 301.
Truesdell, William, 205.

Trumbull, James, 290.
Turrell, Samuel. 279.
Tuttle, David, 203 ; Edmond, 241 ; Enoch, 267 ; David. 269 ; Nathan. 291 ; John, 231 ; Selleck, 290 ; Eli. 297 ; Ebenezer. 297 ; Wid. Abigail, 297.
Van Antwerp, Nicholas. 250.
Wareing, Edmund. 194; Michael. 223; Eliakim, 225 ; Joseph, 231 : Joseph, Jr., 241 ; Eliakim, 249 ; Isaac, 264.
Wusson, Robert, 259 ; Robert, Jr., 259.
Waterbury, Thaddeus, 279.
Weed, Nathan. 225 ; Daniel, 263, 264 ; Ebenezer, 296.
Webb, Richard, 188.

White, Peter, 231 ; Samuel. 279 ; Samuel. Jr., 279 ; Stephen, 230.
Whitlock. Hezekiah, 295 ; Daniel, 286.
Whitney. John, 189 ; John. 192 ; Richard, 195 ; Joseph, 197 : Henry, 199; John, Jr., 202 ; Josiah. 208 ; Joseph, 213 ; Elijah. 217 ; Hezekiah, 217 ; Abraham, 227 ; David. 234 ; Benjamin, 236 ; Timothy, 236 ; Benjamin, 231 ; Ebenezer, 237 ; David, Jr., 238 ; Asa. 298.
Wicks, Stephen. 283.
Williams. Nathan, 255.
Wilson, John. 266.
Wilson, John. 264.
Wood, Samuel. 196 ; Stephen, 299.
Young, Richard, 265.

INTRODUCTORY.

THE TIME OF SETTLEMENT.

TRUMBULL, in his History of Connecticut, vol. i., p. 115, says, that in 1640, " Mr. Ludlow made a purchase of the eastern part of Norwalk," " Capt. Patrick bought the middle part of the town, " and that " *A few families seem to have planted themselves in the town about the time of these purchases.*" On p. 202, under the date of 1651, he says, " Though the eastern and middle parts of Norwalk had been purchased more than ten years, yet there had been only *a few scattering inhabitants* within its limits." Trumbull is minute and accurate in his dates concerning the purchases, and in the date of the order of the General Court for the settlement [1650]. In addition to the public records, he had access to other sources of information, which are now lost, viz. the " Manuscripts of Rev. Moses Dickinson," to which he refers, p. 202. But on what authority he says that " A few families seem to have planted themselves in the town about the time of these purchases" [1640], and that at the time of its regular settlement [1651], there were " a few scattering inhabitants" within the limits of the town, I know not. I find no recognition of the presence of such prior inhabitants on the

2

town records. On the 15th of February, 1651, the planters were here, as appears from the deed from RUNCKINHEAGE. Some of them, at least, were probably here the year before. There is a tradition that several of them spent the winter here.

THE FIRST MINISTER.

In the great Bible of Capt. Hezekiah Betts, who died in 1837, aged 77, I find, among other historical memoranda, entered by his own hand, that THOMAS HANFORD began to preach to the people of Norwalk about the year 1648. As Capt. Betts was so curious about such matters, and so accurate, I had entertained no doubt that his record was correct, and so published it ; but as the people who agreed for the settlement with Mr. Ludlowe, in 1650, engaged to " invite an orthodox and approved minister with all convenient speed," it is clear that Mr. Hanford was not here in 1648. Trumbull is doubtless correct, when he says, p. 299, " the same year [1652] Mr. Thomas Hanford began to preach at Norwalk, and some time after a church was formed in that town, and Mr. Hanford ordained pastor."

THE NAME.

The common tradition concerning the name, is the account given by Barber in his Historical Collections, p. 392, that the name NORWALK is derived from the one day's " *North-walk*" that limited the northern extent of the purchase from the Indians. It is wonderful that so awkward and improbable a fancy ever gained credit. Norwalk is the old Indian name. The Indians were called " the Norwake Indians'" and the river bore the

name of " Norwake River," when the English first
came to these shores. Mr. Ludlowe's purchase in 1640
was from " The Indians of Norwalke," and the land is
described as lying between " the twoe rivers, the one
called the *Norwalke*, the other *Soakatuck*."* In the
earliest town records the name is written *Norwalke*
(the *w* probably silent, as in Warwick). Our aged
people retain the ancient (and probably true) pronunci-
ation, *Norruck*. Bradley's Register says that the early
Colony Records call it *Norrwake*.

THE RECORDS.

The first record of town proceedings is under the date
of 1653. The first book of grants and deeds is entire ;
but it was evidently not begun till some 20 years after
the first settlement. From 1653, the record of town
proceedings appears to be full and complete. The first
books are much worn, and in some places the writing is
so much defaced as to be illegible. The remaining
books are in a good state of preservation.

The early Church Records are irrecoverably lost. Phebe
Comstock, aged 83 years, informs me that she used
often to visit at Dr. BURNET's, and at one time desired
to see the Church Records. Dr. BURNET threw open a
book-case, and said : " There : whenever any of my parishioners wish to consult the Church Records, there
they are at their service." She often consulted them.
There were three large folio volumes, one kept by each
of the three ministers, Mr. HANFORD, Mr. BUCKING-
HAM, and Mr. DICKINSON ; each volume filled with writ-

* It is a pity that the unmeaning name of WESTPORT was ever
substituted for the old Indian name of SAUGATUCK. If I were an
inhabitant of that town, I would never cease to petition the Legislature till they changed it back again.

ing.   She says that after Dr. BURNET's death, in 1806, these volumes were left in a basket in the old parsonage, and were gnawed and eaten through and through by rats, and quite destroyed.   The TOWN RECORDS* are invaluable.

PLAN OF THE ANCIENT SETTLEMENT.

The ground-plot (except the river and salt-meadows) is taken from an actual survey by THOMAS BENEDICT, 3d.† The division of the lots I have made out from the "TABLE OF HOMELOTS," compiled from the records. As these records were not made till some twenty years after the settlement (some of them much later) during which time several changes had occurred ; as neither the length nor breadth of any lot is mentioned, and the quantity given only by estimate ; and as some of the original grants were never put on record, and are mentioned only incidentally in the boundaries of the other lots, it will readily be seen that there was no small difficulty in making out the plan with desirable accuracy. There are, however, several fixed landmarks : the roads and the coast are the same.   The site of the meeting-house is certain.   The lots correspond with the description in the "Table ;" they fill up the space assigned. There are other corroborative evidences of the accuracy of the plan.   I showed to an aged descendant of the Fitch family, the lot which THOMAS FITCH bought of

* But they are kept in a wooden building, without any security against fire; and should a conflagration occur in that long and hazardous range of wooden buildings, they will, in all likelihood, be destroyed.

† The map of the parts east of the river up to the churches is from a survey of Mr. BENEDICT's.

EDWARD CHURCH. "Oh, now I remember," said she, "that my grandfather used to call it ' the Church lot,' though I had entirely forgotten it." In making out the plan I found it impossible to fill out the space south of MATTHEW SENTION's and GEORGE ABBOTT's lot, without making some proportionably too large. I took the plan to several aged people, who at once told me that the open space below these lots lay open to common even within their recollection. Mr. SAMUEL FITCH went with me on to the ground, and pointed out the boundaries. I flatter myself that whoever will compare the plan with the "TABLE OF HOMELOTS," and then go over the ground with the plan open in his hand, will be satisfied with its general accuracy.

THE FIRST SETTLERS.

There is no complete list of the original settlers, but a Table of " Estates of lands and accommodations" in 1655, contains the names of the following inhabitants.

ABBITT, GEORGE	KELLOGGE, DANIEL
BEACHAM, ROBERT	LUPTON, THOMAS
BECKWITH, STEPHEN	MARVIN, MATTHEW, SEN.
BOWTON, JOHN	MARVIN, MATTHEW, JR.
CAMPFIELD, MATTHEW	MORE, ISACKE
ELI, NATHANIEL	MARSH, JONATHAN
FITCH, THOMAS,	MORGAN, WIDOW
GRIGGORIE, JOHN	OLMSTED, RICHARD
HALES, SAMUEL	RICHARDS, NATHANIEL
HALES, THOMAS	RUSKOE, JOHN
HAITE, WALTER	SENTION, MATTHIAS, SEN.
HAIES, NATHANIEL	SENTION, MATTHIAS, JR.
HANFORD, THOMAS REV.	SENTION, MATTHEW
HOMES, RICHARD	SEAMER, THOMAS
KEEILER, RALPH	WEB, RICHARD.
KEEILER, WALTER	

In a List of accounts in 1654, are the following names which do not appear in the preceding list of Estates, viz. :

BRYANT, ——	RAIMENT, RICHARD
CHURCH, EDWARD	SEAMER, RICHARD
FITCH, JOSEPH	WHITINGE, GILES
NASH, EDWARD	

And in 1656 the following :

MORGAN, OWEN	REID, WILLIAM

And in the Table of Home Lots, the following : some of whom must have come in several years later.

BENEDICT, THOMAS, SEN.	HAIES, SAMUEL
BENEDICT, THOMAS, JR.	LOCKWOOD, EPHRAIM
BENEDICT, JOHN	KETCHUM, JOSEPH ⌐
BETTS, THOMAS	KEELER, JOHN
BUSHNELL, RICHARD	PICKETT, JAMES
CAMPFIELD, SAMUEL	PLATT, JOSEPH
COMSTOCK, CHRISTOPHER	SENTION, MARK
CRAMPTON, JOHN	STEWART, ROBERT
FITCH, THOMAS, JR.	SMITH, SAMUEL
FENN, JOSEPH	TAYLOR, THOMAS
GREGORY, JOHN, JR.	WARD, THOMAS.
GREGGORIE, JAKIN	

The following notices of the first settlers of Norwalk, I find in the " Catalogue of the Names of the First Puritan Settlers of the Colony of Connecticut,"—" By R. R. Hinman. Hartford, 1846."

" ABBOTT, GEORGE, 1648."*

" BECKWITH, STEPHEN, 1649."

" BELDING, JOHN" (son of John of Wethersfield, who died 1677).

* Date of the first mention in the Colony Records.

" BENEDICT, THOMAS, 1662."*

" BETTS, THOMAS, Guilford, 1650" (Mr. Hinman refers to Widow Betts, 1639, and John Betts, 1648).

" CAMFIELD, (or Campfield,) MATTHEW—a magistrate and judge ; not only a leading man there, but in the Colony.—One of the signers of the petition to King Charles II. for the Colony ; in 1662, appointed with Gold and Sherman to hold courts at Fairfield.

" ELY, NATHANIEL" Hartford, 1635,—constable, 1639, " one of the settlers of Norwalk, but afterwards removed to Springfield, Massachusetts."

" FITCH, THOMAS,—a brother of Rev. James, at Saybrook, and of Joseph, of Windsor.

" GREGORY, JOHN—a deputy, 1662-3.

" HOYT, WALTER, Windsor, 1640. ▬

" KEELER, RALPH, Hartford, 1639, viewer of chimneys in '45.

" MARVIN, MATTHEW—surveyor of highways at Hartford in 1639, and '47 ; an original proprietor and settler in Hartford before '39 ; removed to Norwalk, deputy to the General Court from Norwalk in '54.

" OLMSTED, RICHARD, Hartford, 1640, constable '46, fence viewer '49, deputy in '62-3 ; moved to Norwalk and was made a military officer. In 1661 was appointed with John Banks, and Joseph Judson, who were appointed by the General Court, to run the lines between Fairfield and Stratford."

" RICHARDS, NATHANIEL, of Hartford—in the Colo-

---

* Of Thomas Benedict, a much earlier account is given among the family records of Norwalk in this work.

Mr. Hinman says, that Robert Lockwood came to Connecticut from Cambridge, and was probably one of the settlers of Norwalk. I do not find that this is so; perhaps this is the origin of the family.

ny in 1639 ; constable in '41 and '49, orderer of the
town in '44, deputy in 43.

" SENCHION, OR ST. JOHN, MATTHIAS, 1640.

" SEYMOUR, RICHARD, Hartford, 1639, chimney
viewer in '46.

" WEBB, RICHARD, Hartford, 1639,—on the first
Grand Jury at the General court in the Colony in 1643.
Also a juror in '43-4, selectman in '48, surveyor of high
ways in '49. He soon after removed to Stamford, was
made free there in '62."

The following additional particulars concerning some
of the first settlers are taken from the 1st book of
Grants and Deeds.

" ELIZABETH WEBB, relicke of Richard Webb," in
1677, employed her " Beloved brother John Gregory
to make an agreement with Thomas Butler of Hartford,
and his wife," they " laying claime to the estate of
my deere husband, Richard Webb, deceased,—"fol. 51.

RICHARD HOMES, of Stratford, Oct. 12, 1657, bought
of Alexander Bryan, of Milford, the home-lot which was
Thomas Smith's: and March, 1663, the lands of Stephen Beckwith, planter, of Norwalk.

MATTHEW CAMPFIELD, late of Norwake, now resi-
dent in Newarke, in the Colony of New Jersey (gave a
deed) to his son Samuel, April 1, 1669.

SAMUEL HALES, now of Weathersfield, late of Norwake, sold to John Platt, May 14, 1669.

THOMAS BARNAM, of Fairfield, had a grant before 1663.

JOSEPH SMITH, late of Long Island, bought of Samuel Campfield the north part of his home-lot in 1675.

SAMUEL SMITH, in 1672, a parcel of land in Indian-
field.

SAMUEL BELDING, Feb. 28, 1673, bought two parcels of land in the Neck planting-field.

JAMES PICKIT, in 1674.

THOMAS BETTS, JR. (fol. 55), in 1677, bought of Benjamin Fenn, of Milford, the house and home-lot formerly belonging to his brother, Joseph Fenn.

RICHARD RAYMOND, removed to Saybrooke, gave a deed to his son John: in 1677 empowered his " well beloved brother Thomas Betts, of Norwalk," to record all his divisions, &c. : and in 1676, gave by will all his lands in Norwalk " unto those children which my son John Raymond allready have or may have, by Mary Raymond his present wife."

JOHN REEDE, " of Rie," bought of Richard Homes.

" James Miller, and Martha his wife, of Ry, in the county of Fairfield," Dec. 26, 1681.

ANDREW MESSENGER, June 28, 1686 (fol. 85), bought land of Walter Hoyt.

SAMUEL CAMFIELD's house and four acres, between Thomas Betts and Ephraim Lockwood, Dec. 17, 1681.

THOMAS HYATT, in 1679, bought land of James Miller (James Miller and Martha his wife, of Rye, Dec. 26, 1681).

JONATHAN PERKINS, bought of Nathaniel Richards, Feb. 23, 1677.

FORT POINT.

In 1689, John Gregory gave a deed to his son Thomas, of a piece of land " Lying on the West side of Norwalke Towne plott, 2 acres—bounded East by the common land banck ; West, Norwalk river ; South by the poynt of common land where the Indian Fort formerly stood; North by Thomas Betts' Marsh Meadow."

2*

NORWALK.

TABLE OF ORIGINAL GRANTS OF HOME-LOTS TO
THE FIRST SETTLERS.

COMPILED FROM THE RECORDS IN THE FIRST BOOK OF GRANTS
AND DEEDS.

Note.—These records appear to have been made some twenty
years and more after the grants. They are generally without date,
interspersed with other records from 1670 to 1690. Probably some
original grants were never put on record; they are incidentally
mentioned in the boundaries of other grants. The estimated quantity, and the boundaries are given; but not the length of any of
the boundaries. Over some of the records, another hand has inserted the date 1652. The book is complete : the folios being numbered from 1 onward.

GRANTEES.

Richard Olmstead, 4 acres 1 rood.
Bounded east by Common land, west by Town's High-
way, north by Thomas Hale's home-lot, south by
Nathaniel Eli's home-lot.

**Thomas Fitch (purchased the lot laid out to Edward
Church in 1655), 4 acres.**
Bounded east by Town Highway, west by Daniel
Kellogg's home-lot, north by Nathaniel Richard's
home-lot, south by Matthew Marvin, Sen.'s, home-
lot.

Nathaniel Eli (sold to Thomas Betts), 4 acres 2 roods.
Bounded east by The Common, west by Town
Highway, north by Richard Olmsted's home-lot,
south by the other Highway.

**Samuel Hales (sold to Robert Stewart of Milford, in
1660), 4 acres.**
Bounded east by The " Commoninge," west by Highway, north by " The Commoninge," south by Mathias Sention's home-lot.

John Platt (in 1663), 4 acres 2 roods.
Bounded east by Highway and Common land, west
by Ephraim Lockwood's home-lot, north by Samuel
Camfield's lot, south by Thomas Fitch, Jr.'s, home-lot.

Isacke More (sold to Mark Sention in 1660), 4 acres.
Bounded east by Town Highway, west by " The
Coafe [cove] bancke," north by George Abbott's
home-lot.

Richard Seamer (afterwards his son's, Thomas Seamer, by exchange).

Bounded east by The Common, west by Town's Highway, north by Town's Highway, south by Richard Webb's home-lot.

John Bowten, 4 acres.

Bounded east by Mr. Hanford's and John Ruscoe's home-lot, west by Highway, north by Highway, south by Thomas Lupton's home-lot.

Matthew Marvin, Sen., 4 acres.

Bounded east by Town's Highway, west by Daniel Kellogg's home-lot, north by Thomas Fitch's home-lot, south by Meeting-house yard and Matthew Marvin, Jr.'s, home-lot.

Thomas Lupton, 4 acres.

Bounded east by Richard Homes and Mark Sention's home-lot, west by Mathias Sention's home-lot and Common, north by John Bowten's home-lot, south by George Abbott's lot.

Jonathan Marshe, two parcels, 4 acres.

The Greater—Bounded east by Highway, "the coafe bancke" of Norwalk River, north by the Commoninge, south by Thomas Ward's home-lot. The Less—Bounded east by Commonage, west by the aforesaid highway, north by Commonage, south by Commonage.

Walter Haite, 4 acres.

Bounded east by Town Highway, west by "the Common by the bancke coafe" [cove], north by Mathias Sention's home-lot, south by George Abbott's home-lot.

Nathaniel Richards, 4 acres 1 rood.

Bounded east by Town Highway, west by Norwalk River "coafe bancke," north by Isacke More's home-lot, south by Thomas Fitch's home-lot.

Matthias Sention, Sen., Bought of Mr. Steeile of Farmington, who married the widow of Richard Seamer, 4 acres (granted in addition 1, April 6, 1661), 5 acres.

Bounded east by Common land, west by Town's Highway, north by Samuel Hale's home-lot, now Robert Stewart's, south by Matthew Camfield's home-lot.

Ralph Keeiler, 4 acres 1 rood.

Bounded east by Common and Neck fence, west by Town Highway and Edward Nash's home-lot, north by Richard Webb's home-lot, south by Town Highway and Edward Nash's home-lot.

Mr. Thomas Hanford, 4 acres.

Bounded east by Town's Highway, west by John Bowten's home-lot, north by Town's Highway, south by John Ruscoe's home-lot.

Nathaniel Campfield, 5 acres.

Bounded east by Common, west by Town's Highway, north by Matthias Sention's home-lot, south by Richard Olmsted's, that was Thomas Hale's home-lot.

Samuel Campfield (apparently in 1670), 4 acres.

Bounded east by Brooke swamp of common ground, west by Common Highway, north by Ralph Keeler's home-lot, now Thomas Betts', south by John Platt's home-lot.

Thomas Benedick, Sen. (recorded March 1, 1669–70, having possessed it some years before), purchased of Mr. Hanford 1 acre 1 rood, of John Ruscoe 2 roods, of John Bowten 1 rood—4 acres.

Bounded east by Mr. Handford's and John Ruscoe's, west by John Bowten, north by Town Highway, south by Richard Homes.

Samuel Haies (two parcels, the last a piece of salt meadow in the rear of the first), 5 acres.

Bounded east (first) by Common Highway, west by "The bancke," north by Common land, south by Ralph Keeler's home-lot, that was Thomas Ward's. Salt meadow—Bounded east by Bank of Sd. home-lot, west by "Norwalke river coafe," north by "Coafe of sd river up to the bancke," south by "the creeke."

John Gregorie, Sen. (4 acres granted, bought 4 acres of Stephen Beckwith), 8 acres.

Bounded east by Town Highway, west by John Raimond's, north by Mr. Haies' lot and John Benedict's lot that was George Abbott's, south by Highway runny by "the coafe bancke," 'and John Gregorie, Jr.'s.

John Gregorie, Jr., received from John Gregorie, Sen., of the above, 1 acre 2 roods.

Richard Web, 4 acres.

> Bounded east by Common land adjoining the neck, west by Town Highway, north by Thomas Seamer's home-lot, south by John Raymond's home-lot that was Ralph Reeler's.

Daniel Kellogg, 4 acres.

> Bounded east by Matthew Marvin, Jr.'s, Matthew Marvin, Sen.'s, and Thomas Fitch, Sen.'s, home-lots, west by Joseph Fenn's home-lot and a bank of common land, north partly by Nathaniel Richard's home-lot, and by the " coafe bancke," south by Town Highway.

Matthew Marvin, Jr., 3 acres 2 roods.

> Bounded east by " Meeting-house greene," west by Daniel Kellogg's home-lot, north by Matthew Marvin, Sen.'s, home-lot, south by Town Highway.

Christopher Comstock, January 27, 1661 (then of Fairfield, bought of Thomas Betts, " being then a planter inhabiting in Norwalke," his " house, home-lot, &c., with haffe the land lying to the said house, laid out to said Betts, or belonging to the accommodation of Nathaniel Eli," folio 13), 4 acres.

> See " Nathaniel Eli," who sold this lot to Thomas Betts, which Thomas Betts, in 1661, sold to Christopher Comstock.

Ephraim Lockwood, December 30, 1664 (folio 13)—bought the home-lot of Jonathan Marshe ; " For and in consideration of one mare and sucking colt,"—" his howse with the shelfes, dress boards, &c." also the yards, hovells, and tenn fruit trees growing upon the orchard ; and also the home-lot containing one acre more or less."

> For boundaries see Jonathan Marshe.

Thomas Betts (bought Nathaniel Eli's home-lot ; sold half to Christopher Comstock ; also bought house and home-lot of Ralph Keeler—recorded about 1660), 4 acres.

> Bounded east by Common upland, west by Common Highway, north by John Keeler's home-lot, south by Samuel Campfield's home-lot.

Thomas Ward, of Norwalk (September 1, 1665, sold

to Ralph Keeler his " dwelling howse and howses,
&c.," reserving " the workshop for the abode of his
wife, if she shall have occasion, till the 27th of Sept.,
1666," said Ward reserving to himself "to take away
at his pleasure, the locks upon the dwelling howse
doares, and the younger nursery trees, and twoe boards
lying upon the coller beames"—folio 2,).

> Boundaries not given save on the north, which is
> bounded by Jonathan Marshe.

Thomas Benedict, Jr. (bought of Joseph Fenn, 1671,
" now home-lot, lyinge by the side of the creeke or
river called the Coafe"), 4 acres.

> Bounded east by Highway leading to the point, west
> by "Bancke of the coafe," north by Joseph Fenn's
> land adjoining to his home-lot, south by Cartway
> leading out of Daniel Kellogg's meadow.

Richard Raimond (inhabitant of Salem, in the juris-
diction of Mattachusetts Bay, bought of Ralph Keeler, October 20, 1662, " My howseing, contained at
present in my home-lott, or cow yard," &c., " the
howse, flores, doares, glasse windows, shelfes, or ought
else necessarily fastened together"), 4 acres.

> Bounded east by John Gregorie's lot that was George
> Abbott's, west by Common land, north by John Bene-
> dict's that was George Abbott's, south by "A High-
> way running to the sea bancke."

Jakin Greggorie (in 1666, grant of home-lot upland
and loe-land), 4 acres.

> Bounded east by Common upland, west by Common
> Highway, north by Common upland, south by Tho.
> Tayler's home-lot.

John Platt, of Norwalk (bought of Thomas Lupton,
March 9, 1665, sold in 1674 to John Bowten), 4 acres.

> Bounded east by "Reere of Thomas Lupton's house-
> lot and Richard Homes's, west by Matthias Sention's
> land, north by John Bowten's land, south by George
> Abbott's land.

John Crampton (" because he was a souldier in the late
Indian war," 1679), 3 acres.

> Bounded east by Highway, west by Samuel Benedict's
> home-lot, north by Thomas Betts, Sen.'s, home-lot,
> south by James Miller's home-lot.

Thomas Fitch, Jr. (May 20, 1671, bought of Samuel Camfield) home-lot, 5 acres.

> Bounded east by Upland of the common, west by Town Highway, north by Joseph Sention's lot, south by Richard Olmsted's.

Samuel Smith ("sonne" to Matthew Marvin, Sen., hath given him by said Marvin, August 20, 1674, folio 61, "haffe my home-lot and halfe my orchard as it lyeth").

Joseph Ketchum, 6.

> Bounded east by Ephraim Lockwood and common land, west by Thomas Taylor's home-lot and common land, north by Highway, south by James Picket's land.

Thomas Taylor (home-lot of upland and lowland, A.D. 1670), 4 acres.

> Bounded east by Common land, west by Common highway, north by Jakin Gregorie's.

Robert Stewart (Jan. 22, 1674, bought the "200 pound lot granted to Richard Bushnell").

> Bounded east by Lands of Samuel Camfield, west by Lands of Samuel Camfield, north by Lands of Samuel Camfield, south by Common Highway.

John Ruscoe (original grant, but recorded February 9, 1683), 4 acres.

> Bounded east by Town Highway, west by Lot formerly Thomas Lupton's, north by Mr. Handford's home-lot, south by Richard Homes' home-lot.

At a meetinge heild the 27th of March, —65, granted and voted unto Tho. Betts a home-lott of 4 acres, lyinge next to Ralph Keeiler's home-lot, the said Tho. Betts having at the saied meetinge resigned that home-lott lying by Will Ruscoe's unto the Towne's hands.

At the same meeting granted and voted unto Mstr. Ffenn that home-lott lyine by Will Ruscoe's home-lott, which Tho. Betts hath resigned up.

THO. BENEDICT, senr., in 1669, bought of Samuel

Campfield his houselot, granted him by the town, between Tho. Betts and Ephraim Lockwood.

MR.. BUCKINGHAM's home-lot, 4 acres: bounded E. by land of Tho. Betts, & the common fence, W. by Town's highway, N. by home-lot of Tho. Seamer, S. by home-lot of heirs of John Raymond, senr., decd. (The lot originally laid out to Richard Webb.)

John Nashe (in 1688, a grant in the rear of Robert Stewart's).

> Bounded east by common land, west by Robert Stewart's home-lot.

James Pickett (home-lot in 1672), 4 acres.

> Bounded east by Common Land, the said lot taking in the Water Brook, west by Common Highway, north by John Keeler's home-lot, that was Edward Ketcham's, south by Judah Gregory's home-lot.

Samuel Benedict (in 1678, a home-lot upon Dry Hill), 4 acres.

> Bounded east by Highway that leadeth to said hill, west by Town Highway, south by Thomas Benedict, sen.'s, homelot.

John Benedict, in 1678, home-lot upon Dry Hill), 4 acres.

> Bounded east and west by Highway, north by Robert Stewart's lot, south by Thomas Betts, sen.'s, lot.

Thomas Benedict, Jr. (home-lot between Rayle Hill and Strawberry Hill), 4 acres.

> Bounded east by Highway upon Strawberry Hill, west by Highway leading to the old Common Highway, north by Samuel Smith's lot, south by John Gregory, sen.'s, lot.

Joseph Platt (Recorded Jan. 11, 1699, grant of 16 acres lying at W. Rocks, west side of Highway leading up to said Rocks).

> Bounded partly by land of James Miller, north by Ebenezer Sension, west on Highway, south partly by land of Samuel Betts and James Miller.

Samuel Smith (Feb. 20, 1680, grant of home-lot adjacent to Strawberry Hill), 4 acres.

> Bounded east by Highway, west and north by Highway, south by Thomas Benedict, jr.'s, lot.

Samuel Sention (May 12, 1682, bought home-lot of James Jupp), 4 acres.

> Bounded east by John Gregory, sen.'s, lot and Common Land, west by Common Land, north by John Bowten, sen., that was George Abbott's, south by Highway running by the " Coafe Bancke,"—said lot purchased by Jupp of Richard Seamer.

James Beebe (home-lot, fol. 58, between two hollows in the land that lies against Judah Gregory's and John Hoyt's on the left hand of the Path or Highway leading to the Mill), 2 acres.

> Bounded east by Path or Highway, west by the Bank, north by a Hollow and Common Land, south by a Hollow and Common Land.

NOTE.

The several grants made to each person, previous to the recording—about 1670 to 1690—are generally recorded together. Thus: after the record of Rev. Mr. Hanford's home-lot, follow records of several parcels of land granted to Mr. Hanford, e. g.:

acres.	roods.	
10	2	at Pine Hill and Soakatuck Plaine.
6	0	in the Neck.
5	1	Neck and Fruitful Spring.
4	2	Coast Division.
1	0	Planting Field
1	0	Meadow.
2	2	Meadow Field.
2	1	Other side of the River.
5	0	Meadow at Barren Marsh.
4	2	Upland plain of the Meadows.
0	0	Out-meadow.
6	0	Neck Planting Field.
35	0	Saukatuck Hill.
6	3	Indian Field.
4	0	Rayle Hill: and so on for all the original planters.

DEEDS.

INDIAN DEED TO ROGER LUDLOW.

[East side of Norwalk River.]

A copyie* of a deede of *sale* made by Norwalke Indians,
unto Master Roger Ludlowe, of Fairfield, as followeth,
26th February, 1640.

An agreement made between the Indians of Norwalke
and Roger Ludlowe : it is agreed, that the Indians of
Norwalke, for and in consideration of eight fathom of
wampum, sixe coates, tenn hatchets, tenn hoes, tenn
knifes, tenn sissors, tenn jewse-harpes, tenn fathom
Tobackoe, three kettles of sixe hands about, tenn look-
ing glasses, have granted all the lands, meadows, pas-
turinge, trees, whatsoever their is, and grounds betweene
the twoe Rivers, the one called Norwalke, the other
Soakatuck, to the middle of sayed Rivers, from the sea
a days walke into the country ; to the sayed Roger
Ludlowe, and his heirs and assignes for ever ; and that
noe Indian or other shall challenge or claim any ground
within the sayed Rivers or limits, nor disturb the
sayed Roger, his heirs or assignes, within the precincts
aforesaid. In witness whereof the parties thereunto
have interchangeably sett their hands.

the marke   ROGER LUDLOWE.

Witnesse

Thos. Ludlowe   Tomakergo

Tokancke   the marke of

the marke of

the marke of   Mahachemo, Sachem

Adam   prosewamenos   the marke.

* These "copies" were recorded in the Book of Deeds in the
year 1672.

INDIAN DEED TO CAPT. PATRICK.

[Of the meadows and uplands, adjoininge, lyinge on the west side of Norwake River.]

An agreement betwixt Daniell Patrick and Mahack-
em, and Naramake and Pemenate Hewnompom indians
of Norwake and Makentouh the said Daniell Patricke
hath bought of the sayed three indians, the ground called Sacunyte napucke, allso Mccanworth, thirdly Asum-
sowis, fourthly all the land adjoyninge to the aforementioned, as farr up in the cuntry as an indian can goe in
a day, from sun risinge to sun settinge ; and twoe Islands
neere adjoining to the sayed carantcnayueck, all bounded on the west side with noewanton on the east side to
the middle of the River of Norwake, and all trees, meadows, waters and naturell adjuncts thereunto belonginge,
for him and his forever ; for whith Lands the sayed indians are to receive of the sayed Daniell Patricke, of
wampum tenn fathoms, hatchetts three, howes three,
when shipps come ; sixe glasses, twelfe tobackoe pipes,
three knifes, tenn drills, tenn needles ; this as full satisfaction, for the aforementioned lande. and for the peace-
able possession of which the aforementioned mahache-
mill doth promise and undertake to silence all opposers
of this purchase, if any should in his time act, to witnesse which, on both sides, hands are interchangeably
hereunto sett, this 20th of Aprill, 1640.

wittnesses,
Tobi ffeap
John How

marke.

mamechom

marke naromake.

pomenate
his

marke.

A copyie of the agreement and articles made between
Roger Ludlow, of Fairfield, and Nathaniel Eli, and
Rithard Olmested, with the rest, for the settlinge and
plantinge of Norwalke.

Articles of agreement made between ROGER LUD-
LOWE of Fairfield, esquire, of the one parte, and NA-
THANIEL ELI of Hartford, in the River of Connecticut,
RITHARD OLMSTED of the same, in the behalfe of them-
selves, and RITHARD WEBB, NATHANIEL RITHARDS,
MATHEW MARVIN, RITHARD SEAMER, THOMAS SPEN-
CER, THOMAS HALES, NATHANIEL RUSKOE, ISACKE
GRAVES, RALPH KEELER, JOHN HOLLOWAY, EDWARD
CHURCH, JOHN RUSKOE, and some others about plant-
inge Norwalke, over the 19th day of June, 1650.

Inprimis, the sayed NATHANIEL ELI and RITHARD
OLMESTED, doe covenant and promise and agree, that
they will set upon the plantinge of the sayed Norwalke,
with all convenient speed ; will mowe, and stacke some
hay upon the sayed Norwalke this winter, to the end
that they may, in the spring next at the farthest, breake
up some ground to plante the next season, followinge ;
and that then they will begin to build and inhabite
their-with some considerable companie, and to invite an
orthodoxe and approved minister with all convenient
speede that they may be ; and that the plantation shall
not be taken up under thirtie approved families, in a
short time to be settled their, and so to continue ; and
that, or the like considerable companie ; and that they
will not receive in, any that they be obnoxious to the
publique good of the Commonwealth of Connecticut.
And upon that consideration the sayed Roger Ludlowe

is willinge and doe agree to surrender the purchase of
the sayed Norwalke, whith he bought of the Indians,
of the sayed Norwalke, some years since ; which cost
the sayed Roger Ludlowe fifteen pounds, some years
since ; as by the purchase will appeare ; whith sayed
fifteen pounds is promised to be payed to the sayed
Roger Ludlowe or his assignes by the sayed Eli and
Olmested their assignes, shortly after the first plantinge
thereof, with consideration for the sayed fifteen pounds
from the disbursinge thereof unto that time ; as also that
the sayed Roger, shall have a convenient Lott, laied out
for his sonnes, accordinge to the vallue of 200lb. in
the proportion of Rates as they goe by themselfes ; and
that it shall be one of the first ; the publique charges
beinge borne by the sayed Lott, and proportinabley by
themselfes ; and that it shall be one of the first Lotts
that shall be Laied out. Witness our hands,

                                        ROGER LUDLOWE.

CONFIRMATION OF CAPT. PATRICK'S PURCHASE.

A true and perfect Copyie of the confirmation of the
    purchase of the meadows and lands adjoininge ly-
    ing eupon the other side of Norwake River.

Memoranda. Wheareas Aashowshack and Chachoamer, Indians, are the survivinge propriators of the Land
lyinge on the other side of Norwake River, whith sayed
Land was fullie bargained for, and sold unto Captaine
Patricke of Greenwich, and whereas the sayed Aashowshake and Chachoamer, doe testifie and affirme, with
other Indians, that their was left unpayed by the sayed
Captaine Patricke twoe Indian coates, and fowre fathom
of wampam, now these are to certifie, that I Annanupp,
Alias Parrott, so named and knowen to the English,

have by order and Appoyntment of the Aashowshake
and Chachoamer, received of Mstr. Stephen Goodier,
of new Haven, marchant, the sayed two coates, and
fowre fathom of wampam ; and doe by their order and
in their names, hereby acquitt and discharge the sayed
Mstr. Stephen Goodier, of all dues or demands or any
claims to be made by us, or any Indians what soever,
unto any farther thinge or things in or about the sayed
purchase of Lande made firmely by Captaine Patricke,
a˜d now hereby confirmed unto the sayed Mstr. Goodier,
a l his heirs, and assignes: in witness where of I the
saͿed Annanupp, Alias Parrott doe hereby sett my hand
the first day of July, 1650.

Witnesse
JOSHUA ATTWATER.   the marke [mark] of Annanupp.
THOMAS KIMBERLIE.

the marke [mark] of Anthitunn.

Memorandum. Their is a counterpart of the aforesayed written artickles and agreement and subscribed,
by Nath'n Eli and Rithd Olmested.

A COPYIE OF THE ASSIGNMENT OF NORWALKE, PURCHASED
BY MSTR LUDLOWE, UNTO NORWALKE INHABITANTS,

Aprill the 13th 1654.

Memorandum. That the sayed Roger Ludlowe, doth
by these pressentes, assigne and sett over unto Nathaniell

Eli and the rest of the Inhabitants of Norwalke, all my title, interest, claime and demands whatsoever to the plantation of Norwalke and every part thereof, and doe acknowledge my selfe satisfied for the same, Witness my hand the day and year above.

R^d LUDLOWE.

This Indenture made the 15th of February 1651, Between RUNCKINHEAGE, PIAMIKIN, and MAGISE, and TOWNTOM, and WINNAPUCKE, and MAGUSHETOWES, and CONCUSKENOW, and WAMPASUM, and SASSEAKUN, and RUNCKENUNNETT, and POKESSAKE, and SHOAKE-CUM, and SOANAMATUM, and PRODAX, and MATUMPUN, and COCKENOE-DE-Long-Island, Indians, of the one Partie, and RICHARD WEB, NATHANIEL ELI, MAT-THEWE MARVEN, senr., NATHANIEL RICHARDS, ISACKE MORE, THOMAS FITCH, THOMAS HALES, RICHARD HOLMSTED, RICHARD SEAMER, RALPH KEELER, MAT-THEW MARVEN, junior, NATHANIEL HAIES, EDWARD CHURCH, JOSEPH FITCH, Planters of Norwake, for the use and behalfe of said Town, WITNESSETH, that the said Runckinheage, and Piamikin, (&c. &c.) * * * * HAVE, and in and for the consideration of Thirtie Fathum of Wampum, Tenn Kettles, Fifteen Coates, Tenn payr of Stockings, Tenn Knifes, Tenn Hookes, Twenty Pipes, Tenn Muckes, Tenn needles, to them in

hand paid, Have, and Every of them, for themselves
and their heyers, Granted, Bargained, Sold, assigned,
Enfeoffed, and confirmed; and by these Presents doth
Bargain, grant, sell, enfeoffe, assigne, sett over, and
confirme, unto the said Richard Web, (&c. &c.) * * *
all their lands called and known by the name of Runckinheage, Rooaton, or by whatsoever name or names the
same is called or known, Lying and bounded on the
East upon yᵉ land purchased of Captain Patriarke,
so called, on the West bounded with the Brook called
Pampaskeshanke, which said Brook and pássage, the
Bounds West, Extendeth up into the Country by marked
Trees; and so far as the said Runckinheage, and the
rest above mentioned, hath any Right and proprietie;
and the aforesaid Land bounded with the Brook called
as aforesaid Pampaskeshanke, from the aforesaid passage and path down along to the Sea.   And the aforesaid Land bounded on the South with the Sea; and on
the North the Moehakes Country; with all the Islands,
Trees, pastures, meadinge, water, water courses, Rights,
members, and Appurtenances whatsoever, To Have
and to Hold, and quietly and peaceably injoy, all the
aforesaid lands, &c. * * * unto the aforesaid Richard
Web, &c. * * * * * and to their heyers forever.   And
the aforesaid Runckinheage and Piamikin, and Magise,
and Townetom, Winnepucke, Magushetowes, Conkus-
kenow, Wampasum, Sasseakun, Runckenunnutt, Pokessake, Shoakecum, Soanamatum, Prodax, Matumpun,
Cockenoe-de-Longe-Island, Do by these presents, acknowledge to have received the aforesaid Thirtie fathum
of Wampum, &c. * * * * in full satisfaction.   In
witness whereof the above said parties have for them-

selves, and every of them, sett to their hands, the day
and year above written to this present Indenture.
Signed and delivered in the presence of
STEPHEN BECKWITH,
SAMUELL LUMES,
SAMUEL ELY.

Runckin   his   heage,
        mark.

his

Piamikin,
        mark.

his

Conkus   kenoe,
        mark.

his

Sasse   a kum,
        mark.

his

Wam   passum,
        mark.

his

Sassa   kun,
        mark.

his

Magi   se,
        mark.

his

Winna   pucke,
        mark.

his

Towne   Tom,
        mark.

his

Pro   dax,
        mark.

Pokassake,

Runc   kemunutt.

Recorded February yᵉ 24th, 1708-9.
Pr. JOHN COPP, Recordr.

3

PATENT.

Whereas the Generall Court of Connecticut have formerly granted unto ye proprietors inhabitants of Norwalk, all those lands both meadow and upland, within these abutments, upon the Sea on the South, and to runn from the sea towards the north, full Twelve miles, and abut on the Wilderness on the North, and on Fairfield bounds on the East, and on Stamford bounds on the West, the said land having been by purchase or otherwise lawfully obtained by the Indian native proprietors; and whereas the proprietors Inhabitants of Norwalk have made application to the Governor and Company of the Colony of Connecticut assembled in Court May the 14, 1685, that they may have a pattent for confirmation of the aforesaid lands to them so purchased and granted to them as aforesaid, and which they have stood seized an· quietly possessed of for more than twenty years last past, without interruption; NOW, for a more full confirmation of the aforesaid Tracts of land, as it is butted and bounded aforesaid, unto the present proprietors of the Township of Norwalk,—KNOW YE that the said Governor and Company, assembled in Generall Court, according to the commission, and by virtue of the power granted to them, by our late Sovereigne LORD KING CHARLES the *Second* of Blessed memory, in his late patent bearing date the three and twentieth day of Aprill in the fourteenth year of his said majesties Reigne, Have given and granted, and by these presents do give and grant, Ratifie and Confirme, unto Mr. Thomas Fitch, Mr. Thomas Hanford, Capt. Richard Olmstead, Mr. Thomas Bennedick, Mr. Walter Hoyt, Mr. Matthew

Marven, Mr. John Ruscoe, Mr. Nathaniel Hayes, Mr.
Daniel Kellog, and Mr. Thomas Seamore, and the rest
of the present proprietors of the Township of Norwalk,
and their heirs and assigns forever, and to each of them,
in such proportion as they have already agreed upon
for the division of the same, all that aforesaid tract and
parcell of land as it is butted and bounded; together
with all the woods, upland, arable lands, meadows,
pastures, ponds, havens, ports, waters, rivers, adjoining
Islands, fishings, huntings, fowlings, mines, mineralls,
quarries, and precious stones, upon or within the said
tract of land, and all other profits and commodities
thereunto belonging, or in any wise appertaining ; AND
do also grant unto the afore named Mr. Thomas Fitch,
and Mr. Thomas Hanford, * * * * * * &c., that the
aforesaid tract of land shall be forever hereafter deemed,
and reputed, and be, an entire township of itself—To
HAVE and to HOLD the said tract of land, &c., * * * *
* * * * * * according to the tenour of his majestie's
manor of East Greenwich in the county of Kent in yᵉ
Kingdom of England, in free and common soccage, and
not in cappitee nor by Knight service ; they yielding
and paying therefore to our Sovereigne Lord the King,
his heirs and successors, only the fifth part of all the
Oar of Gold and Silver which from time to time, and
at all times hereafter shall be gotten, had, or otherwise
obtained ; in lieu of all rents, services, duties, and
demands whatsoever according to CHARTER. IN WIT-
NESS whereof, we have caused the seal of the Colony to
be hereunto affixed, this eighth day of July, 1686, in
the second year of the Reign of our Sovereigne Lord
JAMES the Second, by the grace of God, of England,

Scotland, France, and Ireland King, Defender of the Faith, &c.

ROBERT TREAT, Governor.

March 30th, 1686, pr. order of the Governor and Company of the Colony of Conecticot, signed

Pr. me JOHN ALLYN Secretary.

The above written is a true coppie of ye original, being examined and compared therewith, July 8th, 1686.

A true copie of ye Record,

ELEAZAR KIMBERLY, Secretary.

Recorded Dec. 21st, 1708,

Pr. me JOHN COPP, Recorder.

TOWN RECORDS.

EXTRACTS FROM THE TOWN RECORDS OF NORWALK.

Swine in the Planting Field.

At a meetinge 9th of May, 1653, it is agreed and ordered, that if there shall be found any swine in the*——— and planting field without youkes on, such*——— have been agreed upon formerly, that it shall*——— lawful for any inhabitant to kill any of such aforesaid swine being found in the above said woods, after the date hereof, provided the person killinge any such swine shall immediately endeavour to informe the owners of such swine, that they may take them and make meate of them ; and this order to continue untill the companie shall repeale it.

Mr. Hanford s House.

Desember the 18th, 1653, agreede by the Townsmen about Mstr. Hanford's house with Ralph Keeiler and Waltar Haite as followeth, viz. : Ralph Keeiler is to fell all the Timber, and hewe what is to hewe, and frame all. The timber to be laied by and shinckles to be laied by in*———, and he to raise the house, and to hange the shinckles with pinnes, and*——— them*——— in clay and to make the morter, and* ——— house is to be in lenth 26 feete, and bredth 16 ——— and for the saied worke, he is to have ——— in wheate at the marchants price,——— rest in current pay, and he is to finish the ——— by the 10th of Aprill next ; and the said*——— is to do all the ——— worke belonging to the ——— Frame, in such convenent time as may sute ——— Keeiler, for which worke he is to have ye ——— for which worke he is to

* Obliterated.

put it in his rates, ——— provide 800 of board, at 7s a
hundred for it im——— Uppon further consideration
the aforesaid frame is to be 31 foote in lenth, and 18
foote in bredthe, and Ralph Keeiler is to have 20 more;
and Math. Marvin, Jr. now hath undertaken to lay in
2000 of good suff——shinckles at Ralph Keeilers ready
to have at ———.

The Pound.

It was ordered and voted allso at the foresaied
meetinge, that there shall be a good and sufficient pound
or pinnefold erected and sett up, as soon as the season
will permitt; at the place where the Townsmen shall
appoynt, the saied pound to be thirtie foote square, six
foote in height, six rayles in every lenth; the sayed
rayles to be 11 foote in lenth, and the postes to be
about 10 inches square; and for the saied pound the
Towne are contented, and doe promise to pay, to any
that shall undertake to finish, sayed pound, the some
of Twoe pounds.

Memorandum : that in regard there is a convenience
to have the saied pound made and that with expedition,
—Nath. and Math. Camfield, Nath. Richards, and
Thos. Fitch have undertaken to have the saied pound
maid accordinge to the agreement.

Felling Timber.

Agreede and voted at the aforesayed meetinge, that
if there shall be any timber felled in any of the commonage belonging to the TOWN of NORWAKE ——— or
uncorded beyond the space of three mounthes, from the
date hereof, that is to say Desember 29th 1653, then it
shall be lawfull for any planter to use and carry away
the said timber as their proper owne.

Agreed and voted also that if any timber shall be found in the commonage aforesayed, lyinge and continuinge above three mounthes after it is hewen and corded, that then allso it shall be lawful and free for any inhabitant or planter to take it and carry away, as their propper owne.

Agreed and voted at the aforesaied meetinge that if any inhabitant shall fall or cause to be fallen any tree into any common cart way, and not cause said tree to be removed within the space of ——— howres, so as it to be noe annoyance to the saide cart way, that then it shall be lawful for any of the inhabitants to remove the saied tree, and — planter that did fall the saied tree ——— to the ——— that removed the tree the some of ——— in good current pay.

Burning the Woods.

And that the Townsmen shall see the woods burned in the fitting season; and of the time of burninge to give convenient notice to the inhabitants that they may secure their fences.

Town Officers in 1654.

At a meten helde by the inhabitants of Norwake on the 13 April 1654, when they maid choyce of Mr. Fitch and Goodman Moore to be townsmen for the insuen yere; at the same time they chose—Ely as constable for the ensueng yere.

Making Drains.

At a meetinge holden the 24th of Aprill, 1654, it was ordered and agreed and voted that there shall be a drain made through every man's lott in the meadows— and of the lottes in the meadows on the other side— that whenever those men that are chosen to appoynt the same, and also the breadth and depth of the same —to be made as such indifferent men chosen—appoynt; provided also that whenever the saied draines are to be made, there shall be allowance afforded to every man, in meadow, for the losse of the ground by reason of the said drains; also that the same drains are also to be kept and sustained by the owners thereof, for perpetual —as they were appoynted; and those men that are to vewe and appoyent the saied drains—Mr. Camfield, Nath. Eli, Tho. Fitch.

Allotments of Land.

Ordered allso that the allotments to beginne to be layed out as following : Videlicett to beginne—at the end of the hither plaine where John Greggory mowed the last yeare, &c.

The Mill.

Ӻ At a meetinge held the 6th of January, 1654, it was voted and agreede, that the*——— mill shall desist* ——— and not to be carryed on, and Richard Web, Tho. Fitch, Nath. Richards, shall send upon the first opportunitie to Leeiftenant Swaine, and acquaint him with the minds of the Towne concerning saied mill.

Voted, ordered, agreed, and concluded at the aforesaied meetinge, that the three undertakers of the mill in the behalfe of the Towne, with Leeiftenant Swaine, should with all convenient speed agree with the said Leciftenant Swaine for the desystinge and leavinge of the said mill, as well as they could ; and what charges the saied agreement amounted to, the said Towne would satisfy & pay.

* Obliterated.

Townsmen in 1655.

At a meetinge held the 29th of March 1655, voted and agreed that Richd. Web, and Richd. Seamer, are chosen Townsmen for the ensuinge yeare.

Agreed and voted also at the saied meetinge that Waltar Haite and Ralph Keeiler are to worke the fence for the yeere ensuinge.

Agreed and voted that Robt. Beacham is Gate Keeper for the yeere ensuinge,

The Town Herd.

At a meeting held ye 30 of May 1655, agreed and voted that all dry cattle excepting 2 yeer ould heffers shall be herded together on the other side of Norwake river ; and ther keep by the owners of the cattle; every man keping according to his proportion of cattle ther herded. It is also agreed at ye same meeting that for the lodging and wonting of ye sayed herd in the place fore named there shall be a pound erected by the first Wednesday in June, every man sending in help for ye efecting of the pound according to his proportion of cattle there herded. It is also agreed that there is* ———— to be employed in keeping the herd*———— but suficient able man. It is also agreed that whosoever, after lawfully warned, shall neglect his day in keeping, shall forfeit five shillings to ye use of the towne, and for every our that a man is defective after sun halfe an our hye, by not going forth of the towne to the keeping of his herd, he shall forfeit six pence for the town's use.

Fetching the Smith's tools from Hartford.

At the same meeting agreed and voted, by the towne of Norwake to give Matthew Camfield and Nathaniell

* Obliterated.

3*

Hayes six and twenty shillings for the fetching of the
tools pertaining to the Smith from Hartford, and is to
be payd the next rate.

The estate of lands and accommodations ———— in the hands of
as followeth [in 1655].

	£ s.		£ s.
Mstr. Hanford,	300 00	Matt. Marvin, jr.,	139 10
Nath. Eli,	293 00	Thos. Hales,	118 00
Math. Campfield,	283 10	Walter Haite,	obliterated.
Nathl. Richards,	282 00	Dan. Kellogge,	"
Rich. Web,	255 10	Nath. Haies,	"
Isacke More,	252 00	Jonath. Marsh,	"
Math. Marvin, sen.	279 00	Ralph Keeiler,	"
Sam. Hales,	250 00	John Bowton,	"
Tho. Fitch,	314 00	Richd. Homes,	"
Richd. Olmsted,	219 10	Mathew Sention,	"
Mathias Sention,		Steph. Beckwith,	"
sen.,	189 00	Thos. Seamer,	"
John Griggorie,	188 10	Thos. Lupton,	"
Robt. Beacham,	173 00	Wid. Morgan,	"
John Ruskoe,	150 00	To dispose of,	200 00
Math. Sention, jr.,	150 00		
Ralph Keeiler,	150 00	Summ total is	5475 00
Geo. Abbitt,	75 00		

Ladders provided.

At a meetinge holden the 21st of January, 1655, by
the inhabitants of Norwake, voted and agreed that
every householder shall provide, erect, and sett up a
good and sufficient ladder reaching up to the chimney
above the house, the said ladder to be made and sett
up within one mounthe after the date hereof, and that
if any householder shall be defective herein, the said

householder shall ——— of five shillings to the use of
the town.

At the same meetinge, it was fullie agreed, voted and
concluded, between the inhabitants of Norwake of the
one syde, and Waltar Haite of the other syde, that
the said Waltar Haite is to erect and sett up a good
and sufficient gate leading into the meadows of the
other side, &c. * * * *

Feb. 5, 1657.   Voted and agreed that Robt. Beacham shall enjoy and possess that parcell of lande lyinge
betweene his home lott and the Coafe Bancke, as his
owne ; being given and granted by the Towne at the
saied meetinge ; and the saied Robt. Beacham has
promised and ingaged to keepe and maintaine the gate
leadinge into the necke for the yere ensuinge.

March 5, 1657.   At the saied meetinge, Isacke
More, Matth. Sention, Mark Sention, Ed. Nash, with
consent of the Towne, have undertaken to make and
provide a good and sufficient wolfe-pitt upon the other
side in some convenient place, &c.

(1657.)   Memorandum.   That Jonathan Marsh does
ingage to build a corne mill ——— and sufficient ———

Memorandum.   That Jonathan Marsh is to have
———upland to be laied out adjoininge to the mill

At a Towne meetinge held the first day of March,
— 58, agreed with Goodman Marsh about grinding
our corne, and he hath agreed to attend the towne 3
dayes in the week, that is to say, the 2d, the 4th, and
the 6th day of the week, and these days he is to attend,
that we may have ——— to fetch and carry corne to
the mill.

The Indians.

At a Towne meetinge the 18th of Aprill, 1655, voted and ordered Leeiftenant Olmsted and Thos. Fitch are to take care and look after the Indians ———— are permitted to plant butt such as properly belongs to the towne ; that those that doe plant doe speedily make up the fence, and so allso keep it up sufficient, and allso that noe Indian ———— within a quarter of a mile of the towne.

Nails for the Meeting House.

At a Towne meetinge heild the 22d of May, '55, voted and instructed ———— the Townsmen to procuer nayles, with all speed, for the meeting house, and at as reasonable rate as they can—Towne's account. Allso, Thos. Fitch, sen. and Leeiftenant Olmsted are desired to be helpfull unto Nath. Richards in—the procuringe helpe for the making up the mill Damne.

The Cows to Pasture.

Memorandum.   The cowe keeper began to herd the cowes the second Monday in May, being the 8th or 9th day ; and the dry hearde began to be driven out by 3 men—to Rooton, that was Marke Sention, Math. Sention, and Waltar Haite ———— to be allowed 6d. a turne.

Admitting Mr. Reed.

¨ At the aforesayed meeting, voted and agreed that Math. Reed is admitted to come into the towne as an inhabitant.

Must come to Town Meetings.

Anno 1656, April 1st.   At the same meeting agreed and voted, that all the inhabitants of Norwake

shall all be present at the town meetings lawfully warned, and answer to their names, upon the forfeit of 12
pence a man, on such default; and there remayn till
the townsmen or townsman shall —— the meeting,
upon the same forfeit.

Mr. Hanford's Salary.

At a meeting held by the inhabitants of Norwalke
(1656), agreed and voted, that Mr. Handford shall
have three score pounds allowed for the yere insuing,
by them for his rate, and he is to be paid as followeth:
30 pounds in wheat, and pease, and barley, at the prices
——4 shillings per bushell for wheat and barley, and
for pease, 3 shilling per bushell. The other 30 pounds
is to be payed, 8 pounds in —— and the other 22
pounds is to be payed in beefe and pork at the common
currint prise that it brings, when it is dew.

The Meeting House.

At a meeting of the Inhabitants of Norwake, the 3d
of January (1659) agreed and voted, that there shall be
a meeting house built by the joint concurrence of the
inhabitants, 30 foot in length, and 18 foot in * * * to
be set upon posts in the ground, 12 foot in length, that
there be 10 foot distance from the ground to the ——
to the effect of the building, the inhabitants —— having engaged 48 days worke, which each is to performe
as he may be called thereunto by —— chosen and appointed by the towne—to call them forthe, provided
that the said men give warning two days at least before-
hand.

Wolf-pits.

At a meeting held on the 16th of September, 1659,
voted and agree that it shall be lawfull for any person

or persons to make any wolfe pitt or pitts in convenient places, and what wolfes shall be taken and killed by the sayed persons, they shall be allowed for every wolfe 10s. by the towne.

Clapboarding the Meeting-house.

At a meeting held the 12th of December, 1660, the towne hath agree with Mṛ. Fitch, and Goodman Richards, and John Rusco, to claboard the meeting house with inside so hy as the window; to find the bords, and to have 3*l.* 6*s.* for the doing of itt ; this worke to be don by the last of January next.

Difficulty with Fairfield.]

At a meeting held the 6th of May, 1664, voted and agreed, that the deputies made choice of to attend the general court —— are authorized by the said vote, that if they have an opportunitie to issue the difference between the Towne of Faierfield and ourselves concerninge the bounds, they are impowered to issue the same, either by agreement with them according to former propositions propounded unto them, if accepted, and if not accepted, then to issue it in the court if it may be ; and Thomas Fitch is voted to be assisting in the business, &c.

At the same meeting, voted that the Townsmen are hereby empowered to hier a man, or man and horses, at the towne charge, for the sending for Mstr. B——, and bring him again to Faierfeild, for so many times as he may be procured, while Mstr. Handford is absent.

Addition to the Meeting-house.

At the same meetinge (1664), voted and agreed, that there shall be an addition made and sett up, to the meeting-house, and that —— ende sett up and joined unto the fore part of the meetinge house, the sayed building to be in bredth 20 or 22 foote, and in lenth 16 foote at least ; and the towne engages, and every person to worke twoe days a man, if need be ; and there being appoynted Thomas Fitch, sen., and Mathew Marvin, sen., to call out so many men as they think fitt ——— to fell and cutt the timber, and allso to summon each to drawe the saied timber.

Nath. Richards buys the Mill.

At the same meetinge, the Towne doth approve and consent unto Nath. Richards of his purchasinge and buyinge of the mill and land, both upland and meadow of Jonathan Marsh ; the saied Nath. Richards being to give and pay unto Jonathan Marsh for the sayed mill and all that belonges unto the sayed mill, with the upland and meadow, being 6 akers and 2 roodes of upland lying upon the mill hill, and 3 parcells of meadow, and called Cranbury swamp, &c.

Henry Whitney's Mill.

At the sayed Meetinge (July 24th, 1665), Henry Whitney hath agreed and Ingaged with the Towne, to make, build, and erect a good and sufficient ground corne mill, and that at the mouth of Norwake River by the falles ; and that upon certain conditions, which conditions are to be fullie drawn up, by Thomas Fitch, Leeiftennant Olmsted, Mstr. Fenn, Mr. Whitinge, to confirme * * * signed by the Towne or thosse they shall depute their * * * which conditions were fully agreed upon at the sayde * * * betweene the Towne and Henry Whitney * *

Also at the sayed meetinge the Towne voted and granted unto the said Henry Whitney a Homelott, con-

sistinge of twoe akers, the sayed lott to be layed out
upon the mill plaine upon the right hand of the path
leading down to the old mill, being over the Runlett
2 or three rodd from the sayed Runlett and also from
the cart way ; and so the grant of the other Lott is relin-
quishede.

Beating the Drum.

Also (1665), Walter Haite has undertaken to beate
the drumm for meetings when all occasions required, for
which he is to have 10s. Also Tho. Bennidict has undertaken to have the meeting house swept for the yeere
ensuing ; he is to have 20s.

How to deal with the Stamford men.

It was also voted and agreed, August 26, '66, that
such men of our inhabitants as doe goe to cutt hay on
the other side five mile river, the towne will stand by
them in the action to defend them, and to beare an
equall proportion of the damage they shall sustaine upon
that account ; and if they shall be afronted by Stamford men, the towne will take as speedy a course as they
can to prosecute them by law, to recover their just
rights touching the lands in controversy ; and also they
have chosen and deputed Mr. Thomas Fitch to goe with
the sayed men when they goe to cutt or fetch away, to
make answer for and in behalfe of the towne, and the
rest to be silent.

Mending the fences.

At a towne meeting in Norwalk, March the 20th,
1667, it was voted and ordered that it shall be left to
the townsmen from yere to yere, to appoint a time or
day, at or before the 10th of March, for the securing of
the fences on both sides, and that they shall give notis

to all the inhabitants the night before ; and the drumb to be beten in the morning ; which shall be accounted sufficient warning for every man to secure his fence, or else to beare his own damage.

Fetching the Cows.

At the same meeting (Oct. 17th, 1667), voted and ordered, that after the field is cleared, the townsmen shall hier Steven Beckwith, or some other man, to fetch the cowes out of the neck; and that he that shall be hiered shall give warning by sounding a horne about twelve of the clock, that he that is to accompany him may repaier to him.

Wolves.

Also at the same meeting in Norwalk, Oct. 28, '67, it was voted and ordered, that the townsmen, for every wolfe that shall be kild in this town, eyther in pits or otherwise, the head or eares being brought and shewed, after this present day till the town rates are made for the defraying such charges, shall have twenty shillings for every such wolfe.

Training.

At a meeting of the inhabitants of Norwalke, May the 7th, 1668 ; being met together upon an occasion of trayning, and having some other business to transact touching towne officers, did unanimously agree, that what orders should be made and concluded of at the aforesayed meeting, should stand in as full forse as if it had bin legally warned.

Keeping the Young People still in Meeting.

At a meeting of the inhabitants of Norwalk, July the 13 : '68, Tho. Lupton was chosen to look after the young people in the meting house on the Lord's day,

and to doe his best indevor to kepe them from playing
and unsivill behavor in time of publik worship.

The Herdsmen.

At a towne meeting in Norwalk, March the 16, 1668,
it was voted and agreed, that there shall be two herdsmen hired, one to keep the dry heard and the other to
keep the milch heard for this whole somer.

At the same meeting it was voted and agreed that
Steven Beckwith is to keep the milch heard this somer,
and is to have twelve shillings a week for his paynes;
and half a pound of butter for every cow as part of his
pay, and the rest in wheat, pease, indian corn, at 4s. 6d. ;
3s. 6d, and eight groats pr bushell.

Difficulty with Stamford.

Sept. 30, 1668.   Voted and ordered that the deputies that ar chosen to goe to the court in October next,
shall doe there best indevor that the diferance betwen
Stamford and Norwalk may be brought to an issue.

At the same meeting it was voted and ordered that it
shall be left to the towns men to send a letter to Stamford to signifie the towns intension about the difference of
Bounds.

Making a fence for a winter wheat-field, Anno 1668.

Dec. 4, 1668.   It was agreed and concluded that a
fence shall be made and sett up for yᵉ taking in of a
winter wheat field, which sayd fence is to begin at the
gate by goodman Nash his house, and to Run along by
the highway that goes to stony hill, and to end at the
creck that comes in between Matthue Camfield his Island, and Nathaniell Richards out meddow, which fence
is to be made good sufitient fence ; cyther postes and

Rayls, or stones or logs ; but not hegg ; and this to be
finished by the last of September next ensueing, and to
be layed out and divided by Mr. Fitch, Daniell Kellogg,
and Christopher Comstok ; and also it was concluded
that the first lott should begin at the gate ; which first
lott was drawn by

1. Matthew Marvin, sr.	16. Christopher Comstok,
2. Samuel Sension,	17. Mr. Fitch,
3. Robert Stewart,	18. Nathl. Hayes,
4. Samuel Camfield,	19. John Gregory, sen.,
5. Tho. Lupton,	20. Mark Sension,
6. Tho. Fitch,	21. John Raymond,
7. Tho. Seamer,	22. Widdow Webb,
8. Edward Nash,	23. Matthew Marvin, junr.
9. Mr. Hanford,	24. Nathl Richards,
10. Matthias Sension,	25. Richard Olmstead,
11. Tho. Bennydick,	26. John Bouton,
12. George Abbet,	27. John Gregory, junr.,
13. Walter Hayte,	28. John Platt,
14. Tho. Betts,	29. John Ruscoe,
15. Daniell Kellog,	30. Richard Wholms,

31. Matthias Sension, junr.

Ralph Keeler did promise and ingage to fence forty
Rodd of the aforesayd fence provided that he may sett
it up against his own land.

Ash House.

At a towne meting in Norwalk, January the 22d, '69,
it was voted and granted that Thomas Oviet of Milford
shall have liberty to set a house by the water side before
John Gregory's, senr., to put ashes in.

The Indians.

At the same meeting it was voted that Mr. Fitch,

and Matthew Marvin, junior, are desired and apointed, ,
and it is left to their discretion, to treat with the In- -
dians touching the lands between the West branch of *
Norwalk river and Saketuk river; to git it to be marked *
out and bounded twelve miles up the contery at the *
least, and that it may be dun and finished according to .
law, and being so bounded and marked, the Indians are *
to have their 4 coates.

Four Coats to Mamachimon.

Dec. 25, 1669. Voted and concluded that Mamachimon shall have fowre cotes paid to him by the *
towne, when he shall have settled the bounds of the land *
up the country, 12 miles at the leaste, against all claims
whatsoever.

Undivided Lands.

At the same meeting voted and agreed that all the
lands within the bounds of Norwalk that are at present
undivided, shall for futor be divided onley to such as are *
the present proper Inhabitants of this towne, according
to estate given in, only excepting ye division of six acors
the 100 to home lots already granted.

At the same town meeting voted and ordered, that
until such time as ye Indian fence be made up so as to
serve the feild, their shall not any of our inhabitants let
any Indian have any parte of his property neither less
or more to plant upon, eyther on this side or the other,
upon the penalty of 20ƒ an acre so sett; and so propor-
sionaly for every greter or lesser quantity; and the same
order to stand in force against any person that shall
either hier or exchang any land of the Indians for the
futor; and this to stand in force from yere to yere until
it be repealed.

At the same meeting it was voted and ordered that

the corne feilds on both sides ar to be layd in by the
next thirsday com senit, and the fences to be made up
sufficient.

Indian Land.

At the same meeting it was voted and ordered that no
person or persons whatsoever inhabiting in this towne
shall for futor improve any land of the Indians within
the indian feild eyther by hiring, or exchanging gifts,
or any other way, under the penalty of twenty shillings
an acor yerly, for every acor so improved, and so for
every greator or lesser quantity.

At a towne meting in Norwalk, Aprill the 12th, 1670,
it was voted and agreed that the order yt was made
March 15th, '69, to prohibit exchanging of lands with
the Indians, shall be suspended for the next somer, &
that any that have a mind to exchange with them may
soe do ; but not to hold it any longer than the next
Indian harvest, and then the aforesaid order to stand in
as full forse as before.

Boundaries.

At a town meting in Norwalk, June the first, 1670, it
was voted and ordered that Licutent Olmsted and John
Gregory, senr. ar to be joyned with Mr. Fitch and
Mathu Marvin Jun. to git the bounds marked out between Norwalk river and Saketuk river as is expressed
in a former order ; and being so done to such satisfaction as their is exprest in that former order, the Indians
are to receive six cotes at the town's charg.

Treating with Stamford.

At the same meeting voted and agreed that Mr. Fitch
and leuetent Olmsted and Daniel Kellogg are chosen a
commitee to goe to Stanford to treat with the inhabitants

their, to se if they and we can come to a loving and
neighborly issue and agreement, about the division of
bounds betwixt them and us ; and the said committee
is to make these propositions to the men of Stanford,
eyther to divide betwixt five mile river and pine brook ;
that is to say in the middle betwin both ; or else to divide in the middle betwin Saketuk River and the bounds
betwin Stanford and Greenwig.

John Gregory.

At the same meting it was voted and concluded that
their shall be two men chosen to prosecute the case
against John Gregorie, senior, as touching the lands he
howlds from the right of James the Indian, eyther by law
or otherwise, as that they may howld and maintaine
the rights which the town ———— or any other land
which he claims in the like natuer, as the island called
Cokkanus Island.

Town Officers in 1670.

At the same meting [Feb. the 21, 1670] Matthu
Marvin, Junior, chosen to swepe the meating house, and
to have 20s for his pains, and Walter Hayte chosen to
beate the drume, and to have 10s for the sayd imployment; Tho. Bennydick senr. chosen towne clerk, and to
have 20s for his pains ; Mr. Fitch & John Bouton chosen
survaiors, Leuten¹ Olmsted, Ensign Tho. Fitch, Nathaniell Richards, Daniell Kellogg & Tho. Bennydick,
senr. chosen celect men.

The Guard.

At the aforesayed meting it was voted and ordered
that it shall be left to the five men, to procure a hand-
some and convenient seate made and sett up in the meting house, for a garde to sitt in, in the most suitable
place, with all such conveniances for their Arms as they

shall jug necessary, and the charg to be borne by the towne.

Burning the Woods.

At the same meeting voted and agreed, that the townsmen shall hier a man to burn the woods, onely they shall not give above 12s for that cervice.

Cover over Mr. Hanford's Desk.

At a town meeting in Norwalk November 17th, 1670, it was voted and agreed that there shall be a man or men hired to make a comely and convenient cover over Mr. Hanford's desk, in the meting house, at the town's charge.

The Bridge.

At the aforesayd meeting [Jan. the 1st, 1671] it was voted and agreed on that there shall be a bridg made over Norwalk river ; the charg shall be born according to the list of estates then in being of every inhabitant in the town of Norwalk.

At the same meting voted that it shall be left to the select men in this town, to improve their best skill to see what will be contributed by the severall towns adjacent towards the building of a bridg over Norwalk river; it was further voted that the select men shall send to serjent Andrues of Newhaven, to git him to come over to give us advise about the bridg, & the town will bear the charg of his coming and going.

Recompense for bad coats to Mamachimon.

Feb. 9th, 1671.   Voted and agreed that inasmuch as Mr. Fitch have given a rate to Mamachimon to make him a recompense for the badness of the former coats he received, that the prise of it shall be put into this town rate that now is to be made.

Division of land, and laying out Home-lots.

At the same meeting voted and agreed that Nath. Hays & Tho. Fitch, Junr, shall fall in with the rest of the inhabitants in the last devision that was agreed on to be layed out, notwithstanding their former gratuety; onely they are to take it up in the woods, becase they have received already in the neck.

(John Platt & Thomas Bennydick, senr. were to lay out the last division, according to the grant; and also to lay out the home-lots.)

It was voted and agreed that only the proper inhabitants that are now in being shall have a home lott, and all such shall Injoy one according to a former order.

Agreed on that all those men that now draw lots with their neighbors, shall stand to their lotts that now they draw.

Agreed on that the first lot shall begin at the hether end of Drye Hill, as soon as the hill shall be found capable of lotting, by those that are to laye out the lotts, and on this side the hill by the path that goes to Cramberry plain, and so back againe on the other side of the hill homward, & so all the rest of the land in that order.

Agreed that those that do not draw lots with the rest of their neighbors shall take them up with their devision of six acors to the hundred; if it be their to be had; if not, then they shall fall in with their neighbors whear they shall end, or at the side of them, whear it shall be most convenient.

Further agreed that it shall be left to the 3 men that are to lay out the lotts, that they shall size them so as they may be made most equall, according to their best discression.

The Estates of lands & Accommodations of ye town of Norwalk.

IMPRIMIS:

	£					
John Gregory, senr.,	253	10	0	George Abbet,	075	00	0
Nath. Hayes,	115	00	0	Walter Hayte,	192	00	0
Tho. Lupton,	070	00	0	Mathias Sension,	145	00	0
Richd Holmes,	150	00	0	Ralph Keiler,	053	10	0
John Ruscoe,	150	00	0	Samuel Hayes,	100	00	0
Mr. Hanford,	300	00	0	John Hayte,	100	00	0
Tho. Bennydick, sea.,	150	00	0	Tho. Betts,	146	10	0
John Bouton,	100	00	0	Sam. Bennydick,	050	00	0
John Bennydick, jr.,	150	00	0	Ephraim Lockwood,	070	00	0
Daniel Kellogg,	125	00	0	Tho. Fitch, jr.,	150	00	0
Math. Marvin, junr.,	139	10	0	John Platt,	168	13	4
Mr. Tho. Fitch, sen.,	314	00	0	Samuel Sension,	100	00	0
Nath. Richards,	268	00	0	Robbart Steward,	200	00	0
Mark Sension,	252	00	0	Jonathan Pirkins,	10	00	0
James Sension,	175	00	0	James Picket,	10	00	0
Mathu Marvin, sen.,	169	00	0	Samuel Keiler,	53	10	0
Thomas Gregory,	50	00	0	Peter Lupton,	50	00	0
John Olmsted,	50	00	0	Frances Bushnell.	10	00	0
Andrew Messenger,	25	00	0	James Olmsted,	50	00	0
Saml. Camfield,	233	00	0	James Bennydick,	37	00	0
Richard Olmsted,	119	10	0	Danl. Bennydick,	36	00	0
Christopher Comstock,	146	10	0	Joseph Gregory,	50	00	0
Tho. Seamer,	100	00	0	John Nash,	50	00	0
Widdow Webb,	255	00	0	Tho. Hiet,	5	00	0
John Raymond,	150	00	0	Steven Beckwith,	5	00	0
Edward Nash,	166	10	0	John Crampton,	3	6	8
John Keiler,	050	00	0	James Miller,	80	00	0
John Gregory, jr.,	50	00	0	Thos. Barnum,	40	00	0
Judah Gregory,	50	00	0	Thos. Betts, jr.,	10	00	0
Jakin Gregory,	50	00	0	John Belding,	3	00	0
Thomas Tayler,	55	00	0	William Lees,	3	00	0
Samuell Smith,	70	00	0	Saml. Belding,	3	00	0

Estate for the Children.

At the aforesaid meeting voted and agreed on, that every one of our inhabitants that have not as yet had any estate for their childring, shall have five pounds for every childe now in being ; to be added to their father's estate, & this is to take place in the land that is now to be layed out in ye Indian feild, and not before.

Tavernkeeper.

At the same meeting Christopher Comstock was chosen

4

and approved of to kepe an ordinary for the entertayning of strangers.

Chesnut Hill.

At the aforesayed meeting, March 19th, 1671, it was
voted and agreed on that Chesnut Hill is to be resarved
for a feild for the Indians, if need be, and if they shall
except of it.

˙Cockenoes Island.

Allsoe at the same meeting [Feb. 20th, 1672], it was
voted & agreed on that the sayd Island called Cockenoe,
is to lye common for the use of the towne as the other
Islands doe.

The Children of the Town.

John Gregory, Jr. have		Tho. Bennydick, Jr.,	2
childring	3	Daniel Kellogg,	6
John Gregory, Sr.,	1	Math. Marvin, Jr.,	6
Nath. Hayes,	7	Geo. Abbot,	7
Tho. Lupton,	2	Maths. Sension,	7
Rich. Holms,	2	Keilers,	3
John Ruscoe,	5	Samuel Hayes,	1
Mr. Hanford,	6	Jachin Gregory,	2
Tho. Bennydick, Sr.,	6	Tho. Tayler,	2
John Bouton,	5	Judah Gregory,	3
John Hayte, ⸺	1	Samuel Camfild,	1
Thos. Betts,	8	Tho. Fitch, Jun.,	4
Ephraim Lockwood,	3	Tho. Seamer,	7
John Platt,	3	John Raymond,	1
Samuell Sension,	2	Edward Nash,	2
Robbart Steward,	5		

The soldiers in the Indian war.

At a Town meetinge January the 12th, 1676, the
Towne in consideration of the good service that the

souldiers sent out of the towne ingaged and performed
by them in the Indian warr, out of respect and thank-
fulnesse to the sayed souldiers, doe with one consent
and freely, give and grant unto so many souldiers
as were in the service at the direful swamp fight,*
twelve acors of land ; and eight acors of land to
so many souldiers as were in the next considerable service ; and fowre acors to those souldiers as were in the
next considerable service ; the sayed souldiers having
libertie to take up the sayed granted lands within the
bounds of the town, provided that it be not upon those
lands that are prohibited, and also such lands as are
pitched upon before the date hereof by the proprietors or
proprietor ; provided also the sayd grant is only to such
souldiers as shall within one yeere, and possess and improve the sayd lands.

John Roach, a soldier in the "direful swamp fight."

Whereas the towne of Norwalke having given and
granted unto John Roach as a gratuety being a souldier
in the late Indian war, the parcell of land, consistinge
of twelve acres more or less, layed out upon the West
side of the West Rocks so called, &c.

Daniel Benedict, a soldier in the swamp fight.

Granted by the plantation unto Daniel Benedict as a
gratuity, being a souldier in the Indian warr, twelfe
acres of land, and lyeth in three parcels ; whereof one
parcell lyeth upon the hill and plaine of the other side
of Norwalke River, not far distant from the West side
of the cart path leading to the meadow field &c.   Feb.
16, 1677.

Thos. Gregory, a soldier in the Indian war.

Granted by the plantation unto Thos. Gregory as a
gratuety, being a souldier in the Indian warr, eight
acres of land, and lyeth in two parcells, the first parcell

* See page 66.

lying upon the West Rocks, containing six acres, &c. Feb. 25, 1677.

Thomas Hyatt, a soldier in the Indian war.

Feb. 19, 1682. The Towne granted unto Thomas Hyatt, libertie to resign seven acres of land which the town hath formerly granted him respecting as he was a souldier in the Indian warres, and he had taken up the same upon Clapboard Hill, soo called; namely to resign the same up to the towne, so as to take it up elsewhere.

Joseph Platt, a soldier.

Feb. 21, 1698. Granted unto Joseph Platt, as he was a souldier out in the service against the common enemie, the Town, as a gratification for his good service, do give and grant unto him ten Acres of land, to take it up a mile from the town, and wheare it lyes free not yet pitcht upon by any other persons.

Jonathan Abbot, a soldier.

Allso granted unto Jonathan Abitt as he was a souldier, ten Acres of land, to be taken up whear it lyes free not yet pitched on by any persons.

For a man sent out to the warres.

Feb. 21, 1698. The town granted to James Betts, as he sent out a man into the warres, and was at charge and expense of money on account of hireing; the towne does grant unto the sayd James, five acres of land, &c.

Saml. Keeler, a soldier in the swamp fight.

Granted by the plantation of Norwalke, unto Saml. Keeler, with respect to his service, as he was a souldier in the late Indian warr, one parcell of land lying upon Clapboard Hill, so called, containing twelfe acres more or less; and lyeth bounded East and West the com-

mon, North Tho. Hyatt Land, South Ebenezer Sention Land. Recorded May, 1681.

John Crampton, a soldier in the Indian war.

John Crampton hath granted him by the towne as he
was a Souldier in the late Indian warr, two Roodes of
land more or less, and lyeth bounded in the East by the
high way, West Saml. Bennydict's home lott, North Tho.
Betts house lott, South, James Miller's house lott.

John Crampton hath granted him by the towne, as
he was a souldier in the late Indian warr, eight acres
foure roodes of land, more or less, and lyeth upon the
est branch of Norwak River, not far distant from that
meadow called Webbs meadow &c.

James Jupp, a soldier in the Indian war.

James Jupp hath granted him by the towne, as he
was a souldier in the late Indian warr, eight acres of
land, and lying upon the hill called Clapboard Hill, &c.

John Belding, a souldier.

Dec. 12, 1676.   Granted unto John Belding the remainder of the swamp that shall be left, when his
Father Hales is laid out, and to be a part of the land
that he is to have for his being a souldier.

Jonathan Stevenson, a souldier in the direful swamp fight.

Feb. 20, 1677.   Granted by towne vote unto Jonathan Stevenson libberty to take up 4 acres of his
twelve acres given him by the town for his being a souldier ; and that against Tho. Hiet's home lot, on the
East side of the aforesaid Hiet, joyning unto him ;
onely due care is to be taken by them that lay it out,
that the towne be not deprived of the benefit of the
springs for their cattel in the winter season.

"THE DIREFUL SWAMP FIGHT." [See p. 63.]

[This was in king Philip's war. After some successes
of Philip, there was a general rising of the Indians
against the English, for an extent of nearly three hundred miles. The Indians were perfectly acquainted
with the situation of every English settlement. They
lurked at every unguarded pass—crept by night into
their barns, gardens, and out-houses—concealed themselves behind fences—laid in wait in the fields. The
whole country, save some few towns, was a wilderness.
Parties of Indians would plunder and burn a town, carry
the inhabitants away captive, and then retire into the
forests and swamps. Brookfield had been burnt; Hadley, Deerfield, and Northfield had been attacked, and
numbers killed : Captain Lathrop and ninety or a hundred men had been ambushed and slaughtered between
Hadley and Deerfield. Springfield had been attacked
and partly destroyed. The Narragansetts, who had
made a treaty with the English, now harbored their enemies ; and many of their warriors, after having been
engaged in these marauding expeditions, had returned
wounded. There was the clearest evidence that the
Narragansetts were preparing to join openly in the war.
They could muster two thousand warriors, and had a
thousand muskets. Should the Indians all engage in
the spring, in such a warfare as they had hitherto carried on, there was scarcely any hope, but that nearly all
the English settlements must be cut off in detail, without the possibility of successful resistance.

It was therefore determined to attack them in the
winter, though such an enterprise was full of hazard.
Should any disaster befall the troops of the colonies, it
might be difficult or impossible to send them succors or

supplies, on account of the deep and pathless snows,
and the exposures of the winter and the wilderness, besides the danger from the Indians. But dreadful necessity compelled them to make the attempt.

Massachusetts furnished 527 men, Plymouth 158,
and Connecticut 300 men, and 150 Mohegan and Pequot
Indians. The Connecticut troops had marched from
Stonington to Pettysquamscot. Here they expected
shelter, but the Indians had burned the buildings and
killed the inhabitants only a day or two before. This
was on the 17th December. The weather was cold and
stormy. The next day they marched, and formed a
junction with the Massachusetts and Plymouth forces.
Here again they were obliged to spend the night un-
covered in the open field. The next morning, at break
of day, the army marched towards the Narragansett
fort, which was in a deep tangled swamp, fifteen miles
distant. The snow was deep, and the weather extreme-
ly cold. At one o'clock they reached the enemy's fort.
It was on rising ground, in the midst of the swamp,
surrounded with palisades, and, outside of these, with
a hedge of brush a rod thick. The only entrance
which appeared practicable, was over a log which lay
five or six feet from the ground; and this entrance was
defended in front by a fortress of logs, " and on the
left by a flanker." The Massachusetts troops, who
were in front, mounted the log and rushed on. A few
entered the fort. The fire from the loghouse and
flanker was so hot, that a sufficient number could not
force their way through to support them, and those who
had entered were cut down. The deep snow, and the
tangled thicket, rendered it impossible for the whole
body of troops to come up at once ; and it was a considerable time before all could be brought into action.

At length, the Connecticut troops, who formed the rear, mounted over the log and rushed into the fort. Some others forced their way to the opposite side of the fort, and succeeded in making good their entrance, while the attention of the enemy was engaged in front. A long, bloody, and dubious conflict ensued; but the enemy were at length overcome; and what were not killed in the battle fled to the swamp. Three hundred Indian warriors perished on the spot. Many were wounded, and perished from their wounds and from the cold. Nearly the same number were taken prisoners. It was a dreadful day.

The victory was dearly bought. Six captains fell in the action, and eighty men were killed or mortally wounded. One hundred and fifty were wounded, who afterwards recovered. After burning the fort, and all that it contained, the little army, just at the setting of the sun, carrying about two hundred dead and wounded, marched ⸢back to their head-quarters. The night was cold and stormy. It was midnight before they got in. None could have their wounds dressed till they reached their head-quarters. Many died, who might otherwise have recovered. Many perished with cold and fatigue. Well might the fathers of this town call it " *The direful swamp fight.*"]

The Watch.

At a towne meeting November y⁰ 9, 1677, it was agreed that yᵉ watch should be laied down, until such time as there is more danger apering; and that we will stand by yᵉ constable if any trubble should arise upon that account.

The Miller.

At yᵉ aforesaid meeting, it was voted and agreed on between the towne and the miller, John Whitne, that the

townsmen are to carry their corne to the mill upon the
third and sixt days of the weak, comonly called tus-
day & friday ; which days he is to attend to grindin,
& if the sayd John can clere the mill of the corne that
is brought in the aforesaid two days or before, then the
rest of the days of the week he may take to attend to
his own occasions ; but if he cannot clere the mill of
the corne then seasonably brought in, he must clere it
before he leaves.

Saw Mill.

Also at y⁰ same meeting, granted unto Richard
Holms liberty to erect, set up, and improve a saw mill
upon five mile river, and liberty for timber one mile on
this side of yᶜ sayd river ; onlly the sayd Richard is not
to pass over y⁰ sayd grant to any but such as the town
shall approve of; this saw mill is to be set up &
finished within two yers after this date, or else it is
forfit ; and the said Richard is to sell his boards and
planks to the townsmen as the doe at other towns to
their neighbors, and whear their are saw mils.

The School.

At a towne meting May the 29th, 1678, voted and
agreed to hier a scole master to teach all the childring
in the towne to lerne to Rede and write ; & that Mr.
Cornish shall be hierd for that cervice, & the townsmen are to hier him upon as reasonable terms as they
can.

New Meeting House.

At a towne meeting Desember 17, 1678, it was voted
and agreed that the towne will leave the diference
about where the meting house shall stand that is now to
be erected, to three honest indiferent judisious men ;

4*

and they are to vew the places in controversy, and to
hear all Resons & arguments on both sides, & the
towne ingages to sit down satisfied with there detar-
mination, as to the place of its standing.

And further it was voted and agreed, that the honered
deputy Governor, the honered Major Goold, with the
Reverend Elder Buckingham, shall be the men that the
towne shall put this matter of difference too, respecting
the place whear the meting house shall stand. At the
same meeting voted and agreed, that the meting house
that is to be erected shall be forty foote square, &
sixtene foote betwin joynts, & the Rofe of the sayed
house to be built after the manner of Faierfild meting
house.

Tavern Keeper.

At the same meting, Mathias Sention was chosen to
keep an ordinary for the entertayning strangers, &c.

Meeting House Committee.

Also voted and agreed (Jan. 31st, 1678), that the
six men that were formerly choosin to oversee the work
aboute the meting house as a commite for that cervice,
should now be named and recorded; that is to say, Mr.
Fitch, senr., Thos. Bennydick, senr., Nathaniel Hayes,
John Bouton, John Platt, Thos. Fitch, junr.

Building the Meeting House.

At the sayd meting, the towne by a vote doe give
and grant unto the above sayd commite full power to
let out the said meting house that is to be erected,
according to their best discression; & the dimensions
formerly agreed on; as may best advantage the sayd
work; and in the same to have respect to the inhabitants for to improve them, both hands and carts, as

they are capable of, so as may best advantage the work. And allso to set a prise of their work by the day, eyther in the labor of a man, or carting. Allso provided that what hands or carts are warned out to the work, & shall not attend to the work, having two days warning, by the committee or any one of them by appointment from the rest, the laboring man shall forfeit two shillings by the day, and a temo fower shillings; and what charges shall arise upon the sayd work, the town ingages to discharge it by way of rate.

Allso at y⁵ said meeting it was voted and agreed that it shall be left to the commite that is to overse the work, to take the next convenient seson to send for the Jentlemen yᵗ is chosen to put an end to our diferences about the meting house, & to take care for their comfortable and honorable entertainment; and what chargis shall be expendid aboute it shall be defrayed by the towne.

Beating the Drum.

At a towne meting—February y⁵ 18, 1678, ———— Robbart Stuard ingages yᵗ his son James shall beate the drumb on the Sabbath and on other ocations; is to have it for that cervice.

Working at the Meeting House.

At a towne meetting held at Norwalk March 4th, 1678 or '79, it was voted that the Comitty Chosen By the Town, viz.: Mr. Fitch, Thomas Bennydick, senr., Nathaniell Hayes, John Bouton, John Platt, Thomas Fitch, junior, should goe on with the worke Comitted to them, in refferance to the meeting house, and to goe on with the worke forthwith, according to their best Discression.

Cedar Shingles.

At the aforesayed meeting it was voted and agreed that the Comittee shall and may gett or procure Ceader shingles for the Meeting House, if they can be procured upon Reasonable tearmes.

Site of the Old Meeting House.

At the afore said meeting (23 April, 1679), it was voted and agreed by the inhabitants of the town of Norwalk, that all the common land commonly known and called and improved for a meeting house yard, wheare the old meeting house now standeth, Bounded on the south by Mr. Hanford's Lott, on the North with Mathew Marvin, senior's Lott, on the east with Thomas Seamer's Lott, on the West with 'Mathew Marvin, Junior's Lott, shall, as at this present it is, for ever be improved for that end and use; namely of setting up a meeting house there; unless that every particular proper Inhabitant shall freely consent to any other improvement thereof.

At the same Meeting it was allso voated and agreed by the towne that all that Common Land, commonly known and called Goodman Hoyt's hill; every part and parcel of it, shall, as heartofore, forever for the future, be common, and not be improved to any other use; unless it be for the setting up of a watch house there; without the consent and approbation of every Individual proper Inhabitant.

Meeting House Committee.

At the same meeting it was voted and agreed by the towne that Daniel Kellogg shall be joyned with the comittee in the acting and transacting of the business and worke committed to them in carrying on of the worke of the meeting house, according to the former order of the towne in that case.

The Committee strengthened.

At a Towne meeting October the 4th, 1679, it was voted and agreed that there shall be suitable persons chosen to strengthen the committee to carry on the worke of the new meeting house.

At the aforesayd meeting, October 4th, 1679, voted and agreed, that ——— Haite and Robbart Stewart are added unto the committee ——————— as committee men for the carrying on the worke of the new meeting house, and to have equall power with the rest of the committee that was formerly chosen for the aforesayd worke.

Stray Horses.

At the aforesayd meeting, the town did Declare and manifest they would stand by the act of the select men in the act of selling the stray horses for the use and bennefitt of the Towne. At the aforesayd Meeting it was agreed and voted, that the Money for the stray horses souled, shall be improved for to Defray Townes Charges; and the overplus to remaine in the Treasurer's hand for the use of the Towne.

Warning to Town Meetings.

At the aforesayd meeting, it was voted and agreed that if the select men shall be necessitated to send to Peter Clapum to warne him to meetings, those that are sent shall be allowed one shilling for every warning.

At the aforesayd meeting it was voted and agreed that the Towne would stand by Samuell Smith Towne Treasurer, in case of need, to straine any that either neglect or refuse to pay.

The Watch.

At the sayd meeting (Feb. 20, 1679) the Towne engageth to bare the Constable harmless from any damage

in forbareing the watch until such time as ye constable
with ye select men shall see cause for to sett up a watch.

Pounds.

At the sayd meeting it was voted that those pounds
as are now erected within the Bounds of Norwalk, shall
returne to the towne.

At the aforesayd meeting it was voted and agreed
that there shall be noe pound or pounds either begun
or perfected for that end, for to catch horses, within the
bounds of Norwalk, on the pennalty of 20s a weeke, soe
long as they are soe improved, without the approbation
of the towne.

Marking Colts.

At the aforesayd meeting it was voted and agreed that
Jachīn Gregory, John Hayt, John Keeler, and Joseph
Gregory shall be the masters or overseers of those
pounds lieing by five mile river side, who are to be sworne
to a faithfull performance of the trust committed to
them ; who are to mark all colts and yeerlings as they
apprehend belong to the owners of such mares as shall
be brought in, with their owners markes, and also they
are to bring in all such strays, or unmarked horses, as
they shall take in those pounds, unto the towne.

Unmarked Horses.

At the afforesayd meeting it was voted and agreed
that all unmarked horses, as either have been sould or
shall be for the future sould, the one half of the prices
for which they are sould for, shall be to those by whom
they are taken; the other half of the price to the use
and benefitt of the towne ; and none of those horses that
are taken, are to be any way marked or disposed of out
of the pound without the approbation of the Master or
masters of the pound, on the pennalty of the forfeiture of
twenty shillings.

Determining the place for the New Meeting House

At a towne meeting held the 3d of May, 1679, there was a writing Presented by Mr. Thomas Fitch, senr., and Thomas Fitch, Junr, unto the towne to be read; and was read; which they did say and affirm was the award and determination of the Gentlemen, namely, Major Treat and Major Gold, Respecting the place for the setting up of the new meeting house.

At a towne meeting held at Norwalke June the 2d, 1680, voted and agreed by the towne that they doe close in with, and accept of, the act of the Generall Court in refference to a lott for the settlement of the place of the new meeting house.

At the afforesayd Meeting, agreed and voted that the towne will choose some honest, Judicious, Indifferant men, for to see this act of the Generall Court, in refference to a lott for the settlement of the place of the meeting house put into execution; and it is also left to the select men to procure those men; and the time when the matter shall be put in execution in case of need.

Bridge.

At the afforesayd meeting (December the 28th, 1680), John Whittney, James Pickett, Thomas Bennidick, Junior, were chosen a committee to determin the place of erecting a Bridge over Norwalk River; they or any two of them concurring as to the place, whither at the great rock below the lower cart path; or Below the falls; and the abovesayed committee have power to call forth and improve hands and teames for the carrying on and finishing the sayed Bridge: viz. a sufficient horse bridge; and that with as much expedition as may be convenient.

Beating the Drum.

Zerubbabell Haite hath undertaken to beate the drumne for publick meetings, and also for such stray horses as are brought in to be sould, for which he is to have fourteen shillings ; and ten pence a time that stray horses are brought in to be sould.

Town Drum [1681.]

At the aforesayed meetinge, the towne by voate ordereth the select men to purchas of Francis Bushnell a drum for the towne's use ; and also the Traine band to have the use of the same a convenient time, untill the said companie shall procuer one ; and provided the sayd drum can be procured upon Reasonable Tearmes.

Removing the Desk and Seats of the old Meeting House to the new one.—Beginning to meet in the new Meeting House.

At a Towne meeting in Norwalk, held the 8th of November, 1681, the Towne agreed and voted with a unanimous consent, that with all convenient speede, the committee for the new meeting house have power to, and are desired and ordered, with the help of such inhabitants as at the present meeting engaged one day's worke upon —— to remove the deske, and seates, and plankes of the ould meeting house to the new meeting house, and theeir to fix them as well as the same will accomodate the sayd new meeting house ; and the Towne for the future to meet in the sayd new meeting house, to weight upon the Lord in his divine publique worshippe as opportunitie presents.

Keeping Order in Meeting in the year 1681.

Thomas Barnum was chosen and appoynted, for to oversee and to keep good Decorum amongst the youth in times of exercise on the Sabbath and other Publique meetings; and the Towne doe impower him if he see any disorderly, for to keep a small stick to correct such with; oneley he is Desired to doe it with clemency; and if any are incoridgable in such disorder, he is to present them either to their parents or masters; and if they do not reclaime them, then to present such to authority.

Attending Town Meetings.

At the same meeting it was voted and agreed by the towne, that all persons that are members of Towne Meetings, that shall neglect to attend meetings when they are legally warned, within one houre after the time prefixed by those that warne them, they shall pay one shilling as a fyne, &c.

Fining the Majority for unlawful acts.

At the same meeting it was voted by the towne that all that land yett lying in Common; namely a full mile out round from the corner of Richard Olmsted's common fence and a mile out round from the house of William Lees, the sayd land to ly for ever in Common; and if the Major part of the towne shall give, grant, or sell any land now soe lying in common within the sayd limits, they shall pay five shillings a rod, for every rod so given or sould, and so proportionably, for any other quantitie, they shall pay it to the Minor part of the towne.

At the same meeting it was voted and agreed by the Towne, that there shall be a division of six acres to the hundred granted to all the inhabitants, without the limits of the mile excepted in the former order; to take it up where they can find it; provided they are not to prejudice any highway into the woods or to men's peculiar proprieties already taken up; only those as have a former grant of land and have not yett taken it up, they have a month's time to pitch where they can find it, beyond the limitts before expressed; viz. a mile, and then this order to take place.

Selling the Old Meeting House.

Feb. 19, 1683. The Towne voted to make sale of the old Meeting House; and forthwith at the sayd meeting the Towne sould the sayd house unto Josiah Gregorie for the some of fowre pounds, to be payd to them in one yeere, in currant marchantable pay, for the use of the towne.

New Seats in the New Meeting House.

At the aforesaid meeting, the towne voated to have the meeting house seated more comfortable seates, according to the forme the seats are at the present; much as to the same manner, both for order and forme.

At the aforesaid meeting, the town voated the former committee that were improved to finish the meeting house, as now to goe on to new seating the sayd house compleatly and sufficiently, according to their discretion; the forme of the same above sayed being described; giving and granting unto the sayd committe full power to improve the inhabitants, their persons, and Teemes to carry on the worke, and to procuer materialls where it may best be had; and to make rates for the defraying the charge.

Sending a man to Hartford.

Desember the 16th, 1684. The Towne voted and agreed to improve Samuel Hayes with as much convenient speed as may be to travell up to Hartford ———

what light and guidance may be had ——— counsell about ——— lands that is in controversy between the Towne and Fairfield, &c.

A Cattelog of a division of land agreed to be layd out at three acors to the hundred; with the severall lotts as they were drawn by the inhabitants.

		Mark Sension,	21
Imprimis :			
Robbart Steward,	1	Samuel Hayes,	22
Ralph Keiler,	2	Thomas Seamer,	23
John Keiler,	3	James Sension,	24
John Gregory, senr.,	4	Nathaniel Richards,	25
Christopr Comstock,	5	Tho. Betts,	26
John Platt,	6	John Bennydick,	27
Samuel Camfield,	7	Lieutenant Olmsted,	28
Ephraim Lokwood,	8	Edward Nash,	29
John Gregory, junr.	9	Daniel Kellog,	30
Tho. Bennydick, junr.,	10	Matthu Marvin, sen.,	31
Richard Holms,	12	Matthu Marvin, jun.,	32
Samuell Bennydick,	13	John Ruscoe,	33
Thomas Lupton,	15	George Abbet,	34
John Bouton,	16	Mr. Hanford,	35
John Hayt,	17	Matthias Sension,	36
Mr. Tho. Fitch,	18	Thomas Fitch,	37
Samuel Sension,	19	Nathaniel Hayes,	38

John Raymond, 20.

A Cattelog of the Home lots agreed on to be layd out upon Drye Hill, Rayle Hill and Strabery Hill, with the order as they were drawn by those as are to injoy them, &c. &c. [Catalogue omitted.]

School.

August the 20, 1686. Voted by the towne that they would hyer a schoole master for a Quartere of a yeere;

and allow him wages after the Rate of thirty pounds a yeere, which is to be payd by the inhabitants according to their lists of estate.

At the same meeting the towne by vote did leave it with the select men or the major part of them, for to hyer a schoole master ; and allso to obtaine a house for that use, and to fitt it with conveniences for schooleing.

Seating the Meeting House.

December the 24th, 1686.   Voted and agreed by the towne that the seating of the meeting honse shall be for the generallyty to be seated according to the lists of estates by which the men payd in the defraying the charges about the building and finishing the said house.

At the same meeting the towne did manifest that the seat or pew under the Pulpitt shall be sequestered for such as are orderly constituted or officiate in the place or office of a Deacon or Deacons.

At the same meeting the towne did vote John Gregory, senr. and Mr. Fitch, and Thomas Betts, senr., for to be seated in the round seat.

At the same meeting the towne did vote that their should be five more seated in the round seat with Mr. Fitch, John Gregory, and Thomas Betts, senr., and fowre in the seat behind, and five in the long seats throughout. And also the cross seat to be reputed the third seat of the long seats, and foure to sitt in the sayd seat.

Seating the King's Commissioner.

At a towne meeting held in Norwalk, December the 28, 1686, At the sayd meeting the towne by vote did add one more person to every seat than is expressed in a former vote, bareing date Decemb^r 24, 1686.   At the same meeting the towne did vote Mr. Thomas Fitch, for to be seated in the meeting house in the upper great round seat, as he is the King's Commissioner.

At the same meeting the town made choyse of John Bouton, senr. for to help in seating the meeting house, in the roome of Mr. Fitch, he refusing to attend the sayd work.

Feb. 18th, 1686.   Zerubbabell Hoyt did ingage to — beat the Drum and maintaine it, and that on all publique occasions; and to sweep the meeting house for the yeere insuing, and is allowed for his labor two and forty shillings.

Mr. Hanford growing old.

March 25, 1686 or 87,.. The towne did by vote manifest and declare that they doe desire Mr. Hanford to proceed in the worke of the ministry, and therein to continue in the sayd work, untill the Lord by his providence shall dispose of him otherwise ;—promising to indeavor to our ability for to give him due incouragement.

Deputy to the General Court.

At a towne meetting held in Norwalk, May the 9th, 1686, voted and agreed by the town to allow Samuel Hayes, who is elected deputy for the towne for to attend the generall court, the said Samuell Hayes is allowed thirty shillings for himself to be paid as the country Rate is payd the next yeere, and tenn shillings fore his horse, journey, &c.

Line between Norwalk and Fairfield.

At a towne meetting held in Norwalk, June the 27, 1687.   Whereas we having received a note from Captain Samuel Eells, Captain Beard, and Mr. Judson, in order to the measuring of a seventh mile as some ungroundedly call it, and likewise a dividend lyne betweene Fair-

field and Norwalk : Whearfore the towne by these presents by vote doth declare that they shall not comply
nor agree with the aforesayd persons, viz. Captain Eells,
Captaine Beard, Mr. Judson, as a committee, or any
other persons in the measuring of any mile, or running any dividend lyne upon any land of ours lawfully
purchased by us; Allso doe hereby forewarne any person or persons on any land of ours soe to do at present.

Lands sequestered for the Indians.

December 12, 1687.   Voted and agreed that three
acres of land shall be sequestered for the Indians on
the other side of the river, lying on the left hand of the
roade leading towards Stamford.

Division of Over River Land.

[Dec. 12, 1687.   All common land Over the River,
leaving sufficient for highways, to be laid out by lot, to
the inhabitants, according to their estates.

Three score acres of the same sequestered for the
Indians.

A division granted of 20 Acres to the hundred.

Nathl. Hayes, and Sergt. John Platt, a committee to
lay out the division ;—lots to be granted to those only
who are proper inhabitants.   Samuel Keeler allowed to
" come off " from the division Over the River, and to
" pitch at the foot of the hill on the right hand of the
path commonly called Ponasses."   Also Jachin &
Thos. Gregory, " liberty to come off from their division,
and to take on the West side of the path—" bounded
North by Ponasses path ; " also Richd. Cosiar—1 1-2
acres on the north side of the path commonly called
Ponasses.]

The number of Lotts and the order as they were drawn, of that Division of Land over Norwalk River, below the path leading to the Meadow field.

William Lees,	1	Robert Stewart,	27
Samuell Smith,	2	John Lockwood,	28
William Sturdivant,	3	Ralph Keeler,	29
Tho. Betts, sen.,	4	John Ruscoe,	30
Matthias Sension,	5	Daniell Kellogg,	31
John Gregory, jun.,	6	John Platt,	32
Mark Sension,	7	John Bennidick,	33
James Stewart,	8	Widow Lupton,	34
Tho. Benidick, jun.,	9	Saml. Betts,	35
Saml. Hayes,	10	Thos. Benedick, sen.,	36
John Betts,	11	Edward Nash,	37
John Abitt,	12	John Keeler,	38
Mr. Thomas Fitch,	13	John Whitney,	39
John Crampton,	14	Thos. Betts, jun.,	40
Walter Hoyt,	15	Christopher Comstock,	41
John Gregory, sen.,	16	Joseph Ketcham,	42
John Belldin,	17	Mr. Thomas Hanford,	43
Matth. Marvin,	18	Daniel Betts,	44
Frances Bushnell,	19	John Reed, sen.,	45
Nathl. Hayes,	20	James Olmstead,	46
John Raymond, sen.,	21	Thos. Fitch, jun.,	47
Thos. Hyett,	22	Thos. Barnum,	48
James Jupp,	23	John Bouton, senr.,	49
George Abbitt,	24	Elizabeth Sension,	50
Thos. Seamer,	25	Andrew Messenger,	51
Richd. Holmes,	26	John Bouton, jun.,	52

The Estates of Commonage of the Inhabitants of Norwalk, Presented and Accepted by the towne, January the 3d, 1687.

	£	s.	d.		£	s.	d.
John Gregory, jun.,	100	00	00	John Keeler,	100	00	00
John Gregory, sen.,	243	00	10	Jonathan Rockwell,	50	00	00
Joseph Gregory,	100	00	00	Richard Cosiar,	50	00	00
Nathl. Hayes,	215	00	00	Daniell Betts,	69	06	02
Thos. Lupton,	150	00	00	Ralph Keeler,	170	10	00
Richd. Holmes,	155	00	00	Thomas Betts, sen.,	196	10	10
John Ruscoe,	250	00	00	Samuel Betts,	324	06	02
Mr. Hanford,	300	00	00	James Betts,	59	06	02
Theophilus Hanford,	50	00	00	Ephraim Lockwood,	120	00	00
Thos. Benidick, sen.,	153	00	00	John Lockwood,	50	00	00
John Bouton, sen.,	184	15	00	John Platt, sen.,	268	13	04
John Benidick,	100	00	00	Ebenezer Sension,	130	00	00
Thos. Benidick, jun.,	100	00	00	James Jupp,	55	00	00
Thos. Betts, jun.,	99	06	02	John Crampton,	53	06	08
Daniel Kellogg,	96	00	00	Thomas Hyett,	55	00	00
Matthew Marvin, sen.,	264	05	00	Elisabeth Sension,	150	00	00

Samuel Smith,	204	15	00	Robert Stewart,	225 00 00
Mr. Fitch,	364	00	00	Andrew Messenger,	225 00 00
John Fitch,	117	00	00	Thos. Fitch,	200 00 00
Joseph Ketcham,	117	00	00	John Olmsted,	150 15 00
Mark Sension,	302	00	00	Christopher Comstock,	201 10 00
George Abitt, sen.,	125	00	00	Daniell Comstock,	60 00 00
John Abbitt,	50	00	00	Thomas Seamer,	181 15 00
Walter Hoyt,	242	00	00	John Raymond, sen.,	200 00 00
Zerubbabell Hoyt,	50	00	00	John Raymond, jun.,	50 00 00
Matthias Sension,sen.,	195	00	00	Edward Nash,	216 00 00
Matthias Sension, jr.,	50	00	00	John Nash,	100 00 00
Samuel Keeler,	103	10	00	John Bouton, jun.,	50 00 00
John Beldin,	170	00	00	James Browne,	50 00 00
James Stewart,	50	00	00	Samuell Hayes,	150 00 00
Steven Beckwith,	54	00	00	Samuell Belldin,	63 00 00
John Whittney,	110	00	00	Peter Clappum,	100 00 00
William Sturdivant,	160	00	00	Thomas Murwin,	100 00 00
Samuel Camfield,	155	00	00	Jonathan Abbitt,	50 00 00
Thomas Gregory,	100	00	00	Saml. Benidick,	50 00 00
John Reed, sen.,	125	00	00	Thomas Barnum,	40 00 00
William Lees,	103	00	00	Frances Bushnell,	10 00 00
Jachin Gregory,	100	00	00	James Benidick,	f 37 00 00
John Betts,	69	06	02	Danll. Benidick,	36 00 00

Fortifying the Meeting House.*

At a towne meeting held in Norwalk, Aprill the 30, 1690, the towne voted and agreed, that the Meeting house should be the place to be fortified, and a garrison to be erected in order to the security of the towne.

[The committee for " carrying on this work were Serjt. John Platt, Serjeant John Belldin, John Ruscoe, and Saml. Hayes." These had power to proportion to every inhabitant his allotment of work, and to take

* This was just after the destruction of Schenectady and Salmon Falls. The country was in great alarm; the frontier towns were everywhere in peril. A special Assembly had been called on the 11th of April, which determined that there was a necessity for the utmost exertions to prevent the settlement of the French at Albany, " It was ordered that a constant watch should be kept in the several towns, and that all the males in the colony, except the aged and infirm, should keep watch in their turns. If the aged and infirm were more than £50 in the list, they were to procure a man in their turns, to watch and guard in their stead."

them in " the order of house rows ;" beginning " at
John Gregorie's" and " so along that row," and " the
first man's proportion to begin at the south gate, and
so goe along in the same order."]

School Keeping.

Feb. 21, 1692.   Thomas Hanford, junior, was chosen
to the work and imployment of a schoolemaster, for to
learn childeren for to reade and write, and to begin present on that work, and to continue on sayd work one
moneth ; and then at the beginning of next somer, to
enter the sayed work againe, and in case hee and the
towne can agree, for five months more.   And he to be
allowed and payd one pound, ten shillings for each
moneth that he shall attend to the sayd work and imployment.

Killing Wolves.

June 7, 1693.   Agreed and voted that there shall be
allowed and payd unto any person who shall kill any
wolfe or wolves within the bounds of the towne, the sum
of 12s. more than is allowed to be payed by the towne.
This order to stand in full force a twelvemonth.

Death of Mr. Hanford.

At a towne meeting, Dec. 26, 1693, voted and agreed
for to allow unto Mrs. Hanford, widow of Mr. Thomas
Hanford, deceased, for his labor and work in the ministry the sum of sixty pounds the yeere expireing the
first of March next.

Distributing Mr. Hanford's Estate.

Distributed to Elnathan Hanford for his part and
portion out of his father's estate, viz., ye Reverend Mr.
Thomas Hanford, late of Norwalk, deceased, viz. :

To one eighth part of the Home lott or
    Homestead,   -   -   -   13*l*. 15*s*. 0*d*.
To pasture lott, -   -   -   -   18*l*. 00 00

To half ye Indian Brook land, - 9*l*. 00 00
To half the Stonny Hill lott, ye cast
   end of it, - - - 10*l*. 00 00
To thirty acres and half at White Oak
   Shade, - - - - 7*l*. 13*s*. 00

List of Voters at Town Meetings.'

On the 4th of December, 1694, an order was taken
" that all persons who are members of town meetings, who have a vote and suffrage in towne affaires"—who should not attend town meetings when
legally warned, and within one hour after the time,
should pay a fine of two shillings.

[The following is the roll, with the names checked according as they were present or absent at some subsequent meeting.]

John Gregory, jun.	Ebenezer Web,
Nathll. Hayes,	Thomas Hanford,
James Hayes,	Daniell Betts,
Richd. Holmes,	Ralph Keeler,
John Ruscoe,	James Betts, }
Thos. Ruscoe,	Samuel Betts,
Eliezer Hanford,	Daniel Lockwood,
John Benidick, jr.,	Matthias Sension, jr.,
John Bouton,	John Platt, senr.,
James Browne,	John Platt, junr.,
Thomas Betts,	Ebenezer Sension,
Daniel Kellogg,	James Jupp,
Matthew Marvin,	John Crampton,
Mr. William Haynes,	Thomas Hyatt,
Jonathan Abbitt,	John Stewart,
Samuel Smith,	Andrew Messenger,
Samuel Kellogg,	Thomas Benidick,
Mr. Thomas Fitch,	Thomas Fitch,

John Fitch, senr.
'Joseph Ketchum,
Joseph Sension,
John Abbitt,
George Abbitt,
Zerubbabell Hoyt, ---
Walter Hoyt, _-.--
Matthias Sension, senr.,
Samuell Keeler,
John Raymond, jr.,
John Beldin,
James Stewart,
Steven Beckwith,
Joseph Rockwell,
John Whitney,
William Sturdivant,
Andrew Lyon,
James Sension,
Jonathan Rockwell, —
William Lees,
John Betts,
Jachin Gregory,
John Keeler,
Thomas Rockwell,

John Olmstead,
James Olmstead,
Christopher Comstock,
Samuell Beldin,
Samuell Hayes,
Matth'w Seamer,
Benjamin Scrivener,
David Monroe,
Richard Cosiar,
Thomas Seamer,
Joseph Gregory,
John Raymond, senr.,
Samuell Raymond,
Edward Nash,
John Nash,
Isaac Sherwood,
John Reed, senr.,
John Reed, junr.,
John Butler,
Ebenezer Camfield,
Richard Wood,
Peter Clappum,
Joseph Goldsmith.

Procuring a Minister.

At a towne meeting held in Norwalk, January the 16th, 1694; at sayed meeting, the towne made choyse of ten of their inhabitants as the Towne committee, viz., Serj'nt John Platt, Matthew Marvin, Serj'nt Christopher Comstock, Serj'nt John Bouton, Samuel Hayes, John Benidick, James Olmsted, Ensign John Beldin, Ralph Keeler, Samuel Smith; and comissioned they their said committee, in the behalfe of the towne (viz.)

as followeth ; they are to exercise their best prudence
for to look out for, and endeavor what in them lyeth, in
the use of all lawfull meanes, for to obtaine a faithfull
Minister and Dispenser of the word of the Gospell to
us in this place ; and in order thereunto, they are to
send forth their requests or invitations according to
their best prudence and judgment to that end, either by
writing or by messenger, or both, as the major part of
the committee shall agree ; and they their sayd committee are to order and take care for his entertainment
when obtained ; while the Towne doth hereby engage
for to discharge and pay all necessary charges arising
therefrom.

Repairing the Bridge.

Feb. 20, 1694—5. The towne made choyse of Mat-
-thew Marvin, John Whitney, and Thomas Betts, for to
take exact view of the Bridge over Norwalk River, and
to repaire the same, eyther by erecting a new bridge or
by repaireing the old, according to their best judgment
and prudence in that matter ; desiring them to be as
speedy on the sayd work as may be, and as the season
will permitt ; and they the above named persons are
and have hereby granted them full power for to warn
forth and to call to the carrying on the said work, either
handes or teames, or both, as occasion shall require,
and as they shall see meet for the carrying on and effect-
ing sayed work, for the compleat repayering the sayd
bridge.

Mr. Stone employed as preacher.

At a town meeting held December the 5th, 1694, it
was voted and agreed by the towne, Andrew Messenger was chosen collector for to give notice to the inha-

bitants for the bringing in their proportions when the rate shall be made by the townsmen, and to see that the whole of the thirty pounds due to Mr. Stone for his half yeere's preaching the word, be duly and truly payed according to the towne's engagement with the sayed Mr. Stone ; and the sayed Andrew for to act according to the law directing in such cases.

Obtaining a Minister.

At a Towne meeting held in Norwalk, 2d of Aprill, 1695 ; at sayed meeting it was voted and agreed, and by the towne declared as their mind, that the committee formerly chosen for to act for the towne for the obtaining a minister, have hereby full and free liberty from the towne for to move to whom or whear they shall see cause, for the obtaining of the end premised ; without any restraint or limitation to any person or persons ; this to stand full and good, notwithstanding any former act of the towne contrary to this present order, vote, and declaration of the mind of the town.

Purchasing a Minister's lot.

May 23, 1695, voted and agreed by the towne, that that lott obtained of Joseph Gregory, shall be for the accommidating of a Gospell minister for the towne ; and that it is allso agreed by the towne, that at such time as God shall please to bring in unto us such a minister, then and at that day that he shall be called to office and ordayned pastor of the church in Norwalk, then the aforesayed lott shall be and remaine to him, his heires for ever.*

* This was the lot between Capt. Daniel Hanford's and the residence of the late Hanford Fitch. It was occupied by Rev. Stephen Buckingham. The railroad now crosses it.

At a towne meeting, held July the 2d, 1695, at sayed meeting it was voted and agreed upon by the towne, that that land, pasture, and swamp lying in the generall fiield, granted to the ministery, shall be cleared and fenced, and made for improvement for pasture and meadow.

Also at the same meeting it was voted and allso granted by the town unto the minister, to him and his heirs, a parcell of salt marsh meadow lying in the bounds of Norwalk, and that over the river on the west side of the towne, &c.—the sayed parcell of meadow the towne en gages for to fence and make capable of improvement, &c.

Also, at the same meeting, the towne by vote hath given and granted to the minister ten acres of land for plowing, and that in the township of Norwalk on the east side of the brook called the north brook, and on the North East part of Mathew Marvin's Boggy Meadow, to be to him and to his heires for ever.

The Minister's Firewood.

At a towne meeting, July 17, 1695, it was voted and agreed by the towne for to allow and freely give Mr. Buckingham his firewood annually, and at all times, soe long as he shall continue to carry on the work of the ministry in Norwalk.

Minister's Salary.

Also at the above meeting (July 17, 1695), it was voted and agreed by the towne, for to allow and pay 80*l.* per yeer, after the two first yeeres abiding with us, unto Mr. Steven Buckingham, respecting his carrying on the work of the ministry. The said 80*l.* to be annually payed by the town by way of proportion; extraordinary cases only excepted.

The Minister's House.

December 18, 1695. At the sayd meeting the
Towne did manifest and by vote did agree, that they
would build a house for the minister, with as much
speed as might be with conveniency; and the dimensions of the sayd house are as followeth: two and fourty
foot in length, and two and twenty foot in breadth, and
two story high, or two lofts, and double chimneys; and
a comely porch to syd house; and a seller under one end
of the syd house; and stone the syd seller; the sayed
house is allso to have a comly gett at each end of the
same; and all to be decently finished upon the towne's
cost.

The Minister's Salary.*

At a towne meeting held in Norwalk October the 8th,
1697. At sayd meeting it was voted and agreed by the
towne that the eighty pounds sallary granted to Mr.

' * *The Deed of the Lands granted to Mr. Buckingham as his Settlement,* bears date April 7, 1699.

1. One homelot, 4 acres, bound E. by the land of Thos. Betts &
the common fence partly, W. The towns highway. N. The homelot
of Thos. Seamer. S. land & homelot of heirs of John Raymond,
senr., Decd.—with the house which is now built.

2. Land in the field; swamp & upland 16 acres; one half to him
and his heirs forever; the other half after his decease, to return to
the town.

3. Ten acres of upland lying in the woods; lying near the
Towne over the North Brook so called.

4. Three score acres of land in the woods—bounded by marked
trees, adjoining part of the land of Saml. Hayes, and Ensign John
Beldin, above Chesnut Hill.

5. Salt marsh meadow, 2 Acres, bounded E. by the cove, & N.
& N.W. by the bank of upland. S. by a fence and a small creek
near John Bouton's meadow.

5. Three Hundred pounds right in commonage.

Buckingham, the towne doth agree to pay it as followeth, both for specie and price, vizt.; winterwheat, at five
shillings per bushell, Indian corn at two shillings and
six pence per bushell, Rye at foure shillings per bushell,
porke at three pence farthing per pound; biefe at two
pence per pound; all good and merchantable, and none
of the inhabitants to pay above one third part of their
rate or proportion in Rye.

Allso at the same meeting the towne by their vote
did manifest their desire that the Reverend Mr. Steven
Buckingham should be ordayned pastor of the church in
Norwalk before winter; in case the sayd Mr. Buckingham will please to give the towne a dispensation soe
long as till the last day of May next insueing for the
compleating and finishing the house, and allso till the
next Michaelmast for the fencing and cleareing of the
land engaged by the towne to be fenced and cleared for
improvement.

Concurrence of the Town with the Church in settling the Minister.

Allso at the same meeting the towne made choyse of
Matthew Marvin and James Olmstead for to signifie
unto the Reverend Elders at the time of ordination, the
desire and good agreement of the towne with the church
in the ordayning of the Rev. Mr. Steven Buckingham.

A Gallery in the Meeting House.

Oct. 25, 1697.   Voted and agreed to erect the foundation of a gallery in the meeting house, over the fourth
part of sayd house; speedily, before the ordination if
it can be accomplished.   And have made choyse of
Ralph Keeler, and Samuell Keeler, and John Whitney
to doe the work, and to doe it soe as in their best judgment, best for the strength and conveniency of the gallery, &c.

Entertaining the Elders and Messengers at the Ordination.

Allso (Oct. 25, 1697). The towne made choyse of Matthew Marvin, Serjnt. John Platt, and Samuell Hayes, and John Bennidick and Thomas Betts, who are by the towne desired to take care for the providing of a comfortable entertaynment for the Reverend Elders and Messengers when heare at the time of ordination ; the charge of their entertaynment to be payd by the inhabitants of the towne.

Flax for the Drum-cord.

Allso voted and agreed for to allow to John Crampton for the yeere insucing, for beating the Drum on all publique occasions, and allso to sweep the meeting house, and to keepe the house cleane and decent ; and the towne engages for to allow and to pay unto sayd Crampton two pounds ten shillings for his labour; and the towne allow the townsmen for to furnish the sayd Crampton with soe much flax as may make necessary cords for the towne's Drum ; to procure the flax where they can, and the towne to pay the cost of the flax.

Indian Deed to Mr. Hanford.

Know all men by these presents, that I Winnipank, Indian Sagamour of Norwalk, do freely Give to my beloved friend Thomas Hanford, senior, Minister of Norwalk in ye County of Fairfield, in ye Colony of Connecticut, my Island of Land Lying against Rowerton, containing Twenty acres more or less, with all ye trees, Herbage, and other Appurtenances thereof ; which s^d Island is bounded on ye East with ye Island called Mamachimins, and Chachanenas, and on ye West with the point of Rowerton ; I the said Winnipank Do

5*

by this my act and Deed, Alienate the s⁴ Island from all claims of English or Indians, and as being my peculiar propriety, never by deed of gift, or sale made over to any, but now by this my deed I do give it freely to my beloved friend Thomas Hanford, senr., to possess, improve, to him and his heirs forever. In confirmation of this my act or deed, I have set to my hand & seal this second day of December Anno Domini One thousand six Hundred and Ninety.

The mark of { Winnipank.

Signed, sealed, and deliver-   Winnipank Indian, yᵉ
ed in the presence of   subscriber, acknowledged
JOHN GREGGORY,   yᵉ above Instrument to be
SAMUEL HANFORD.   his free act and deed,
                               before me in Norwalk.

Dec. 28th, 1698, NATHAN GOLD, Assist.

Hungry Spring.

Feb. 23, 1699. Voted and agreed that Thomas Seamer shall be warned for to lay open to the use of the towne the Spring called Hungry Spring; for free passing of man and beasts to the sayd spring; he to remove any fence or incumbrance in the way to sayd spring, that is or was by him sett up or erected.

The price of fire wood.

Feb. 23, 1699. It was voted and agreed that all persons as carry fire wood to Mr. Buckingham, shall be allowed for each load of wallnut wood three shillings and six pence, and for each load of oake wood is allowed two shillings and six pence.

Building a school house.

November 27, 1699. Agreed that the towne would build a schoole house as soon as may be with conveniency ; and the dimensions of sayd house is agreed to be as followeth : the length 20 foote ; the breadth thereof eighteene foot; and at least six foot betweene joynts &c. &c.

Certain Town Charges in 1699.*

	s.	d.
Burning the woods, Serjt. John Platt one day,	2	6
Saml. Belden one day burning woods—one day	2	6
(and so of seven others in succession.)		
Samuell Smith for towne barres . . .	2	6
John Platt for a pound of butter . .	0	9
The widow Hyett a 3d part of a wolfe . .	3	4
Allowed to James Hayes for flax 2 pounds for the Towne's Drum delivered to John Crampton,	2	0
Samuel Keeler for mending the towne barres	1	6

Charges for wolves.

	£	s.	d.
Ensigne Belden, five wolves . . .	2	10	0
Samll. Beldin, one wolf		10	0
Saml. Hayes, one wolf		10	0
Josh. Rockwell, one 3d of a wolfe . .		3	4
Tho. Gregory, one wolfe . . .		10	0
Saml. Smith, one wolfe		10	0
Elizar Hanford, one wolfe . . .		10	0
Ebenezer Sension, a 3d of one wolfe . .		3	4

Powder and Lead.

April 10, 1700. It was voted and agreed by the inhabitants and hearby declared as the towne's act, that there shall be a rate made and levyed forthwith, for the

* The town clerk had turned over several leaves, and made this record out of its order.

procuering of powder and lead for the towne store or
magazine; to be levyd in money, a halfpenny on the
pound.

Certain Town Accounts.   Dec. 30, 1701.

	£	s.	d.
Joseph Ketchum, for running the lyne be-twean Stamford and our towne,	0	3	6
Itm. One day burning woods,	0	2	6
Allso half one side of the pound: allso some rayles carrying to the towne Barres,— all	0	9	0
Allso, a pint of rum,	0	1	0
Samuell Keeler, one day burning woods,	0	2	6
His horse to the Court at New Haven,	0	7	0
Allso one day renewing the bounds of the purchase ; him and his horse,	0	4	0
Allso a pint of rum,	0	1	0
Samuell Hayes, his horse to Hartford,	0	10	0
One third of a wolfe,	0	3	4
Samuel Beldin, two-thirds of a wolf,	0	6	8
Serj't. John Raymond, one-sixt part of a wolf,	0	1	8
Zerubabell Hoyt, half one wolf, ———	0	5	0
' Allso burning the Islands,	0	0	18
Matthias Sension, for beating the drum,	1	2	6
Allso a drum-cord,	0	3	0

John Copp, Schoolmaster.

Dec. 30, 1701.   Voted and agreed by the towne that
they would have a schoolemaster for the next yeere insueing in case he can be obtained.   Allso voted and
agreed that Mr. John Copp shall be the person for that
work in case he can be obtained on reasonable termes.

Allso voted and agreed, that for the paying of the
charge of a schoolemaster shall be as followeth: that all
children from the age of five yeeres old to the age of

twelve yeeres, shall all pay an equall proportion; excepting the feamale; all that doe not goe to schoole,
and all youths above the age of twelve years as goe in
the day, shall pay equally with the others above sayed;
and all night schoollars shall pay a third part soe much
as the day schoolers; and the schoolers to pay fifteene
pounds; and the remaynder of the charge of schoole
master's sallary shall be payd by the towne according
to their list of estate in the publique list of the Col-
lonie.

Payment of the Town rate in 1701.

Voted and agreed, that the town rate shall be payd
in maner as followeth, vizt, in wheat at 5s. per bushl,
Indian corne at 3s. per bushell, flax at 9d per pound,
oats at 1s 8d, rye at 2s. 6d, Barley at 3s. per bushell,
and not to pay to any, above a third part of their debt
in flax, oats, Barley, but 2 thirds of all be in wheat or
Indian corne.

The Islands.

Whereas the inhabitants of the towne of Norwalk,
have had possession of severall Islands lying adjacent
to their township, and allso improvement of them forty
yeares, and longer, without being interrupted by any
persons laying claime and prosecuting their claime in
due forme of law, the sayd towne having had quiett
possession long before the sayd law of possession was
enacted, and ever since; the select men and justice doe
in the name of sayd towne and for their behoofe, enter
and record unto the sayd towne, them, their heires and
assignes for ever; namely Cockenoes Island known by
sayd name, and Mamachimons Island, and the Long
Island, and Camfield's Island, known by sayd names,
and all other Islands lying in or adjacent unto the
towneshipp of Norwalk; to the legallity of this record

we whose names are hereunto sett and subscribed, our
names and hands.

JAMES OLMSTEAD, Justice and Recorder.
SAMUEL SMITH,   ⎤
THOMAS BETTS, |
SAMUELL BELDEN,   ⎬ Townsmen.
SAMUELL BETTS, |
SAMUELL MARVEN.   ⎦

Recorded this 4th day of January 1702—3.
(From Book 2 & 3.)

Sitting in the Deacons' seat.

Jan. 14, 1702. The towne did, by their vote, allow
John Gregory, senior, liberty to sitt in the Deacon's seat
before the pulpitt, for the advantage and benefitt of his
hearing the word preached.

Allso at the above sayd meeting the towne did by
vote grant and allow, unto Matthew Marvin, liberty to
sitt in the Deacon's seat before the pulpitt for the benefitt of his hearing the word preached.

Horse sheds by the Meeting house.

Jan. 14, 1702. Granted liberty to those inhabitants
out-dwellers, for to erect shelters for their horses for
the Saboath and publique occasions, by Matthias Sension's jr. Lott in the common, not to hinder or obstruct
his passage to his barne and yard, or to his shop.

In case of fine by the Sergeant Major.

Feb. 26 ; 1702, it was voted and agreed by the towne
that in case the present select men shall be fyned by
the Serjnt. Major, for the townes defect in not having
their proportion of armes and ammunition in their
towne stock according to law, the towne engages to pay
the fyne, and that by way of rate.

The meeting-house bell.

Feb. 3, 1703. The towne voted that the Bell should
be fetcht from Ralph Keeler's and forthwith hung up in

the meeting house for to be wrung ther for the probation of the goodnes of the Bell.

At the same meeting the towne made choyse of
Ralph Keeler and James Stewart to hang the bell in
the meeting house, and to doe all that is necessary respecting the hanging the sayd bell, and allso to put a
new tongue into the bell if it shall in there judgments
soo need it.

Ringing the bell, and beating the drum.

Dec. 1704. William Lees did engage with and unto the towne to beat the Drum or ring the bell, and that
on all publique occasions. And also to sweep the meeting house every week decently ; and the towne engages
to allow and pay unto sayd Lees the next yeere the sum
of one pound ten shillings.

Fetching arms from Stanford.

Allso the towne engages to pay any damage that may
be done, or happen to be done, in the armes that are to
be fetcht from Stanford ; and allso to pay those persons
as shall fetch them, reasonable satisfaction for their
labor.

Seating the meeting house in 1705.

Voted, that the meeting house shall be seated with
as much conveniency as may be ; and that the order or
method of seating the meeting house shall be in the act
of the towne bareing date Feb. 21, 1698 ; only further
agreed that noe person shall be degraded, or brought
lower than they are now seated.

Also voted and agreed that the first long seat in the
gallery of the meeting house shall be accounted and
deemed as the fifth long seat below, and those as sitt
below have liberty there to sitt still.

Also that there shall be twelve men seated in the long

seat of the gallery; namely, the first seat of the gallery.

Also, there is to be two seats of the gallery seated on the woman's side of the gallery, if need be.

Allso, the towne made choyse of Thomas Betts, senr., Samuell Smith, senr., and Ralph Keeler, senr., they to seat the meeting house according to the order of the towne.

Seating the Meeting House in 1706.

The towne made choyse of a committee, vizt.; James Olmstead, John Benedick, senr., Samuel Smith, senr., Zerubabell Hoyt, Thomas Betts, senr., Ebenezer Sension, Joseph Platt, persons with whom the towne have left that affaire, vizt., the seating of the meeting house; and they the sayd committee to order and determine that matter according to their best discretion; they to have respect to age, quality, and the estates of persons in the publique list, and the towne to abide their determination.

Allowance to Mr. Buckingham instead of his yearly Firewood.

Feb. 28, 1706–7. Voted and agreed by the towne, to allow Mr. Steven Buckingham twenty pounds pr. year, to be paid in specie as his rate is to be payd in, he freeing the towne from the obligation they are under, in finding or providing his firewood.

Mr. Buckingham's agreement thereto.

The town of Norwalk, performing their above mentioned engagement, as to summ and price, are now freed from the obligation concerning fire wood to me.

S. BUCKINGHAM.

Cutting Sedge.

Dec. 18, 1707. The Towne by their present act, do prohibit any person or persons cutting any sedge or Crick-thatch, on any of the towne's right, before ye first day of September, annually; and if any person shall presume to act contrary to this act, he or they shall, after the first half load, forfitt twenty shillings for every half load; to be paid by the person or persons delinquent, half to ye use of ye town, the other half of said twenty shilllings to the complainer who shall prosecute the same to effect.

School Keeping in 1707-8.

Feb. 10th, 1707–8. Voted and agreed, that there shall be a schoolmaster hyred according to law.

Also, voted and agreed, that ye school master Hired shall attend and keep ye schoole two months on this side of the river, and one month on ye other side.

Also granted liberty to those our inhabitants over the river, to erect a schoole house in a convenient place, not prejudissing the highway.

The Town keeping good hours.

Also voted (1707–8), and agreed, that there shall be no votes passed nor any grants made by the towne, nor any record made of any votes, after nine of the clock at night.*

* "In 1708, John Belden, Samuel Keeler, Matthew Seymour, Matthias St. John, and other inhabitants of Norwalk, to the number of twenty-five, purchased a large tract between that town and Danbury. The purchase was made of Catoonah, the chief sachem, and other Indians, who were the proprietors of that part of the country. The deed bears date Sept. 30, 1708. At this session [1709], it was ordained, that it should be a distinct township, by the name of RIDGEFIELD."— *Trumbull*, p. 460.

Keeping order in town meeting.

Dec. 16th, 1708. Voted and agreed that there shall
be a moderator chosen, who shall have power to put to
vote all matters or affaires that are then in adjitation,
and also to endeavour to keep good order and decorum in
speaking ; and all who are disorderly in speaking, to be
by words corrected by the moderator ; and also that if
any person shall, notwithstanding, be so bold as to proceed in disorderly speaking, when corrected by the moderator, he shall suffer by fyne, imposed on ye delinquent by ye moderator and the majority of the townsmen, to the sum of five shillings, to be leavied by distress on the estate of the delinquent.

Over River Burying Ground.

Dec. 16, 1708. The town grants to ye inhabitants
on the west side of Norwalk River, a piece of ground
for a burying place, on any convenient piece of land in
commons ; and John Benedick, senr., Zerubabell Hoyt,
and Thomas Betts, senr., are appointed a committee to
appoint the place.

Sitting in the great Pew.

Feb. 10, 1708–9. The town votes Mr. Samuell
Hayes into ye great pue, to sitt in upon publique
days, &c.

Stray Jades.

March 4, 1708–9. The town makes choyse of John
Steward to claim and sell all stray jades for the
town (when no better claim appears), that shall be
brought out of ye woods to ye town by the Horse Hunters, and that the horse hunters shall have half of what
ye horses shall fetch, when they are sold.*

* In Hinman's Catalogue of names of Puritan settlers, under
Matthew Griswold, is noticed " A severe lawsuit between said

The Tide Mill.

Dec. 15, 1709. The town grants by a major vote, to Joseph Birchard, Thomas Betts, John Betts, and John Gregory, jr., the liberty to Damm up ye crick lying before ye sd Gregory's, with also the privilege of the stream that runs into ye said crick and through the said damm : provided that they the said Joseph, &c. * * do sett upon the said work in order to the erecting a grist mill upon the damm that they shall so erect, within one year from this date ; and do accomplish the work of the said mill within ye term of three years from the day of these presents ; and so long as they the said undertakers do maintaine a good sufficient grist mill, the said stream shall remain to them and to their successors that shall so maintaine ye same : they to grind all grain into good and sufficient meal for the town, for the toal stated in ye law ; and not to grind for any strainger coming with his grain to said mill, so long as any of ye inhabitants of this Towne's grain is lying in said mill unground ; excepting any of said inhabitants shall allow any strainger their turn.

A Platform to the Gallery.

Dec. 15, 1709. The town by major vote grants to John Bartlet, James Lockwood, and Samuell Keeler, jr., a liberty to erect and build on ye west side of the meeting house, a plattform from ye gallery unto the north

Griswold and Reinold Marvin." " The arbitrators awarded that one half the horses should be equally divided between them, and that the other half should go to the colony, and Marvin should look them up; and appointed a committee to sell the horses and execute the award." Upon this Mr. Hinman remarks : " The arbitrators must at least have resided at *Dutch Point*, if they were not Dutch Justices." This record may explain the matter without the necessity of so uncharitable a supposition. ;

window upon the cross plates; and with others that shall present, for a sufficiency to erect upon the same four pues, which shall remain and continue for their use, to seat themselves in ye time of publique service : and that during the fall term of ye town's pleasure; so that whenever they shall see cause to make any alteration of that matter so as to deprive them of their seats, the town ingages to allow such charge, that the said buildings shall be advantageous to ye town, as by indifferent persons may be adjudged ; they relinquishing all other seats in the meeting house, during ye time of their sitting.

The Meeting House Belfry.

At the same meeting, the town (granted to Samuell Keeler, jr., twenty acres of land in one place, and twenty-six acres of land more, to " take up in ye woods") —upon condition that he the said Keeler do erect a Belfree upon ye top of our meeting house, and compleatly finish the same ; and hang the bell that is now hung upon ye meeting house, or any other that may be obtained seasonably before ye said belfree is finished ; and to cloase ye sides of the upright where now ye bell hangs ; all to be compleated by the last of June next insuing; the town to provide stuff for ye closing ye upright, and to cart the same, with the timber that shall by the said Keeler be prepared for ye belfree, to ye meeting house ; and also find ye nails that will be wanted for ye whole work; also the sayd Keeler to fraim in ye top of ye turret a good sufficient cedar stump to fix a weathercock on, if ye town see cause ; or a pinnicle.

Gregory's Point.

Dec. 29, 1710. (The town granted some land to

John Benedict) "which grant is by way of exchange with the said John Benedict for a free passage for carts, horses and men, as they may have occasion, unto ye point of land extending itself into ye harbor, which passage is limited to ye way that is and hath been improved, along through ye said Bennedick's land unto yᵉ said point, which privilege is to remain to the town forever; which point is known as commonly called GREGORY's POINT."

Seating several persons in the Meeting House.

Dec. 29, 1710.   The towne grants liberty to William Stirdevant, Jonathan Wood, Richard Cosier, Andrew Lyon, John Fillio, Thomas Austin, to sitt upon ye seat joining to the Little pue, in ye North East corner of the meeting House, and their wives to sit on the opposite seat, joyning to yᵉ North West corner of yᵉ meeting house.

Allso———to Samll Carter to sitt in yᵉ seat before yᵉ hinde pillar, with John Marvin, &c., and to James Hayes to sit in yᵉ seat where Lt. William Lees formerly satt.

The Bell rung at nine o'clock at night.

Dec. 11, 1713.   The town grants to Zerubbabell Hoyt twenty-six shillings in pay, or two thirds money, for his ringing yᵉ bell at nine a clock at night, for yᵉ year ensuing; and the said Hoyt ingages to performe the same.

A Highway to Ridgefield.

Dec. 16, 1713.   The town by major vote made choice of Capt. Joseph Platt, Capt. John Raymond, and Ensigne James Stewart, for their committee to make a settlement of a highway or road to Ridgefield, if they and

the committee of Ridgefield can agree ; and doth fully
impower said committee to make restitution to such
persons that s^d highway may take land from within the
limits of Norwalk township.

Attending Meeting in Ridgefield.

March 1, 1713-14. The town by a major vote frees
Jonathan Wood, senr., from paying any rate to ye ministry in Norwalk, for ye future after this year's rate is
paid, provided ye said Wood attends ye meeting in
Ridgefield on ye Sabbath and so long as he continues so
to do.

A Sabbath Day House for John Taylor.

March 1, 1713-14. The town by a major vote grants
liberty to John Taylor to erect a small house for his
family's conveniency on ye Sabbath, on such part, of y^e
town's land near ye meeting house, as ye select men
shall allow or find convenient.

A New Meeting House.

Dec. 11, 1717. The town by a major vote determines to build a new meeting house, of such dimensions
as shall hereafter be concluded upon ; to be erected on
ye north end of Ensign James Stewart's Home lot.

At ye same meeting the town by a major vote grants
a rate of one penny in a pound in money to be leavied
upon the inhabitants of the town, to be collected this
year, and put into ye hands of ye town treasurer, to be
improved by the committee that shall be chosen and appointed for managing ye business of ye new meeting
house.

At the same meeting ye town by a major vote determined that what money is granted by the town, viz.
(ye penny on ye pound) to be colected this year, shall

be layed out in buying nailes and other necessaries for the new meeting house.

At the same meeting the town by a major vote determines that the accomplishment of ye work of s^d meeting house shall be indeavored for within the term of four years.

At the same meeting the town by a major vote determines that what is found necessary to be done in reparing the old meeting house to make it comfortable for the time being until the said meeting house be built, be out of hand done.

Whether to repair the old Meeting House.

Jan. 9, 1718-19. It was proposed by way of vote, that those that were for repairing, and for making an addition to the old meeting house, should signifie their minds by passing out of ye house first, and be numbered ; and that those who ware for erecting a new meeting house, on the place where John Keeler's barn stands, should pass out of the house afterwards & be numbered. Upon tryall of which, those that̄ were for repairing and adding to the old house were in number twenty six that passed out, and Lt. Taylor declared himself to be of that mind though he passed not out. And those that were for the meeting house to be erected as aforesaid, were in number thirty that passed out, and Capt. Platt and myselfe declared to be of ye same mind with them, tho not passing out.

This meeting is adjourned to ye next Monday morning come sevennight at Eight of ye clock in ye morning.   Test, JOHN COPP, *Town Clerk.*

How to settle the difference about the old house or a new one.

At a town meeting convened by adjournment on the 19th day of January, 1718-19, in Norwalk, in the old school House.

The Town by major vote determines to leave the whole affaire of ye present differance in the town respecting the Repairing the old meeting house and enlarging ye same by addition; or the building a new meeting house, and determining the place where the new house shall be erected, unto a wise and judicious committee of three persons hereafter nominated and chosen; all which charge of the s^d committee to be defrayed by ye town.

Upon Tryall of ye minds of ye town upon the above vote, it was proposed that those y^t were of the mind to pass s^d vote into their act, should move out of ye house. Upon tryall of whiche, Forty one persons went out of ye house, and eight persons y^t were not in ye house when ye proposals were made, came to me and declared themselves for ye said act. The negative vote was proposed in ye same manner, and no person or persons appeared to move out; the number of ye persons y^t remained in the house, as near as I could come at, were in number Twenty six.

At ye same meeting, the town by a major vote, made choise of Major Peter Burr, Major Samuel Eals, and Mr. Jonathan Law, Esq., for their committe, with whom they would leave the whole affair of their difference above expressed, and to make a decision thereof.

At the same meeting the town by Major vote Determines that any two of the abovesaid committee agreeing, their determinations shall be as binding to the town to fulfil, as if they all three concurred and signed their result

At ye same meeting ye town by a major vote have chosen Capt. John Raymond, Capt. Joseph Platt, Lt. Matthew Seamer, Ensigne Saml. Comstock, Mr. Samll.

Betts, and Mr. John Marven, a committee to represent ye town in laying before s^d committee the surcomstances of ye town in their present differences.

At the same meeting ye town by major vote makes choise of Mr. Copp to entertain the Get^{h}men Committee afore chosen, when come to town.

At the same meeting the town by a major vote makes choise of John Copp to go forth with ye gentlemen ye said committee in order to obtain their coming over with as much expedition as may be.

At the same meeting, the town by a major vote impowers the town's committee afore chosen to render and pay to ye Gentlemen committee, honorable reward for their service (in these affairs) for the town ; for which the town treasury shall reburst ye s^d charges.

Beginning the new Meeting House.

^{r} At a town meeting convened in Norwalk August 17th, 1720, The town by a major vote resolves and concludes that men shall be hired to raise the meeting house, such men and so many as Mr. Samll. Grummon, carpenter, shall think needfull ; in ye town, and by ye advice of the Committee.

The town, by a major vote, resolves and oblidges themselves seasonably to grant such leavies by way of rate, on ye inhabitants of ye town, as shall be sufficient to discharge all such necessary charges, as the committee appointed to manage that affair of the new meeting house, as already have or shall find needful, to contract for the accomplishment of ye underpining, raiseing, covering, and encloseing s^d house, at or before the first day of March next ensuing the date hereof.

The Town, at ye same meeting, by a major vote,

6

determines that the new meeting house shall be raised
fronting East, and to y° street.

The second School District.

(*Note*. On the 4th of January, 1719-20—the town
voted that the winter school should be kept half of the
time at the old school house, and the other half the
time at the new school house at the North end of the
town.)

January 30, 1720—21. The town by a major vote
determines to have two schools attended and kept for
the year ensuing, one at y° south end of y° town,
and the other at y° north end; at y° two respective
school houses now in being, in y° winter time; and y°
summer schoole at y° south end, and at y° school house
on y° west side of y° river. And y° country money shall
be divided according to lyst by y° military lyne.

Gathering Oysters.

Dec. 4, 1721. The town by major vote prohibits all
persons whatsoever excepting the proper inhabitants of
y° town, rakeing and gathering of Oysters within y° har-
bours, coves, or any other place, appertaining and being
within the limits of our township. And any such person or persons as shall be found rakeing or gathering oysters within y° aforesayd limits, shall suffer the penaltie
of three shillings per bushell.

Right of commonage to all young men arriving at the age of 21
years.

Dec. 4, 1721. The town by a major vote resolves
and determines that a copy of a certain vote passed at
a town meeting convened in Norwalk Dec. 15, 1698, in
the words following, to wit: "Also granted that all the
town born children, shall, as they attain y° age of Twenty one years, all of them have a fifty pound right of
commonage in the town, and also as are twenty one

years of age to have it in this last division granted."
—A true copy of ye town act lost,

Test, JAMES OLMSTEAD, Town Clerk.

Shall be put on record, and be of as good force and efficacy as the original was before it was lost; and that no female shall have benefit by this act, by their being born in ye town.

Selling Oysters to oyster vessels.

April 16, 1722. The Town Resolved, that whosoever of ye inhabitants of the town shall directly or indirectly sell any oysters, or give leave to any vessel, men, or any other person or persons to gett oysters within ye town bounds, or shall carry and put on board any oysters, shall incurr a penalty of five shillings pr. hundred, and so in proportion for greater or less quantites.

Seats taken from the old Meeting House for the new.

March 11, 1722—23. The town gives liberty to ye committee for the new meeting house, to take from ye old meeting house such seats and boards, plank, and other things, that may be needful to use in the new meeting house.

The Town Magazine.

At the same meeting, the town by a major vote determines that a suitable place shall be made in the new meeting house to put ye towns magazine in, and remove the same as soon as may be.

Seating the new Meeting House.

June 3, 1723. The town left the business of seating the new meeting house to a committee of seven ; viz. Capt. Joseph Platt, Lieutenant Samuel Marvin, Serjent John Bennedict, Samuel Kellogg, Lieutenant Matthew Seymor, Captain Samuel Hanford, Mr. John Betts, Sen.

Mrs. Hanford still alive.*

At ye same meeting, the town voted Mrs. Hanford into ye pue with Mrs. Buckingham.

December 11, 1723. The town voted Capt. Samuel Hanford to sit in ye pue with Captain Olmsted and Captain Platt.

No town meeting to be holden in the new Meeting House.

At the same meeting (Dec. 11, 1723), the town by a major vote resolves, that no town meetings shall be warned to convene at the new meeting house, nor attended and held within s^d house; nor that any act or acts of the town shall ever be accounted of any value that shall be passed within the walls thereof. Also determines that no other improvement shall be made there, but what is consistent with, and agreeable to the most pure and special service of God, for which end it was built and now devoted.

Selling the old Meeting House.

At the same meeting, the town by a major vote determines to make sale of the old meeting house. Mr. John Bartlett, Ensign Samuel Comstock, and Mr. James Lockwood a committee to sell and dispose of the same.

A School Dame at Saugatuck.

At the same meeting, the town grants liberty to Drye Brook and Sawkatuck inhabitants to improve a School

* "From the first settlement of the town to 1732, a term of more than 80 years, there was no general sickness in the town. From 1715 to 1719, there died in this large town twelve persons only. Out of the train-band, consisting of 100 men, there died not one person from 1716 to 1730, during the term of 14 years."

"Mrs. Hanford, relict of the first minister of the town, died Sept. 12, 1730, aged 100 years."—(Manuscripts of Rev. Moses Dickinson in Trumbull's History.)

. -

Dame among themselves to schoole their children in ye summer season, and also grant to them their proportion of ye country's money.

At ye same meeting ye town grants that the refuse boards left at ye new meeting-house, be used about ye school-house neerr ye Mill plain.

The old bell hung upon the new Meeting House.

At the same meeting the town by major vote determines to hang ye bell on ye new meeting house, and there to be rung upon necessary occasions until there appear a suitable opportunity to sell the same.

Mr. John Copp in the second pew from the pulpit.

At the same meeting, the town by a major vote grants ye seating of John Copp in ye second pue from ye pulpitt; and his wife in ye third pue on ye woman's side.

Mr. Thomas Fitch in the pew with the Justices.

Mr. Thomas Fitch, Jr., is by major vote of ye town seated in ye pue with the Justices, and the town desires that he would read ye psalme, and set ye tune in ye time of publique service.

Mr. Thomas Benedict to set the Psalm tunes.

December 2, 1724. The town by major vote desires Ensigne Thomas Bennedick, Jr., to sett ye tune to ye Psalme, at such times as that part of service is to be performed in ye publik worship of God; and to read ye Psalms needed, ye town also seats ye said Bennedick in ye 3d long seat at ye end of ye middle alley.

The town votes Mr. Benjamin Lynes into ye pue at ye S. W. corner.

The Parish of Wilton begun.

December 7, 1725. The town by a major vote signifies their willingness that the inhabitants of Kent,

Belden's Hill, and Chestnutt Hill, and so upwards, be-
come a Parish or village by themselves ; if the Generall
Court (upon their application) shall see meet so to establish them ; and in order for ye settling ye bounds of
said village, a committee from each party shall take a
view and present to the town where they think the
bounds should be stated ; that the town may consider
upon it, and, upon their liking, establish the same.

At the same meeting, ye town by a major vote made
choise of ye Worshipfull Joseph Platt, Esq., Captain
Raymond, and Lieutenant Seymor committee for to
joyne with a committee from ye said inhabitants, in
vewing where ye bounds may be best fixt for said upper
village, and make a report to ye town of their opinion
therein.

Stone steps for the Meeting House.

February 18th, 1725-6.   The town by a major vote
determines that they will have stones obtained for ye
makeing of steps at each of ye doars of ye meeting house.
Joseph Platt, Esq., Mr. John Bartlett, and Ensigne
Thomas Bennedick, Jr., to see to ye obtaining of s^d
stones, and get ye steps made, &c., at the town's cost.

Difficulty with the Rev. Mr. Buckingham.

At the same meeting (Feb. 18, 1725-6), the town by
a major vote determines that something shall be done
in order to regulate ye difficulties ariseing in the town
about ye Reverend Mr. Buckingham.

The town by a major vote made choice of Joseph
Platt, Esq., Mr. James Brown, Lieutenant Comstock,
John Copp, Deacon John Benedick, Jr., Mr. John
Betts, Sen., and John Betts, carpenter, Committee to
present the grievances of the town to the ministers of the
county.

Mr. Buckingham's salary stopped.

A bill was brought into ye meeting of ye following tenure, viz. :

Att a town meeting regularly warned by the select men of ye town of Norwalk and convened at the new school-house at the north end of said town, Feb. 18, 1725—6, the town by their major vote agrees and resolves, that for the future no colector in the town of Norwalk shall be oblidged to colect Mr. Buckingham's rate in the specie as hath been usual ; and that the inhabitants of the town shall not be under any obligation, by force of any vote, to pay any provision for the answering of their severall proportions of s^d Mr. Bucking's sallary ; and doe hereby determine and fully agree, that all votes and grants of that kind shall be wholly null and void.

Read off to ye town, put to vote, and passed in the affirmative.

The Association of Ministers called.

Feb. 28, 1725-6.   The town accepts what Mr. Copp & Mr. James Brown (with concurrence of ye rest of ye committee) have done, in obtaining from ye Reverend Mr. Davenport, Moderator of ye Association (ye Reverend Mr. Webb & Mr. Chapman adviseing and consenting therewith) letters of notification to ye ministers of ye county, for an Association of s^d ministers at Norwalk, on ye eighth day of March next ; and resolves to have ye said letters of notification sent to the Reverend persons to whom they are directed ; and make provision for ye entertainment of s^d ministers when they come, which charge shall be defrayed by the town.

The Old Pulpit.

At ye same meeting, the town by a major vote, grants

to the inhabitants of ye upper society the old pulpit upon free gift.

A Minister allowed to Saugatuck.

At the same meeting, the town by a major vote grants to ye inhabitants about Sawkatuck, liberty to improve some meet person or minister of ye gospel to preach among them, &c., they paying their full dues to ye support of ye minister of ye town.

Mr. Buckingham's Letter to the Town.

At a town Meeting convened in Norwalk, March 22d, 1725-6 :

To the Town of Norwalk now conven'd together, I being heartily concerned for ye difficult state of the town, and thinking sincerely within myself, that a loving accommodation of ye difficulties and differences at present between ye town and myself, will be everyway most conducive to ye peace and union of the town, and the satisfaction of every member therein; and so, in the whole, most declarative of the glory of God, and most for the interest of religion, more especially in this place, I thereupon, with Christian concern, move to ye town for an accommodation of ye s^d difficulties.

S. BUCKINGHAM.

The Town most gladly receiving Mr. Buckingham's desire, do heartily fall in with his motion for an accommodation of ye difficulties ; provided the Rev. Mr. Davenport, Mr. Cook, and Mr. Chapman, do propose any meathod for such an accommodation, which they do think to be equivalent to, or may answer, the advice of the late association at Norwalk.

Read off to ye town
and by a major vote past in ye affirmative.

The Council for Advice.

March 30th, 1726.   The town mett, and by a major
vote requests the Reverend Mr. Sacket to joyne with ye
Reverend Mr. Davenport, Mr. Cook, & Mr. Chapman,
in that affair refer'd to them ye last meeting before ye
adjournment.

A Supply for the Pulpit.

The town by a major vote grants to Mr. Thomas
Fitch, jnr., Thirty shillings pr. day for two days and
a half preaching with us in times past ; and also for
what days he may be so improved by us for the future.

The Council.

March the 31st, 1726.   The Town mett, and by a
major vote made choice of Mr. James Brown to offer in
ye town's behalf in ye present affair now before the
Reverend Gentlemen, viz., ye Rev'd. Mr. Davenport,
Mr. Cook, Mr. Chapman, and Mr. Sacket being present.

The Town closes with the advice of Council. ˙

At the same meeting, the town having had read off to
them the advice of ye late association of ye ministers of
ye County at Norwalk, for ye Calling of a council of
the elders and also of the messengers of the churches in
the County ; and also the further advice of ye above
Reverend Gentlemen, to pursue s[d] advice, as most
agreeable to rule and order, and most conducible to an
orderly and decisive determination of our difficulties,
——— the town closes with ye advice afores[d] & by a
major vote determines that a council of ye elders, &
also of the messengers of the Churches in this County
shall be called.

6*

Calling the Consociation.

The town by a major vote determined that a suitable person shall be sent to ye Rev'd Mr. Stodard of Woodbury, Moderator of ye last council in this county, to obtain letters of notification to ye elders and messengers of the churches in this county, to convene at Norwalk on the first Monday evening in May next, according to ye advice and discretion of ye late association at Norwalk; and that due provision be made for the entertainment of ye said council when convened; the whole charge to be defray'd by the town.

The Committee to represent the Town before Consociation.

April 27, Annoque Domini, 1726. (The town appointed Mr. James Brown, Joseph Platt, Esq., & John Copp, their committee to appear in behalf of the town before the Consociation, and to manage the whole affair relating to the difference between ye Rev. Mr. Buckingham & the town.)

The Town dissatisfied with Mr. Buckingham's Conversation.

At a town meeting convened in Norwalk, August 12th, 1726, at ye same meeting, the town by a major vote do signifie their dissatisfaction with the former and latter conversation of the Reverend Mr. Stephen Buckingham, viz.: before and since ye determination of council; as also with the determination of the council in that affair.

At ye same meeting, the Reverend Mr. Buckingham appeared, and read off before ye town then convened the following proposals, and directed in manner following:

Mr. Buckingham's proposal.

To ye town of Norwalk, with ye Church appertaining thereunto :

Being apprehensive of disquietments among many respecting my continuance in ye service and work of ye ministry among you, these are to signifie to you, that if you are disposed, and do so agree to call a consociation of ye elders and messengers of ye churches of this county, whereby I might have a regular discharge from ye work and service of the ministry, and ye care of your souls ; as by a like consociation I was regularly established in, and unto ye same ; and that the said consociation shall allso take cognizance of such publike scandalls that any of ye members of this church may lye under, in breaches of severall commands of the morall law, and other Scripture rules; that so, whatsoever of that nature may appear, may be orderly removed, and y chhs. peace established,—Under which surcomstances once obtained, I shall freely lay down ye work and service of ye ministry among you.

August 12th, 1726. STEPHEN BUCKINGHAM.

The proposal voted to be irregular.

Sept. 14, 1726. The town according to adjournment met, at which meeting it was proposed to the town, whether they would call a consociation according to foregoing proposall of the Rev. Mr. Buckingham, presented to ye town August 12th, 1726.

By a major vote, ye town determines the above s^d proposal to be irregular, and therefore, by a major vote, resolves ye above question in the negative. '

A Committee to treat with Mr. Buckingham, about his salary.

Dec. 1, 1726. The town determines to have a committee chosen to treat with the Reverend Mr. Buckingham, refering to his salary, and the act of the town upon the same, Feb. 18, 1725-6.

Building a town house.

[*Note*. After the town were shut out of the meeting house, they met, generally in ye " North," or " Upper," School House.]

Dec. 9th, 1726. The Town determines to have a house built upon such place as the town by major vote shall agree to determine, that may well entertain the town to meet in at their town meetings, and others as the town shall or may have occasion from time to time ; and also for the entertainment of a generall schoole.

[At the same meeting it was put to vote whether they would build a town house " between the meeting house and Mr. Street's, or whether they would " build an addition to the upper school house ;" upon which 18 voted for the former, and 33 for the latter.]

Mr. Buckingham's " frequent visits at yᵉ house of Mr. Lines."

Jan. 25th, 1726—7. The town determines that some thing shall be done respecting ye yet remaining difficulties about ye Reverend Mr. Stephen Buckingham, in order for the obtaining relief; and in consideration of ye difficult surcomstances of ye church and people of this town, by reason of the sd Gentleman's frequent visit at ye house of Mr. Lines, with some other remarkable occurrances, the town have by major vote agreed that a council of elders and messengers of this county be called, in order to hear the grievances, and quiet the uneasiness of the Chh. and people herein.

At ye same meeting, the town made choice of John

Copp, Mr. James Brown, and Mr. Saml. Betts, committee to represent ye town before s^d council when convened, and to manage the whole affair respecting ye premises aboves^d.

[Soon after this date some drew off to the Church of England, and the First Congregational Society was organized under the style of " The Prime Ancient Society." The Town then ceased to manage the ecclesiastical affairs, and all proceedings relative to such matters, connected with the Congregational Society, will be found under the head of SOCIETY RECORDS.]

Land to Wilton Parish.

At a Proprietors meeting convened in Norwalk, Feb. 1, 1726-7, the proprietors by major vote grant to ye Parish of Wilton, Tenn Acres of land, to be layd out where ye proprietors alow land to be taken up, to be to ye use of ye Presbiterian or Congregational ministery among them forever.

Parsonage.

Feb. 12, 1728-29. The Proprietors grant Tenn Acress of land to be layd out West of ye High way that leads up from Isaaac Hayes's to Strawberry Hill, and North of the high way that lead up by Ebenezer Hyat's lott, towards the said Hayes's, where it can be most conveniently had, and that not prejudiciall to any High wayes ; which Tenn acres of land ye said proprietors grant for the use of a Dissenting Presbyterian or Congregational minister, that now is or shall be improved and ordained to that work in ye ancient and prime society in ye township of Norwalk from time to time.

[At the same meeting the Proprietors granted to the Parish of Wilton, five additional acres: six acres

" Westward of Canfield's Hill;" six acres " about ye
Wolf pits ; and six acres " Where it may be most convenient about ye White Oak Shade, for ye use and Improvement" " of a Dissenting, Presbiterian or Congre-
gationall minister thereabouts Improved and settled in
that work, and so from time to time."]

Grant to Canaan Parish.

April 3, 1732. The Proprietors by major vote grant
to the Inhabitants of Canaan Parish all ye common land
where their meeting house standeth, and Thirty Rods
from the meeting house, that is common and highway
there, so long as they shall support a meeting house in
said place.

Grant to the Church of England Professors.

Feb. 11, 1733-4. The Proprietors by major vote
grant to such persons in the Town of Norwalk that are
professors of the Church of England by law established,
One Rood of land on such part of the plain before Lt.
Lees, as the committee hereafter named and chosen by
sd proprietors shall think most fitting, stake the same
out, for them to build a Church upon, for ye worship of
God in that way ; and for a burying yard ; to be for yt
use forever ; Provided they build a Church on any part
of it.

[Oct. 5, 1750. Nehemiah Mead and Joseph Lockwood, Jr., purchased of the Proprietors a small parcel of
land " Near the Mill Brook, where their Tann fatts now
stand ;" and "At the same meeting the Proprietors by
major vote, grant to ye professors of the Church of
England in Norwalk, seventy one Poles of land adjoining to ye aforesaid land, as ye same is staked out by
sd committee ; who are hereby ordered to execute a deed
in proper form and manner for their holding the same."

A deed of the same is on record in Book of Deeds from 1753 to 1762.]

Sept. 25, 1760. A Deed from the Committee of the proprietors, to the Chh. Wardens of St. Paul's Church, and the rest of the professors of the Chh. aforesaid, "for the use and benefit of a burying yard, a small piece of common undivided land in sd Norwalk, situate and adjoining Northerly and Westerly of the land formerly granted by sd proprietors unto sd professors on which sd Chh. is built, in quantity fifty eight poles of land :" "bounded Easterly by highway and land belonging to sd professors, Southerly by sd land of sd professors, and partly by glebe land and common land, Westerly by sd glebe land, and Northerly by common land or highway."

Deed from the founders of St. Paul's Parish.

(Book of Records from 1740 to 1747.)

* * * Sundry persons, all Professors of ye Chh. of England, * * intending the same * * for ye first Glebe lands to endow sd Certain Parrish Chh. called St. Pauls, in the township of Norwalk * * * * KNOW YE that the sd Saml. Cluckston & Ralph Isaacs, John Belden, Jonathan Camp, * * * * * in great reverence and regard to the Chh. of England as established by law, and her excellent Doctrine, service, unity and order, preferable to any other upon earth * * * * * have founded the Parish Chh. aforesaid * * * * and for the endowment thereof, do by these presents, truly give, grant * * * * * to ye Society for Propagating the Gospel in Foreign Parts, a house and tract of land lying within ye bounds of Norwalk, in ye main street, sd land contains by estimation about one acre, be ye same more or less; and is bounded as followeth, vizt, South and East by high-

way, North & west by common land * * * * * * *
* * * * * in trust * * * to say, as soon as there shall
be a rector according to the order of the Chh. of England * * * ye premises shall be and inure to ye use of
such Rector incumbent and his successors as ye glebe
land of sd Chh. in fee simple forever * * * &c. 25
March, A. Dom. 1747.

Grants to the Professors of the Church of England of land upon
Strawberry Hill.

At a proprietors' meeting, April 6, 1747, Ralph Isaacs
& Saml. Cluckston, who are Church Wardens & have
represented to this meeting that those of the Proprietors
of the Church of England request that the Proprietors
at this meeting would grant to ye s^d Professors of the
Chh. of England, Five Acres of land * * at a place
called Strawberry hill; and this meeting having taken
s^d request into consideration ; being minded to oblige s^d
Professors, Do hereby grant to s^d Church Wardens and
the rest of s^d Professors said Five Acres, to be laid out
by a committee appointed for that purpose, for the support of a missionary settled according to ye canons of y^e
Church of England, from time to time forever.

[June 14, 1748. The Proprietors granted to the same
Two acres and a half, adjoining the above for the same
uses.]

Middlesex.

April 6, 1747. Whereas the Proprietors of Norwalk,
did by their vote ye 12 Feb. 1728-9, vote and grant six
acres of land South East from the land that was called
Woods-land land, Westward of Canfield's hill, for ye
use & improvement of a dissenting Presbyterian or Congregational minister thereabouts improved & settled in

the work & so from time to time ; and there being now
a minister settled by some of the people of Norwalk &
Stamford and the people of Five mile river that have
united with ye people of Stamford, supposing that s^d
land belongs to them for ye support of s^d minister,
and thereupon a question being put to this meeting,
whether s^d land ought to be improved by those of ye s^d
society that lives in ye bounds of Norwalk for ye use
afores^d, passed in the affirmative by a Major vote.

Town House.

Dec. 8, 1746.   The town agreed and voted to erect a
town house on ye southerly side of the road near where
the old town house stood (34 feet long, 24 feet wide).

Soldiers in the French War.

At a meeting of the Inhabitants of the town of Norwalk, Nov. 2, 1757.

Capt. Thomas Benedict is chosen Moderator of s^d
meeting.

At ye same meeting, upon information of 350 Regu-
lars to be posted in this town for Winter quarters, towards defraying the charges of the same the Town by
vote grant a Rate of one penny upon pound of all the
rateable estate.   *   *   *   The Select men   *   *   *
are by vote appointed to take care of the aforesayd Regu-
lars.

Guard House and Hospital.

Feb. 20, 1759.   Voted that the Town shall provide
fire wood, &c., for the Guard House and Hospital ; and
the select men for the time being are appointed to take
care of the same, so far as it relates to the town.

Saybrook Platform.

[One Saybrook Platform given gratis to each minister

in this town ; the select men divide the remaining part
according to list.]

Against Riotous Proceedings.

Nov. 12, 1765. Whereas there have been diverse
routs and tumultuous and riotous assemblies of disorderly people in the land, and some in this colony ; and
there are diverse reports of many threatenings of such
further tumults and riotous assemblies, to the intent of
doing mischief to the persons and properties of diverse
people, and especially against some in the principall
places of rule and government ; all of which are contrary to the peace, and to subvert all order and government ; and whereas the inhabitants of the town of Norwalk, in general town meeting assembled, taking these
matters into serious consideration, think it their indis-
pensable duty to bear proper and publick testimony
against such unlawfull proceedings ; and accordingly do
declare their utter abhorrence and detestation of all
such routs, tumults, and riotous· assemblies, and such
alarming threatenings of mischiefs ; and as they think
themselves bound in loyalty to the King, and for the
security of the privileges of the colony, and of the lives
and properties of ye subjects, do hereby further declare,
they will use their utmost endeavor, in all proper and
legal ways, to prevent and suppress all such disorders,
so far as appertains to them to be aiding and assisting
therein.

Burying Ground on Mill Hill.

(Last Monday of Dec. 1767.) "At the same meeting the Inhabitants by major vote give and grant all
their right and title to the burying place on Whitney's
hill, so called, to ye inhabitants of the First Society.".

Non Importation.

Aug. 20, 1770.   Col. Thomas Fitch chosen moderator of the meeting.   Voted that they will send a committee to N. Haven to attend the general meeting which
is proposed the next day after commencement, to consult affairs relative to importing goods, &c.

(Capt. John Cannon, Col. Thos. Fitch, and Capt.
Benjamin Isaacs were chosen delegates of this town to
attend the general meeting afores^{d}.)

Dr. Thadds. Betts, Mr. Thos. Belden, Capt. Stephen St. John, and Samuel Gruman were chosen and
appointed to draw such instructions as they shall think
proper for the aforesd delegates, and lay the same before this meeting, which is to be adjourned.

The Continental Congress.

Dec. 5, 1774.   Whereas, this meeting have taken into
consideration the matters contained in the association
come into by the Continental Congress held at Philadelphia the 5th day of September, 1774, and approved
of by the lower house of assembly, and recommended by
them to the several towns in this colony, to appoint
committees for the purposes in the eleventh article in
sd association contained—Do approve of the same,
and in pursuance thereof do appoint Eliakim Raymond,
John Cannon, Thadds. Betts, Stephen St. John 2d,
Lemuel Brooks, Eliphalet Lockwood, Nathl. Benedict,
Samuel Gruman, Goold Hoyt, Thos. Betts, Ozias Merwine, Phinehas Hanford, Daniel Betts, jr., Blackleach
Jesup, Ezra Gregory, John Carter, James Richards,
Samuel Richards, Gershom Raymond, Asa Hoyt, a
committee for the purpose in s^{d} Eleventh Article contained, during the pleasure of the town.

County Congress.

Feb. 6, 1775. Doct. Thadds. Betts, Capt. Stephen St. John, Gershom Raymond, and Samuel Gruman, were chosen a committee to represent this town in County Congress.

Donations for the Poor inhabitants of Boston.

At the same meeting, Messrs. Thomas Benedict, Eliphalet Lockwood, and John Cannon, were appointed to receive any donations that may be brought in for the relief of the poor inhabitants of the town of Boston.

The Committee of Inspection.

Feb. 6, 1775. Voted that those persons which have been warned by the committee of inspection, to bring in their arms, shall not vote in choosing a committee of inspection at this meeting.

At the same meeting were chosen Messrs. Phinehas Hanford, Stephen St. John 2d, Thadds. Betts, Nathl. Benedict, Osias Merwine, Lemuel Brooks, Thos. Fitch, Uriah Rogers, Jabez Gregory, Seth Seymore, Timothy Fitch, Danl. St. John, Blackleach Jesup, Danl. Betts, jr., Clap Raymond, Ezra Gregory, James Richards, Moses Comstock, Samuel Cook Silliman, Samuel Richards, and Jesse Raymond, a committee of Inspection during the pleasure of the town.

Be saving of Gun-powder.

At the same meeting, voted, that they disapprove of ye unnecessary use of Gun-powder, and recommend it to the committee of inspection to take care of the matter.

The Nullifiers of Poplar Plain and Norfield.

Jan. 8, 1776. Whereas, information hath this day

been made to this meeting, that there are numbers of the inhabitants of this town, living at Poplar Plain and parts adjacent, have united with numbers of the inhabitants of Fairfield, living in Norfield Parish and the Western part of the town of Fairfield adjoining to this town, and have unwarrantably formed themselves into a body, and call themselves a committee, and being so formed, have resolved and determined that every person that is in debt shall not be liable to be sued for the same, nor be liable to pay any interest on obligations, but be discharged therefrom ; and that justices of the peace shall not sign any writ, or grant any executions, and the officers shall not serve either writs or executions ; and have also in case any creditor shall attempt to sue for his debt or require interest on obligations, or a justice sign a writ, or any officer serve the same, they will unitedly prevent and oppose with all the force and strength they can procure the same.—This meeting, taking into consideration the aforesaid matters of information, and the aforesaid illegal resolves and determinations, are of opinion that the same have a direct tendency to set aside all law, and leave us in the hands of a merciless set of men, and to throw us into confusion and distraction, and to deprive us of all our valuable and constitutional rights. We therefore do hereby vote and agree to use our utmost influence, power, and strength, to disapprove and to discountenance every such illegal measure ; and do everything in our power, unitedly, to aid and assist the authority in suppressing the same in every proper and legal way.

Salt Petre Works.

At the same meeting, the select men are directed to erect Salt Petre works, and carry on the making of Salt

Petre at the expense of the town, agreeable to the law of this colony ; unless some particular person or persons shall appear to do the same.

Magazine.

At the same meeting, the select men are directed to erect a magazine to keep the warlike stores belonging to the town, " and that on the hill between Mr. Leaming's house and Ebenezer Lockwood's."

Committee of Inspection.

May 20, 1776. Whereas, complaint is made to this meeting by the committee of inspection in this town, that some inconveniency has arisen on account of the difficulty of having the major part of said committee collected on sudden and special occasions, voted, that any seven of s^d committee shall have power to act in said capacity on any sudden and special occasion.

Donald McAuley's Salt.

Oct. 14, 1776. Whereas there has been great uneasiness among the inhabitants, with respect to the great rise of salt ; and there being a large quantity in the possession of Donald McAuley of this place, which the inhabitants of this town are necessitated to have for their use at some price ;—the said Donald McAuley therefore came into this meeting, and agreed with the inhabitants, that he would not ask them more than twelve shillings, lawful money, per bushel, out of the said quantity, for their own consumption ; and if the market price shall be less, any time hereafter, he will accept of the same. Upon which the inhabitants consent that any one person may purchase salt of him accordingly.

The Watch.

Oct. 14, 1776. Voted, that the select men give a proper reward, to the persons appointed and ordered by the authority to set the watches, for their service; and draw an order on the town treasurer for the payment thereof.

Allso voted, that the select men make such provision for the watches as they shall think proper in regard to housing.

Cannon and Cannon Ball.

Dec. 2, 1776. The select men are directed to transport six cannon, such as they shall judge best for the defence of this town, from Salisbury; and provide carriages for the same; and also a sufficient quantity of ball for the security of the town.

Monopolies and Oppressions.

March 12, 1777. The inhabitants by vote agree that they will assist the officers of this town in carrying into execution one certain law of this state, entitled an act to prevent monopolies and oppressions, by excessive and unreasonable prices for many of ye necessaries and conveniences of life.

The Guard.

March 12, 1777. The inhabitants by major vote approve of what the authority and select men have done, in regard to hiring 75 men as a watch or guard to this town.

Filling the Continental Battalions.

Whereas, the slow progress made in filling up the continental Battallions to be raised by this state, and the vast importance of their being immediately com-

pleted, &c., was on the 18th day of March, 1777, taken
into consideration by his Honor the Governor and the
Council of safety ; and thereon voted and resolved by
said board, to ascertain the quota or proportion of each
town to complete s^d battallions and to promote and
encourage such enlistment. Lest any should be
embarrassed by a prospect of leaving their families,
without a security of their being properly provided for ;
it is by said board earnestly recommended to the several towns in this state to engage and promise such soldiers as shall undertake in sd service, and have not
time and opportunity to lay out their money, and make
provision for their families (such as have any), that
their said families, on their reasonable request, shall be
supplied in their absence with necessaries at the prices
stated by law ; and that each town severally appoint a
committee for that purpose, to see them provided for
and supplied accordingly, on such soldiers lodging, or
from time to time remitting money to said committee for
that purpose ; and without any additional expense ; and
the necessary expense attending the same, to be borne
by the town respectively, &c ;—It is therefore recommended by this meeting, that all the inhabitants, of
every rank and condition, vigorously exert themselves in
encouraging, promoting, and forwarding the filling up
the quota or proportion ascertained by said board for
this town, in order to complete said Battallions ; and
also voted, that Messrs. Stephen St. John 2d, Thomas
Benedict, Phinehas Hanford, Jesse Raymond, Thadds.
Hubbell, Oliver Whitlock, James Richards, and Nehemiah Benedict, be a committee for the purposes contained in said resolves, with full power and authority to
engage and promise to such soldier as shall inlist in s^d

service, that all matters and things contained in sd resolve respecting them, shall be punctually performed agreeable thereto, and it is recommended by this meeting, that the virtuous sons of liberty cheerfully and readily engage in sd service at this critical time ; so that peace and rest may once more be restored to the United States of America ; by means whereof this meeting have reason, by the blessing of God, to expect the same may be effected.

Messrs Eli Reed, Asa Hoyt, John Gregory, jr., Levi Taylor, Nathan Hubbell, and Moses Comstock, were appointed a Committee to endeavour to find the number of soldiers enlisted in the continental army, in this town, and report to this meeting.

This meeting is adjourned to meet Tuesday, at 2 o'clock.

Met according to the foregoing adjournment. Doct. Thadds. Betts, Moderator, present.

Voted, that it is the desire of this meeting, that the recruiting officers in the Continental service request the several Captains of the military companies, in this place, to warn their respective companies and Householders to muster as soon as may be, to beat up for volunteers ; and the inhabitants are desired to incourage the enlistment by their liberality. The companies and inhabitants of the first society are desired to muster together on the parade of the first company.

Salt brought from Boston.

September 25, 1777. Nehemiah Benedict, Nathaniel Benedict, and David Comstock, were appointed a committee to get what salt there is in the town of Boston, belonging to the inhabitants of this town, from

7

thence, in the best manner they can, at the expense of the town.

Clothing for the Soldiers.

At the same meeting Hezekiah Hanford, John Lockwood, Jr., Hooker St. John, Levi Taylor, Thadds. Hubbell, Abijah Betts, James Olmsted, Samuel Gates, Abijah Comstock, Timothy Reed, Levi Hanford, James Lockwood, and Gershom Richards, were appointed a committee to procure and collect such articles of clothing as is requested by a resolve of the Governor and Council of Safety, for the use of the soldiers in the Continental army, and deliver the same to the select men in order that the same may be forwarded according to said resolve.

Supplying the families of soldiers.

At the same meeting, voted that the Committee formerly appointed to procure provisions for the families of those soldiers which are gone into the army, from this town, go on and procure the same for such families, at the rate set by law ; and in case they are obliged to give more, the select men to order the treasurer to pay the overplus.

Dec. 1, 1777.   Matthew Marvine added to the Committee for providing for the families of those that are in the army.

Considering the Articles of Confederation

At the same meeting, voted Messrs. Thomas Fitch, Thaddeus Betts, Stephen St. John, David Comstock, Joseph Chapman, Nehemiah Mead, and Samuel Gruman, were appointed a committee to revise the articles of Confederation published by Congress, and make report to this meeting which is to be adjourned.

Jan. 13, 1778, at one of the clock, Met according to the foregoing adjournment.

Blackleach Jesup was chosen to supply the families of ye soldiers of the Continental army, in addition to the former committee.

Whereas his Excellency the Governor, on receipt of the articles of the confederation published by Congress, for the approbation of the several assemblies of the United States, sent a copy of the same to this town, in order for the town to show their sense relative thereto.

It is voted by this town, that they are sensible of the great difficulty of concerting any plan of union with so many different states, under so many different circumstances, free from objection, and without being liable to exceptions ; yet the articles contained in said confederation generally appear to this town to be well framed, and calculated to form a union for the general benefit of the whole ; yet, notwithstanding, this town beg leave to submit to ye consideration of the General Assembly whether the method of supplying the common treasury, contained in the eighth article, and the mode of raising a continental army, in the ninth article, is so just and equitable as may be devised.

Voted also that a copy of this be sent forthwith to the General Assembly to show the sense of the town in the premises.

Regulating the price of labor.

March 25, 1778. The select men are desired to procure such a number of the late act of the Assembly printed, respecting the regulations of the prices of labor, &c., with the doings of the authority and select men of this town relative thereto, as that each Householder in this town may be supplyd with one at the expense of this town.

Distributing the State salt.

Aug. 10, 1778. Voted that the select men are desired and empowered to distribute the salt lately purchased by this state for their inhabitants of this town, to and among the said inhabitants, in just proportion according as each man's particular list in the year 1777, and to draw orders on the Town treasurer for the necessary cost arising on such division.

Borrowing money to buy Clothing for Soldiers.

At the same meeting voted, that the committee heretofore appointed to procure clothing for the officers and soldiers in the Continental Army, are desired to procure money on interest, to purchase said clothing as soon as may be; and the select men are ordered to pay the interest and cost of procuring the said money, out of the town treasury.

Giving salt to the families of Soldiers.

August 10, 1778. Whereas on a division of salt belonging to the town, there is yet a small part remains on hand, and the inhabitants agree and vote that the select men shall pay the expense that has arisen on sd salt out of the said remainder; and if there is still any remains, to deliver the same to ye families of such soldiers belonging to this town, as are in the army.

Fines for neglect, when the enemy came to Tarry Town and to Horseneck.

2d Monday in March, 1779. Doct. Betts not being present, Capt James Richards chosen Moderator.

Voted and agreed, that all fines and forfeitures that shall be collected out of the alarm list, and militia companies, and light horse, in this town, for neglecting to turn out at the time the enemy landed at Tarry Town last Decr., and at the time the enemy came to Horseneck last Feb., and shall hereafter neglect to turn out, shall be delivered by the town treasurer to the Captain of the company from which the same shall be collected, and this vote to continue in force during the pleasure of the town.

Depreciation of Continental Currency.

3d Monday in June, 1779, at 4 o'clock.

Col. Thomas Fitch, Capt. Eliphalet Lockwood, and Samuel C. Silliman, Esq.,were chosen committee to meet a County Convention at Fairfield, to consult the address from the Continental Congress respecting the depreciation of the Continental currency, &c.

Classes for providing Soldiers with clothing.

At the same meeting voted that the inhabitants of this town shall be put into as many classes as their cota of soldiers in the Continental Army, and each class to provide clothing for one soldier.

Town House.

At the same meeting (1st Monday of August, 1779), voted to have a town house built as soon as conveniently may be.

(The dimensions to be 45 feet by 30, posts 16 feet; lower story 12 feet in height, a convenient chimney at each end; and to be set on the Westerly part of the Town House Hill.)

Continental Currency.

Aug. 16, 1779. Voted that we will strictly and punctually adhere to the recommendation of s^d convention (of the County)—with respect to putting a stop to the depreciation of the Continental Currency ; and also abide by any such measure as s^d convention shall hereafter adopt for such purpose.

Small Pox.

2d Thursday of October, 1779. Voted that ye Small Pox by enoculation may be carried on for 2 months at the house of Moses Bixbe and Capt. Solomon Morehouse, under such regulations as the law prescribes.

Tax to raise Soldiers.

27th Day of June, 1780. Doct. Thaddeus Betts chosen moderator.

Voted, that they will tax themselves to raise money to hire the number of Soldiers to compleat the quota of this town for the Continental Army.

Voted that Col. Matthew Mead, Capt. Nathan Gilbert, Capt. Saml. Keeler, Lt. James Betts, Capt. Solomon Morehouse, Lt. Jer. B. Ells, and Capt. Danl. Richards, be a committee with full power to enlist such a number of able-bodied men as shall be sufficient to compleat the quota of this town for the Continental Service during the war, or three years resolved by the General Assembly last May ; and that they engage such sums, and in such a way, as their discretion and judgment shall direct, to such as shall appear to engage in said service ; and that the same be done forthwith, and a report thereof be made to this meeting at their adjournment.

Adjourned to meet the last day of the same month.

At the same meeting voted that they will take the late emission of paper money emitted by this state, equal to silver and gold in all payments whatever.

Tax for Provisions for the Army.

(NOTE.—On Aug. 25, 1779, they had levied a tax of two shillings and six pence on the pound to defray the charges arisen and arising on the town.

On the 13th of March, 1680, they had laid a tax of two pence on the pound to hire soldiers for the continental army) now

Nov. 13th, 1780. The inhabitants grant a tax of six pence lawful money on the pound, in silver and gold equivalent, upon the polls and ratable estate of the inhabitants of this town, on the list for the year 1779, to be paid in Beef, Pork, Wheatflour, or money; the beef to be delivered before the 16th day of Dec. next, and the pork and flour, before the 15th of Jan.'y next, to the person or persons that may be appointed to receive the same or the money; the beef, pork, and flour at the prices mentioned in one certain statute law of this State, intituled an Act for Collecting and Storing a quantity of Provisions for the use of the Continental army, and the forces for the defence of this State.

4th day of Dec. 1781. The select men are directed to deliver the sum of ninety pounds in state money, which they have now in their hands, to the collectors and receivers of provisions, for them to lay out in purchasing casks and beef.

The Select men are desired to hire money to procure this town's quota of Soldiers for the Continental Army; and the town engages to indemnify them in doing the same.

The inhabitants grant a tax of one penny on the pound, on the list of 1779, to be paid in wheat & rye flour, and Indian corn, agreeable to one certain statute, &c.

Inimical Persons.

At the same meeting the authority and select men are directed to send for the committee respecting inimical persons, at the expense of this town.

Judgment against Inimical Persons.

We the subscribers, agreeable to an act and appointment of the Honorable Gen'l Assembly, having been called upon and requested by the Civil authority and select men of the Town of Norwalk, to enquire into the character and conduct of a number of persons whose names are contained in a list or roll by them presented to us, as Inimical and Dangerous to the Liberties and Independence of the United States of America; and we having duly examined into the premises, are of opinion that the following persons whose names are hereafter expressed, are inimical and dangerous as aforesaid; and therefore give judgment and order that their names be enrolled in the town clerk's office in s^d town of Norwalk as dangerous and inimical as aforesaid for the purposes mentioned in an act of the Gen'l Assembly of this state, entituled, An Act more effectually to prevent robberies and plunders from our open and secret enemies, vizt. : Obadiah Wright, Nathan Burwell, Jr., Thomas Hanford, Nathan Jarvis, Thomas Fairweather, David Bolt, Peter White, Hezekiah Whitney, 2d, Nathan Gregory, Phillip Scribner, Hezekiah Belden, John Beldin, Edward Nash, Gershom Raymond, James Fillio, William Bolt, Ebenezer Church, David Lambert, Goold Hoyt, Abraham Whitney, John Saunders, Jr., Garner Olmsted, Richard Patrick, Nathan Fitch, all of Norwalk aforesaid; each of the above named persons having first been duly notified and cited to appear before us at time and

place by us appointed for that purpose; to shew reason
if any they had, why their names should not be enrolled
as aforesaid.

Done at Norwalk, this 20th Day of April, A.D. 1781,

By us,   DANIEL SHERMAN,
BENJA. HENMAN,
To the Town Clerk   ANDW. ADAMS,
of Norwalk.   INCREASE MOSELY.

Clothing for Soldiers.

Dec. 4, 1781. James Selleck, Thos. Benedict, Eli
Reed, Ezra Benedict, David St. John, Aaron C. Comstock, & Matthew Merwine, were chosen a committee
to purchase cloathing for the soldiers belonging to this
town in the Continental Army; ———— and directed to
hire money on interest to purchase the same; and the
town engages that the same shall be made good to them,
with interest, as the same was at the time of hiring.

Classes for Raising Soldiers.

At the same meeting the select men and military
officers are to look into the affair of the Continental
Soldiers; and the select men are to class the inhabitants
for such a number as they shall find wanted for the
quota of this town; and also to class the inhabitants
for such a number of soldiers as shall be wanted in a
State regiment at Horseneck for one year.

A Guard for the Defence of Norwalk.

Feb. 18, 1782. Voted that a sufficient number of
men be raised, by inlistment, for a sufficient guard in
this town.

Col. Thos. Fitch, Col. Matthew Mead, Capt. James
Richards, Capt. Eliph. Lockwood, & Mr. Hooker St.
John, were chosen a committee to ascertain the number
7*

of men wanted for a guard, and lay a plan for raising the same.

To the inhabitants of the town of Norwalk now assembled in town meeting: We the subscribers being appointed a committee to lay a plan for raising a number of guards sufficient to defend this town, with a sum of twelve hundred and forty pounds lawful money granted to this town by the General Assembly for that purpose ; beg leave to Report: That there be forthwith raised by inlistment for the town, of six months unless sooner discharged, ninety men including corporals ; and that there be appointed one Captain, and one Ensign for the purpose of defending this town ; and that a Captain have £6 lawful money per month ; an Ensign £3 5 0 per month, a Corporal £2 4 0, and a Private £2 0 0 per month ; and that we find that the said sum will amount, for six months, to the sum of Eleven Hundred and fifty three pounds Ten Shillings: and that 18 be stationed at the lower end of the town on the East side of the river ; and 18 at Ketchum's, one half thereof to keep centry at the going on at Stephens Island ; and 18 at the Old Well, and 18 at Flax Hill, and 18 at Middlesex ; and that officers or privates, at their election, have one half of their wages in provisions at the following prices, vizt. : fresh beef $3\frac{1}{2}$d, salt beef 4d, flour at $2\frac{1}{4}$d per pound ; and that there be a Corporal to each class ; and that the officers be appointed by the authority and select men ; all of which is submitted by your most obed't humble serv'ts.

Increase of Wages to the Guard.

Aug. 1, 1782. Whereas the wages given by this town to the Guard to serve for the defence of this town for the term of five months unless sooner discharged, are found insufficient to induce a sufficient number to engage in s^d service, it is therefore voted and agreed by this town, that the officers already engaged in said service receive, in addition to the wages given, the usual rations for such officers hereafter; and that the soldiers already engaged, receive from this time, in addition, rations as usual, and that those who shall hereafter enlist into s^d service to the 20th of August next, shall receive 40s per month to that time, unless sooner discharged, and rations; and that such a number of s^d guard do duty, in the day time, as the Captain shall judge proper; and at all times when he shall judge it necessary for the safety and defence of the town.

The authority and select men to nominate a Lieutenant to serve in the guard & in this town; and to have his pay and rations in proportion to the other officers. At the same meeting voted that on a complaint being made, to the authority and select men of this town, against any officer or soldier in the guard, of his or their not being faithful in doing their duty, the said authority and select men shall cause the s^d officer or soldier to be called before them and examine into their conduct, and on proof of their misconduct, may dismiss them from service.

Hiring Soldiers.

May 6th, 1782. Voted that there shall be a committee appointed to hire three soldiers to serve in the continental army for the term of one year.

Applying for Relief on account of the burning of the town by the enemy.

Aug. 11, 1783. This town taking into consideration the many and great distresses, difficulties, and losses a

number of the inhabitants have sustained, met with, and
are reduced to, by means of the enemy's burning up,
destroying and plundering them of their most necessary
property during the late war with Great Britain; and the
very great injury and damage done to the town by means
thereof; and that the same was brought on the town
during the course of a war undertaken by the direction
and order of the inhabitants of this State united with
the other States, and the common consent of the inhabitants of this State, for the defence and security of the
common liberties, privileges, and freedom of this
State; in which war it was then understood and fully expected the misfortunes accidentally thrown on any particular part during the course of the war, as it was undertaken for the defence and security of the whole, and
considering that it is altogether just, equitable, and
righteous so to be :—have thereupon agreed and voted
that Col. Stephen St. John, Esq., be agent for the town,
to make use of such measures as he shall judge proper,
by memorial in conjunction with other suffering towns,
or separately, to the General Assembly, or otherwise,
in order to obtain redress of the town's grievances sustained and met with during the course of the war, and
for a repair of the damages done by the enemy, to be
made to the individual sufferers; excepting to those sufferers who are known to be inimical to the liberties and
independence of the United States of America.

Tories.

*Feb. 24, 1783. Put to vote whether those persons

---

*Note.—I copy this record in the order that it stands on the book.
The preceding article is recorded first, though the date is posterior
to this.

which have gone off and joined themselves with the enemy, should return back and inhabit in this town.

Past in the Negative.

(At an adjourned meeting, a fortnight from the above date,)

Eli Reed, Danl. Betts, Jr., James Benedict, Justus Hayt, Saml. Seymore, Lt. Joseph Rockwell, Thomas Betts, Jr., & Enoch Scribner, were appointed a committee to assist the civil authority and select men, in keeping out of this town any suspected or transient persons who shall attempt to reside within the limits thereof; and make information of such persons to the authority and select men; & take their direction in all proceedings with them.

Dec. 1, 1783. [Hezekiah Rogers, Job Bartram, Isaac Keeler, Saml. Deforest, Justus Hayt, Matthew Gregory, Saml. Comstock, Stephen Betts, Eli Reed, a committee] to take directions from the select men of this town, and deal with those persons who have been to the enemy and returned, according to their directions.

Last Monday in December, 1783. Voted that the select men and Committee are to act their discretion respecting those persons which have joyned the enemy, notwithstanding any former votes.

END OF TOWN RECORDS.

A VIEW OF NORWALK, CONN.
From the Rocks.

SOCIETY RECORDS.

EXTRACTS FROM THE RECORDS OF THE FIRST CONGRE-
GATIONAL SOCIETY.

Calling the Society Meeting apart from the Town.

To Lt. Matthew Seymore in Norwalk Greeting, &c.

Pursuant to an act of ye Generall assembly, passed in Oct. 1726, Entitled An act for directing how societies shall meet and form themselves after other societies are drawn off from them. ¯

In his Majestie's name you are hereby required to warn all ye inhabitants of ye Prime Ancient Society in ye township of Norwalk, to meet together on ye first Fryday of March next ensuing ye date hereof, at eight of ye clock in ye morning, then and there to act any thing proper and lawful for them to act when so met to-gether.   JOSEPH PLATT,

Dated at Norwalk, Feb. ye 27,   *Justice Ps.*

Annoque Domini, 1726-7.

(The society met according to the above warning,) made choice of ye Worshipfull Joseph Platt, Esq., Mo-derator.

At the same meeting it was proposed to the society whether any thing should be done about obtaining a suitable person to supply ye vacancy of our pulpit. Voted in ye affirmative.

The society considering ye awfull frowns of heaven upon them for months past, and are still obvious, con-cludes it their incumbent duty to set apart a day for the humbling and abasing their souls before the Lord by fasting and prayer for redress; By their major vote do appoint Wednesday, ye 15th of this instant March for that solemnity; and desire Rev. Mr. Davenport, Mr. Cook, Mr. Sackett, Mr. Hauley, and Mr. Sturgeon, to

grant us their presence and assistance in carrying on ye
work of s^d day.

(Mr. Buckingham's rate due last year voted to be paid
as heretofore, "any act of ye town to ye contrary notwithstanding.")

Association of Ministers.

March 16, 1726. The society determines to have an
Association Quorum, at least of ye Ministers of this
county called, and to associate with us on Wednesday ye
22d of this instant, March, to advise, direct, and guide
us in ye weighty affair before us.

Questions for Advice.

March 23, 1726. According to adjournment ye society met. The Revd Mr. Cooke, Mr. Chapman, Mr.
Sacket, & Mr. Hauley associated with the society.

The society, by major vote, desires ye Revd. Association to give them an answer to ye following question,
viz. Whether it be proper or expedient that ye Revd
Mr. Buckingham be introduced into ye work of ye ministry in this society or not.

The answer from ye Revd. Association.

The Prime Ancient Society in Norwalk moving this
Question for resolution to us ye subscribers associated at
their desire in Norwalk March 23, 1726—7, viz.
Whether, &c.—We are of opinion that inasmuch as
ye Revd Mr. Buckingham hath resigned his pastoral
charge here, considering ye distressed circumstances of
ye place, and that under the countenance of ye late
Council in this place, who also have signified themselves
persuaded that the interest of religion and edification
of souls are the great ends of ye Gospel ministry, and
sorrowfully affected with the consideration of those

ends in this place being greatly obstructed and disadvantaged, We are of opinion that it is not proper or expedient that the sd Revd. Mr. Buckingham be introduced into ye work of ye ministry in this society, for ye reasons above alleged.

SAML. COOKE,
DANIEL CHAPMAN,
THOMAS HAULEY,
RICHARD SACKET.

Advice about procuring a minister.

There was nominated by some persons in the meeting, viz. Mr. John Curtice of Wethersfield, Mr. Gilbert Tenant in ye Jerseys, Mr. Dunbar of Boston, and Mr. Chauncey, Jr., of Hadley ; and ye Society crave of the Revd. Association their particular direction concerning them, or any other that they shall see meet to direct to us as a person to be applyd to, with an invitation to a probationary improvement among us in ye ministry.

The return from ye Revd. Association.

We ye subscribers associate at Norwalk March 23, 1726—7, being applied to by ye Prime Ancient Society in sd Norwalk for advice and direction, &c. * * * We are of opinion that as to Mr. Tennant now in the improvement in ye ministry in the New Jersey, it may not be so proper to make application to him for the supply of a vacancy here for this reason, viz. Because of ye paucity of Gospel labourers in those parts ; which requires us rather to wish their increase than to take any methods for ye decrease of their numbers ; especially considering our ministry from time to time earnestly solicited to send Gospel labourers unto those parts, more than we have been capable of supplying them with ; and do advise that this society would soon as may be, endeavor to inform themselves whether there may be a proba-

bility of obtaining Mr. Dunbar of Boston ; and upon
such a probability attained, to make application to him
for ye purpose afore sd ; and if there shall not be a
probability of obtaining the sd Mr. Dunbar, we advise
that the society make application either to ye said Mr.
Curtice or Mr. Chauncey, as upon consulting the ministers next neighbouring either of them, they may be encouraged.

SAML. COOKE,

DANL. CHAPMAN,

THOMAS HAULEY,

RICHARD SACKET.

Sending for a minister.

May 10, 1727.   The Society * * determines to send
a meet person to Mr. Chauncey Jr. of Hadley, as upon
consulting ye ministers neighbouring to him he may be
encouraged ; and in case Mr. Chauncey cannot be obtained, then to apply himself to ye sd ministers for advice to some other suitable person to apply to, and that
he do his utmost endeavor to obtain one according to
such direction, or to act about ye whole according to the
best of his discretion, to supply ye vacancy in our pulpit, at least for a probationary improvement in the
ministry among us.

* * Mr. James Brown to proceed upon ye business
as above expressed.

Revd. Moses Dickinson invited.

June 26, 1727.   The Society by major vote agree to
give the Revd. Mr. Moses Dickinson a call to supply the
vacancy in our pulpit.

* * Made choice of Capt. Joseph Platt, Esq., to go
to ye Revd. Gentleman, and endeavor to obtain him
pursuant to sd vote.

Made choice of Mr. John Bartlett, Capt. Joseph Platt, and Mr. Thos. Fitch Junr., to provide for, & to treat with ye s^d gentleman when he comes.

Call to Mr. Dickinson.

July 19, 1727. The Society having had report made from ye late Committee of ye circumstances of ye Revd. Mr. Moses Dickinson, who hath been with us upon a probationary improvement, with which report they are well satisfied as to the gentleman's circumstances; and do hereby give the s^d Revd. Gentleman a call to ye work of ye ministry among us; provided ye Revd. Elders now convened in this place give their approbation thereunto, voted in ye affirmative 75, Contra 39.

Advice asked of the Association.

The society determines to move to the Revd. Elders for a resolve respecting the circumstances of ye Revd. Mr. Dickinson, and whether they advise to the call above s^d.

There being severall persons of this Society under scruples respecting the relation they stand in to ye Revd. Mr. Buckingham, that is to say, whether s^d gentleman be regularly discharged from his pastorall relation to y Chh. and people of this place ; the Society taking this matter into consideration, do move to ye Revd. Elders convened, that they would give their opinion in ye premises, that such persons may receive satisfaction in that matter.

Answer of the Association.

July 20, 1727. The society receiving from ye Revd. Elders associated, an answer to ye foregoing matter of scruple, and it was read off as followeth :

A Quorum of Fairfield Association Occasionally convened in Norwalk July 19th, 1727.

Whereas it is Signifyed to us from ye records of ye
Society that there are severall persons of this Society
under Scruples respecting the relation they stand in to
ye Revd. Mr. Buckingham. That is to say whether ye
said Gentleman be Regularly Discharged from his pastorall Relation to ye Church and people of this place ;
and that our opinion in this case is desired.

In answer whereunto we Declare this to be our
Opinion that the Revd. Mr. Buckingham hath been
regularly Discharged from his pastorall Relation to
ye Church and people of this place ; And offer upon it
as followeth ; viz. (1) The Condition of this Church and
people hath been for a considerable time greviously per-
plex^d & Divided ; whereof a very great part have been
so distanced in affection from their Late pastor, that the
Cure of it after a Considerable time of Tryall, hath
appeared even to be Dispaired of ; Whereas also it appeared to us, that Saveing Ends of ye Gospel Ministry
here may not generally be attained, which in ye Judgment of ye late Counsel and in our Opinion is Cause
Justifying ye pastor's Resigning his pastorall Office, as
to ye Exercise of it in ye place of his Improvement ;
We propose the following Scriptures to be well Considered. Ephe. 4 : 11, 12, Our ascended Lord gave ye
gifts of ye Ministry to men for ye Edifying ye Body of
Christ : Where ye Edifying ye Body is expressly Set
down as a main End of Gospel Ministry. Now the prin-
ciple End being Generally Obstructed and that after a
Convenient Time of Waiting, may be well interpreted
as a call from above to ye Minister that hath been improved, Humbly to yield himself to —— that Christ

our Lord and ye Interest of immortal Souls may increase
and flourish ; John 3d, 30th. We have also considered
James 3d, 16th, Where envying and strife is, there is
Confusion and every evil work. Now this we have
thought ye Malancholly Condition of this Place ; &
have been Ready to account the Method of ye Council
in their late Doings accepting ye Revd. Gentleman's
Resignation, & supplying the Sanction of their authority thereunto, to be a proper and probable Remedy
of ye unhappy Distemper of this place. (2) The Revd.
Mr. Buckingham, as we understand, appearing in the
late Council, affected with ye Sorrowful state of ye place
and ye improbability of his future service here, Did
Seriously, Solemnly, & willingly resign his pastorall
Relation to ye Church and people of the place ; which
was in his power to Do so far as Concerns an act of his.
And the s^d Resignation being willingly made by him,
we apprehend no injury Done him, Because an injury to
a willing mind cannot be Done. We propose John 3d,
30th, he must increase, but I must Decrease. Which
example of that Great man, than whom a greater was
not Born of Women, We do understand presidential
even to ye ministers of ye Gospel in our Times, when
this continuing in the exercise the Gospel ministry may
be justly thought to interfere with the Generall Spirituall
good of Precious Souls.

3. The Resignation of ye Revd. Mr. Buckingham in ye
presence of ye society's com'tee, before ye council, ye
authority whereof we suppose not proper for ye good
people of this place to question, who have come into our
ecclesiastical constitution and accepted our articles of
administering Chh. discipline ; yet for ye satisfaction
of any of our people of this place, we mention ye

fifteenth Chapter of ye Acts; and thence observe, that ye council at Jerusalem (ye pattern for Chh. councils in Gospel times) in the difficulties that had arisen, in ye church of Antioch, &c., did undertake to determine that difference, in authoritative way. Acts 15: 2. "To whom we gave no such commandment." Now commandment is a word necessarily implying authority—see also verse 28. " It seemed good to ye Holy Ghost & to us to lay no greater burden," &c.; which expression to us implies authority, carrying an obligation in it on ye Chh. and people that applyd to ye council, see also verse 29; " From which if ye keep yourselves ye shall do well;" whence followeth yt ye Chh., which applied to the council at Jerusalem, if they did not observe the order of council, they should not do well, for that ye conclusion of council were ye highest authority, not to be controlled or disputed.

4. The Resignation of ye Revd. Mr. Buckingham being authorized by his proper judges, that is to say, ye council of ye elders & Chhs. of this county, the bond of his relation to this society, as pastor, is dissolved & ceaseth : (whereupon it followeth that ye bond of ye relation of this Chh. and every member thereof to ye sd Mr. Buckingham, their late pastor, is also dissolved and ceaseth.)

Unto ye above we only add as ye Rev. Mr. Buckingham hath formally declared himself willing to be directed by ye ministers of this county; now then as we account it on his part a good observance of order, for the future to forbear the exercise of ye pastoral office, to say, preaching and administering any sacraments in this place; so also, ye good & Christian people of this place will, in our opinion, show themselves men of order to contribute their part to such a direction of our association.

Our thoughts in relation to ye motion of this society to the Revd. Mr. Moses Dickinson, we offer as followeth, vizt :

That we are all glad of an opportunity now to signify the great respect and value we have for ye Revd. Mr. Moses Dickinson, and the satisfying prospect we have of his well answering ye necessities of this destitute society, and with all cheerfulness assure ye good people thereof, of our good approbation of this society's having their eyes upon the Revd. and valuable gentleman for ye work of ye ministry here, whensoever it appears to us that ye condition or proviso of ye Presbytery releasing him from a pastoral relation to ye people of Maidenhead, &c. appears absolutely & in fact to be by judgment of that Presbytery completed.

A true copy.

SAMUEL COOK, Scribe.

The society by a vote of Eighty eight, none appearing in the negative, do invite and call ye Revd. gentleman to ye work and labor of ye ministry among them.

Agreed and concluded to defray the charge of transportation of ye sd Mr. Dickinson and family, whensoever he may be obtained to move unto us.

(A committee appointed for this purpose and to provide a house, &c.)

* * Appointed ye Worshipfull Joseph Platt, Esq. to attend ye Revd. Mr. Dickinson home into ye Jersies, and also to endeavour the obtaining from ye Revd. Presbytery there, the Revd. Mr. Dickinson's discharge from ye Chh. and people of Maidenhead.

(On the society book is recorded at length the minutes of the Fairfield Association, in a meeting at Wilton,

Aug. 29, 1727, in which they approve of the doings of the council at Norwalk; and it appearing that Mr. Dickinson was now dismissed by his Presbytery, the association advise the society of Norwalk to repeat their call; which they did in full form on the 1st of Nov. 1727.

Difficulty with Mr. Buckingham.

Jan. 10, 1727–8.   The society grants ten pounds to Mr. James Brown, for his service at ye General Court, in answering ye memorial against the select men, preferred at New Haven in October last to the General Court by Mr. Stephen Buckingham. (Also granted 20s. to Lt. Samuel Comstock, which he paid to Mr. Fowler, lawyer, to assist in ye cause abovesaid.)

May 10, 1728.   Made choice of Joseph Platt, Esq., to represent the inhabitants of ye said society, to answer ye memorial of Mr. Stephen Buckingham. Made choice of Thomas Fitch, Esq., Mr. James Brown, and John Copp, Committee to prepare what is needful to be sent to Capt. Platt, who is now at ye said Assembly; by a safe hand, if such can be obtained, or else to send a man directly from hence to Capt. Platt.

At a meeting of ye Prime ancient Society of ye Town of Norwalk, convened May 7, 1729, * * Made choice of Mr. James Brown and Thos. Fitch, Esq., to appear in behalf of the society at the General Court, to be held at Hartford this present month; there to answer a Petition exhibited to sd court against the town of Norwalk, by the Revd. Mr. Stephen Buckingham.

The society impowers Mr. James Brown (that if he finds ye abovenamed Mr. Fitch engaged on ye petitioner's side), to employ or improve (if he see it needful) an attorney at Hartford to aid and assist him in ye premises.

Rev. Mr. Caner of the Church of England.*

Dec. 22d, 1729. The society, by major vote, determines that a receipt from under the hand of ye Revd. Mr. Caner, brought by any of ye church of England in this society (so declaring themselves, and attending as ye law* in that case mentions) for so much paid him as

* At a General assembly held in Hartford, May, 1127, it was enacted * * That, "If it so happen that there be a society of the Church of England, where there is a person in orders according to the Canons of the Church of England settled, and abiding among them, and performing divine service, so near to any person that hath declared himself of the Church of England, that he can conveniently, and doth attend the public worship there; then the collector, having first indifferently levied the tax as aforesaid, shall deliver the taxes collected of such persons declaring themselves, and attending as aforesaid, unto the minister of the Church of England living near unto such persons; which minister shall have full power to receive and recover the same, in order to his support in the place assigned to him."

(The same Act gave power to any society of the Church of England to levy on themselves greater taxes at their own discretion, for the support of their minister.)

"And the Parishioners of the Church of England, attending as aforesaid, are hereby excused from paying any taxes for the building meeting houses for the present established churches of this Government."

The General Assembly held at Hartford, May 8, 1727, enacted, "That where there are such dissenters as are commonly called Quakers, who do attend the worship of God in such way as is allowed by said act [in the 7th of Queen Anne, A. D. 1708], within this colony, or are so situated that they may and do attend the service out of the limits of this government, in any such meeting aforesaid; and shall produce a certificate from such a society, of their having joined themselves to them: and that they do belong unto their society; that he or they shall be excused from contributing to

ho or they are assest by this society, in the minister's
rate of said society; which receipt or receipts, so delivered to ye collector of the minister's rate, shall be a sufficient discharge to ye said collector, as if gathered by
said collector and paid the said Mr. Caner, and
thereby obtained his receipt for the same.

Meeting with the Professors of the Church of England.*

At a meeting of ye Prime Society in Norwalk with the
Professors of the Church of England inhabitants of said
society, legally warned, and being convened at ye old
school house in said society, Feb. 2d, 1746–7 * * * Grant
a rate of one penny the pound on all polls and ratable
estate of all the inhabitants within ye limits of said society, towards completing ye town house ; said house to
be improved for school society's meetings of ye inhabitants in said society, as pr grant of ye town at their
last annual meeting.

the support of the established ministry, and from contributing or
paying any tax levied for the building any meeting house or houses,
in the society where they dwell."

The General Assembly held at New Haven, Oct. 9, 1729, also
granted, "That for the future, the same privilege and exemption
from the charges aforesaid as was granted by this assembly in May
last unto the people called Quakers, is hereby allowed unto them
[the people called Baptists], under the like regulations ; any law,
usage, or custom to the contrary notwithstanding.

" At this time," says Prof. Kingsley, p. 95, " there were in Connecticut, but two or three congregations of Episcopalians, and two
of Baptists, all of which were small ; and no congregation of
Quakers."

* The schools were managed by the Prime Ancient Society;
their votes concerning districts, school houses, &c., at their annual
meetings being put on record from time to time.

8

The authority pew.

Dec. 14, 1747.   Voted, that Saml. Fitch, Esq., shall sit in ye pew next ye pulpit stairs, with the rest of ye authority.

Meeting House Windows.

Dec. 17, 1750.   Determine to glaze the meeting house with sash glass 7 & 9 inches —— * * A committee appointed to perform the same ; and are impowered to sell and dispose of ye glass and lead belonging to ye windows, in order to purchase glass and other materials for ye same.

His Honor, the Governor.

At a meeting of the Prime Ancient Society in Norwalk, assembled Dec. 25, 1754, * * The society by vote manifest their willingness that his Honor the Governor should choose any place in ye meeting house to erect a pew for himself and family.   Ye society send 3 men to treat with his Honor in the affair.

At the same meeting, ye said society grants the head of two fore seats in the meeting house, on ye women's side, to erect a pew for his Honor the Governor to sit in ; which is left to the discretion of David Benedict, Doct. Uriah Rogers, and Mr. Joseph Platt, a committee appointed to build said pew at ye society's charge.

Seating the Justices:

Dec. 10, 1755.   The society by vote desire the Justices to remove and sit in the pew with their wives.

Adorning the Governor's Pew.

At the same meeting, the society desire the committee appointed to erect the Governor's pew to do what they

shall think proper, to adorn the pew where the Governor now sits, in lieu of building a pew.

A colleague for Mr. Dickinson.

[In Feb. 1764, the society, with the concurrence of
Mr. Dickinson, voted to take measures to procure a colleague ; provided that means for the support of such colleague could be furnished by subscription, without laying any burden upon the society as such. In March
report was made to the society that such subscrip-
tions were furnished.]

Rev. William Tennent.

[Mr. Tennent having preached some Sabbaths on probation, the society by vote, unanimously invited him
to settle as colleague with Mr. Dickinson, Nov. 13,
1764.]

Mr. Leaming's Rate.

Dec. 17, 1764.   Thomas Hanford appointed to collect Mr. Leaming's rate.

The Presbytery of New Brunswick.

[Mr. Tennent wished to retain his connection with
the Presbytery; which the society, by mutual understanding, allowed, provided Mr. Tennent should "unite
with us and with the Association in the Ecclesiastical
constitution of the colony." The Presbytery, however,
understood it otherwise, and appointed a time, and a
committee of their own, for the installation. Whereupon, June 12, 1765, after a suitable preamble, the
society voted thus] :—" This society, by a copy from
the minutes of the Presbytery, are informed, that Mr.
Tennent declared his acceptance of the call of the society,
upon condition that he shall still continue a member

of the synod of New York and Philadelphia, and of
New Brunswick Presbytery ; * * * but at the same time
professed his desire and intention to hold communion,
and be in connection, with the Revd. association aforesaid, as far as is consistent with his continuing in his
relation to said synod : and that thereupon the said
Presbytery had presumed that this church and society
complied with the condition annexed by Mr. Tennent,
to his acceptance of their call (which was made on very
different terms) ; and accordingly have assumed to themselves a right to appoint and did appoint the time of instal-
ment, and a committee of their own to officiate therein.
On consideration of all which, this society is of opinion,
that the annexing the condition aforesaid to the acceptance
of the call aforesaid, is a proposal subversive of the foundation on which the agreement and proceeding of the
society were predicated ; and the proceedings of the
Presbytery in consequence thereof is an attempt to draw
the church and society off from the constitution in which
they are united, and to lead them to renounce the rela-
tions they stand in, and esteem too sacred to be violat-
ed ; and do also view such appointment of the time and
persons for installment, as an imposition on the society ;
and therefore is to be treated with neglect. Therefore,
the society do declare, that they cannot comply with the
abovesaid conditions and appointment ; but are obliged
to look on Mr. Tennent's annexing such embarrassment
to his acceptance, tantamount to a denial of the invitation made him, &c., &c. [In consequence of this, the
society appointed a committee to rent the House and
land which they had purchased as a parsonage for the
Colleague pastor. An explanation followed: Mr. Tennent declared that he never expected or intended that

the society should be under the power of the Presbytery; and signified his readiness to accept the call, if this explanation should prove satisfactory. Whereupon the society voted their approval and desired his settlement, adding, in their vote, June 19, 1765, that " Nevertheless, it is expected, that before his installment, a certificate be produced from the Revd. Presbytery aforesaid, of Mr. Tennent's being released from them, agreeably to the tenor of the above proposals, in order to make way for a regular settlement here, and a full union with the association here, on the constitution of this colony.]

Collectors of Mr. Leaming's Rate.

Dec. 16, 1765.   Nathan Burwell, Jr. to collect Mr. Leaming's rate.

Dec. 1766.   Ebenezer Church to collect Mr. Leaming's rate.

Dec. 14, 1767.   Goold Hoyt chosen collector of Mr. Leaming's last year's rate, likewise for the present year's rate.

Dec. 20, 1768.   Asa Hoyt chosen collector of ye Church of England professors.

Dec. 11, 1769.   Garner Olmsted to collect of the Church of England professors.

Dec. 10, 1770.   John Saunders to collect Mr. Leaming's rate.

Dec. 15, 1771.   Matthew Reed, collector of Mr. Leaming's rate.

Dec. 21, 1772.   Micajah Nash chosen to collect Mr. Leaming's rate (afterwards excused and Isaac Camp chosen in his room).

Dec. 13, 1773.   Garner Olmsted chosen collector of tax on ye professors of ye Church of England.

Dec. 14, 1774. Garner Olmsted collector of ye professors of ye Church of England.

Dec. 11, 1775. Daniel Church collector of ye professors of ye Church of England.

Dec. 9, 1776. Saml. White chosen collector of ye Church of England Professors.

Dec. 8, 1777. Barnabas Merwine Collec. of ye Church of England professors.

Dec. 14, 1778. John Saunders collector of Mr. Leaming's rate.

[Before the next annual meeting, the town was burnt by the British; and Rev. Mr. Leaming retired with the invaders to their fleet.]

Repairing the Meeting House.

Dec. 11, 1769. Put to vote, whether the society will repair the meeting house according to the report of those persons desired to view the same ; that is to say, to put on a new roof, and new side the house, and to make new window frames, so far as should be necessary. Passed in the affirmative.

Dec. 15, 1771. The committee heretofore appointed to repair the meeting house, are requested to do the same in the month of May next, &c.,   *   *   and then to colour ye sd house.

Mr. Tennent called to Charleston, S. C.

Jan. 8, 1772. Whereas the Rev. Mr. Treat of New York, applied to the committee of this society, desiring them to call the society together, that he might inform them that a call is presented to the Rev. Mr. Tennent in Charles Town in South Carolina, and to acquaint the society with the reasons for the application made to Mr. Tennent, and also to know whether the society will

concur with Mr. Tennent in calling a council to de-
liberate upon the affairs of the call; and also further
signified that it was the earnest desire of the Revd. Mr.
Tennent that the society should be convened for the
purpose aforesaid; and whereas the society being now
convened in consequence of sd requests; and the Revd
Mr. Treat having informed this meeting of the call from
sd church in Charles Town, &c.

The question was put whether this society will concur
with the Revd. Mr. Tennent in calling a council for the
purpose aforesd. The society having taken these matters into consideration, and seriously deliberated upon
them, are of opinion, that as there doth not appear any
cause arising in the society, or any matter subsisting
between Mr. Tennent and the society that makes it necessary or expedient for the society to desire a council,
Therefore the society Resolve the above question in the
negative.

The Consociation.

Jan. 14, 1772. Whereas the Consociation of the
Western District of Fairfield County, now met in this
society to consider and determine a case of no less importance than the expediency of the Rev. Mr. Tennent's
dismission from the pastoral relation to this church and
society, in consequence of a call, &c., * * * *
have notified this society of sd meeting, so that they
may have an opportunity to be heard if they have any
thing to offer in the case. * * * * Voted and
agreed by this society, that the reasons offered for Mr.
Tennent's dismission are altogether insufficient, &c.,
* * * and that they are entirely against Mr. Tennent's being dismissed, and do not consent to the sd
Mr. Tennent's dismission from us; and that a copy of

this vote be presented to sd council speedily, to signify
our minds in ye aforesaid case.

Mr. Tennent dismissed.

Jan. 22, 1772. [The society considering at length the
reasons offered by the Consociation ; and] " Having
seriously weighed the several matters and proceedings"
with " the effects and consequences which may probably
follow a non compliance," " are of opinion that considering the same, and the steps taken to effect it, has rendered Mr. Tennent's usefulness in this society much less
than it otherwise might have been, if not altogether at
an end, Therefore, in compliance with his earnest request, and in deference to the opinion and advice of the
venerable Council, &c. * *   do signify that if he desires the council to be convened, or shall convene the
same for their approbation thereof, or for his discharge
from any other relation or connexions, this society has
nothing to object.

Supplies for the Pulpit.

[In Oct. 1773, Mr. Cotton was employed to preach
till the next annual meeting ; and on Dec. 13, 1773,
" The committee appointed to look out for another
minister, to preach on probation, are desired to return
the society's thanks to Mr. Cotton, for his good service
here, and to pay him honorably for the same."]

[In Dec. 6, 1776, Mr. Kittletass was preaching here.
In May 11, 1778, The society voted to invite Mr. Fenn
to preach ; in Dec. 1778 to invite Mr. Robinson.   April
1780, The committee were directed to hire Mr. Mour-
dock ; Aug. 27, 1782, to invite Mr. Tullar ; Dec. 9,
1782, voted that Mr. Tullar shall be invited to settle
here as a minister in this society ; but Dec. 26, 1782,

this vote was reconsidered and made void, "by reason
there were but few people at the former meeting."
Sept. 5, 1783, desired the committee to invite Mr.
William Lockwood to preach in the society. June 17,
1784, Mr. Spalding had been employed, and was desired to preach two or three months longer. Dec. 13,
1784, The committee were directed to invite Mr. Sherman to preach on probation.]

Dr. Burnet.

2d Tuesd. in Oct. 1785. The Society called Rev.
Mr. Burnet to be their minister ; to be installed " on
the second day of November next."

The present meeting-house.

The meeting-house now occupied by the First Congregational Society, was completed in the year 1790.

Ministers of the First Congregational Church.

* THOMAS HANFORD, began to preach in 1652 ; Ordained in 1654 and died in 1693, after laboring in the ministry here 41 years.

† STEPHEN BUCKINGHAM, Ordained Nov. 17, 1697.
Resigned Feb. 24, 1727, having labored in the
ministry here about 30 years.

  * Cotton Mather mentions Mr. Hanford in his list of New England ministers who came from England students in divinity, but
who finished their education in the Colonies.

  † Stephen Buckingham is the first name on the Triennial catalogue of Yale College. He graduated at Harvard College in 1693,
and received his second degree at the first commencement of Yale.

  He was a son of Rev. Thomas Buckingham, the fourth minister
of Saybrook, Conn., and Esther Hosmer Buckingham, his wife.
He was born Sept. 3, 1675.

  Rev. Thos. Buckingham, the father of Stephen, was a son of
Mr. Thos. Buckingham, of Milford, Ct., and was baptized Nov. 8,

8*

* MOSES DICKINSON, called from Maidenhead, N. Jersey, and installed in 1727. Died May 1, 1778, in 1646; ordained pastor of the Church in 1670; one of the founders of Yale College; moderator of the Synod which formed the Saybrook Platform in 1708; died April 1, 1709, aged 63.

Mr. Thomas Buckingham, of Milford, father of Rev. Thomas, is noticed in New Haven Records in 1730; said to have come to N. England with Rev. Peter Prudden and others; his name is on record with the first settlers of Milford, Nov. 28, 1638; was one of the "Seven Pillars" at the organization of the Church; died at Boston (whither he had gone on business,) in 1657.

[These particulars concerning the family of Mr. Buckingham, I have received from Mr. Nathaniel Goodwin, of Hartford.]

Inscription on the tomb-stone of Mr. Buckingham.

Here lyes buried the
Body of the
REVD. MR. STEPHEN BUCKINGHAM.
Late Pastor of the First Church
of Christ in Norwalk;
departed this life
Feb. 3d, 1745-6
Ætatis 70.

* Mr. Dickinson graduated at Yale in the year 1717.
Inscription on Mr. Dickinson's monument.

Beneath
this monumental stone
lies interred
the body of the
REVD. MOSES DICKINSON,
Late pastor of the First Church of Christ
in Norwalk,
who departed this life May 1, 1778,
in the 83d year of his age
and 51st of his ministry in sd. church.
A man of a good understanding,
well informed by study,
Chearful in temper, Prudent in conduct,
he came to his grave in full age
like as a shock of corn cometh
in his season.

the 83d year of his age ; having been pastor of the 1st Church in Norwalk nearly 51 years.

WILLIAM TENNENT,* Installed Colleague Pastor with Mr. Dickinson in 1765. Dismissed in 1772, after a ministry of 7 years.

MATTHIAS BURNET, D.D.† Installed Nov. 2, 1785. Died June 30, 1806, in the 21st year of his ministry in the 1st Chh. of Norwalk, and in the 58th year of his age.

ROSWELL R. SWAN,‡ Ordained Jan. 14, 1807. Died March 22, 1819, in the 41st year of his age, and the 13th of his ministry.

SYLVESTER EATON,§ Ordained Oct. 4th, 1820. Dismissed Feb. 29, 1827, in the 7th year of his ministry.

* Mr. Tennent was a son of the famous William Tennent, of New Jersey, who was restored to life after having been apparently dead several days; and after the people had once or twice assembled for his funeral.

† Inscription on the tomb-stone of Rev. Dr. Burnet.
Beneath this stone rests the body of the
REVD. MATTHIAS BURNET, D.D.,
Late minister of the word of God in the first Church of Christ
in Norwalk, who was dismissed from this life's labors on
the 30th day of June, A. D. 1806, in the 58 year
of his pilgrimage, and the 21 of his
ministry in said Church.

‡ Mr. Swan graduated at Yale in 1802. The following is the inscription on his tomb-stone,
Here lies
A faithful and successful
Minister of Jesus,
THE REV. ROSWELL R. SWAN, A. M.,
He was ordained a Minister of the Gospel and settled over the First Congregational Church and Society in Norwalk Jan14, 1807, and died March 22, 1819, in the 41st year of his age, and 13th of his ministry.

§ Mr. Eaton graduated at Williams College in 1816.

HENRY BENEDICT,* Installed, Aug. 13, 1828. Dismissed —— 1832, in the 4th year of his ministry.

EDWIN HALL, Installed June 14, 1832.

THE SECOND CONGREGATIONAL CHURCH was organized Sabbath, Jan. 3, 1836, in the 1st Congregational Church. Sixty-five of the members of said church having previously received a letter of dismission from said church, came forward and gave their assent to their Confession of Faith, and entered into Covenant with each other. All this was done after mature and mutual consultation; in entire harmony, and in accordance with the unanimous votes of the First Church.

REV. JAMES KNOX statedly supplied the pulpit from 1836 to April 1, 1839.

REV. JOHN B. SHAW was stated supply from 1839 to 1841.

REV. FRANCIS C. WOODWORTH was installed Pastor Feb. 9, 1842. Dismissed Feb. 6, 1844.

REV. Z. K. HAWLEY, stated supply from April, 1844, to the present time.

————

THE EPISCOPAL CHURCH.

THE EPISCOPAL CHURCH, ST. PAUL'S PARISH, was incorporated in 1737, and a small building erected, which was afterwards converted into a parsonage, and a larger one, 55 by 42 feet, erected in 1743. In 1779 this was burnt, together with the town of Norwalk, by Gen. Tryon; but, in 1780, when the people had been impoverished and scattered by this disaster, and the removal of their pastor, the Parish erected a temporary

* Mr. Benedict is a native of Norwalk; graduated at Yale in 1822.

Drawn from Nature by E. C. Palmer.

Church edifice; and in 1785, rebuilt upon the former foundation. The building was consecrated by Bishop Seabury. In 1840 the Society unanimously resolved to build the edifice now erected, 77 by 55 feet; tower projecting 9 feet; vestry in the rear 9 feet; height of the steeple 150 feet.

The following is a list of the Clergy who have officiated in this Parish since its incorporation.

In 1737, REV. HENRY CANER,* a missionary of the Society for the propagation of the Gospel in foreign parts.

In 1738, REV. RICHARD CANER.†

In 1749, REV. JOHN OGILVIE.‡

In 1751, REV. JOHN FOWLE.

In 1756, REV. DR. DIBBLE, of Stamford.

In 1758, REV. DR. JEREMIAH LEAMING,§ who was removed by Gen. Tryon in 1779.

In 1780, REV. DR. DIBBLE, of Stamford.

In 1784, REV. JOHN BOWDEN, D. D.

In 1789, REV. MR. FOOT.

In 1790, REV. GEORGE OGILVIE.

In 1797, REV. WM. SMITH, D. D.

In 1800, REV. HENRY WHITLOCK.

In 1811, REV. BETHEL JUDD.

In 1813, REV. MR. JOHNSON.

In 1814, REV. BETHEL JUDD.||

* Rev. Henry Caner graduated at Yale in the class of 1724, and received the degree of D.D. from Oxford.

† Rev. Richard Caner was a graduate of Yale, in the class of 1736.

‡ Rev. John Ogilvie graduated at Yale in 1748; received the degree of D.D. from Aberdeen and from the college at N. York.

§ Rev. Jeremiah Leaming, D.D., graduated at Yale in 1745.

|| Rev. Bethel Judd graduated at Yale in 1797; received the degree of D. D., at Washington College, (now Trinity) Conn.

In 1816, Rev. Reuben Sherwood.*

In 1830, Rev. Mr. Atwater.

In 1830, Rev. Jackson Kemper, D. D.†

In 1835, Rev. James C. Richmond.

In 1836, the present Rector, Rev. Wm. Cooper Mead, D. D.

[The above was furnished by a member of the Episcopal Church, and by him derived from the most authentic sources in possession of the Church. It will be seen that there is a slight inaccuracy in the date concerning Rev. Henry Caner. It is here supposed that he commenced his labors in 1737. The records of the 1st Congregational Society already given, show that Mr. Caner was here in 1729.

The record of the organization of the Prime Ancient Society, shows that sundry persons had withdrawn and organized themselves into another denomination, i. e., as Professors of the Church of England prior to 1726.]

THE METHODIST CHURCH.

The Rev. Cornelius Cook preached the first Methodist sermon in Norwalk, near the New Canaan parish line, in 1787; the Rev. Jesse Lee preached the next sermon, on the 17th of June, 1789, in the highway, near the centre of the town.

The first society or class was formed, probably, in 1790. The numbers, however, and precise date cannot be given, as the earliest records are lost.

The first church edifice was erected in 1816. This building was taken down in 1843, and the present neat and commodious one erected on its site.

From 1790 to 1834, Norwalk was an important appointment on the Fairfield, Redding, and Stamford circuits.

In 1834, the society, having greatly increased in num-

* Rev. Reuben Sherwood graduated at Yale in 1813.
† Now Bishop of Missouri.

bers and wealth, judged themselves able to support regular and constant preaching on the Sabbath. They were consequently erected into a station at the session of the N. Y. Annual Conference in May of that year, and a preacher was appointed to labor with them.

The following is a list of the names of the preachers who have been stationed in Norwalk from 1834 to the present time :

Rev.	LUTHER MEAD,	1834—5
"	DAVIS STOCKING,	1835—7
"	Y. L. DICKERSON,	1837—9
"	CYRUS FOSS,	1839-40
"	WILLIAM THATCHER,	1840—1
"	G. N. SMITH,	1841—2*
"	LABAN CHENEY,	1842--3
"	HARVEY HUSTED,	1843—5
"	W. C. HOYT,	1845—7†

THE BAPTIST CHURCH.

THE BAPTIST CHURCH was organized Aug. 31, 1837, of members of Baptist Churches residing in Norwalk and vicinity.

The Rev. WILLIAM BOWEN was their preacher from the organization of the church until April 1, 1838.

Rev. WM. H. CARD of New York was then invited to preach for one year.

The church edifice was completed and opened for worship, on the 11th of March, 1840.

In Jan. 1840, the church called Rev. JAMES J. WOOLSEY of Philadelphia, to be their pastor.   Mr. Woolsey commenced his labors on the 1st of March, 1840 ‡

* Died in New York, Oct. 22, 1845.

† The above account was furnished by Rev. W. C. Hoyt.

‡ The above facts are from a document furnished by Rev. J. J. Woolsey.

REMINISCENCES.

Mrs. Philips, widow of Ebenezer, aged 84, Feb. 5, 1847. Her brother was in the army, and died of the camp distemper, at Bergen Point, N. Jersey. Her father went to his relief, took the disease, and died soon after returning home.

Her mother moved to South Salem soon after the burning of Fairfield.

Rev. Mr. Leaming was a strong tory. He went off with the British when the town was burnt.

—

Col. Buckingham Lockwood says that he always understood that the first meeting-house stood on the corner north of Dennis Hanford's house; that is, on the south corner of the lot now occupied by Rev. Mr. Ellis. He remembers when the space was all open to the common.

The second meeting-house stood where the widow of John Mallory now lives. He remembers when that lot was all open.

The third meeting-house stood very near the site of Charles Thomas's present residence, on the highest spot between him and Storrs Hall's. The whole lot, including the three lots south, lay open. He remembers the old foundation of the meeting house that was burnt.

At the burning of the town his mother and five children were in Wilton; and on an alarm fled with her children to the woods. This he remembers. His mother spoke of her distress when her children cried for something to eat.

Miss PHEBE COMSTOCK, aged 83 years, Sept. 26, 1846, lived in New Canaan, at Canoe Hill. Used to go over to her uncle's, where they used to climb an apple-tree and see Norwalk very distinctly. Went to meeting at New Canaan. In cases of alarm, which was given by firing three guns in succession, the men left all and hastened to the parade. Such alarms often came. Her father would run in and say, " Now, girls, unyoke the oxen and turn them out," and in less than five minutes would be off to the parade. They used to carry their guns to meeting ; no more thought of going to meeting then without their guns, than we do now without our psalm books. " They never had an alarm without repairing to the parade ; and they did not go slow neither." The alarm at the burning of Norwalk came about day-break. Went to the apple-tree ; saw the flames ; heard the guns. Her father and four brothers were engaged in the defence ; the " dreadfullest day she ever saw ;" the guns kept firing a long time ; " a dreadful fight." She saw the " Red-coats" take up several of their dead or wounded, and carry them to their boats ; saw the steeple of the meeting-house fall in.

ONESIMUS, the colored man, who lives with Miss Comstock, and lived with the former Phebe Comstock, was 84 years old Dec. 4, 1846. When continental soldiers were quartered in town, the chaplain was at Miss Phebe's ; his waiter died, and Onesimus took his place. The soldiers were billeted round, but assembled for roll-call every day. Onesimus was enrolled.

Onesimus, at one time after the town was burnt, went down to get salt hay at Miss Phebe's meadow, not far from the old potter's shop, sometimes called " The Village," below Old Well. Miss Phebe went with him to look out, as the enemy were always lurking round for cattle, horses, and prisoners. Onesimus saw some "Red-coats" stealing along up a creek, and gave the alarm to Miss Phebe. "We put on; we had good horses then, and we ran; we did not go slow." They escaped—gave the alarm at the Old Well—the guard pursued, and took two "Red-coats" prisoners.

PHEBE COMSTOCK used to visit Mr. Hezekiah Hanford's girls down town. At one time, old Mr. Hanford said, "Now, Phebe, I will take you to the spot where the first of your ancestors used to worship God, when they first came to this country." "Pshaw!" said Mrs. Hanford, "what do you want to take the girl down there for?" "Because," said Mr. Hanford, "she takes an interest in these things, and will remember. Our people care nothing about it." He then led her down to the place where the old meeting-house stood, near Dennis Hanford's, and said, "Here your fathers used to worship God: and when the first old shanty became too small, they built another house up there;" pointing to the spot where John Mallory since lived. She remembers well the meeting-house that was burnt in the Revolution. It was larger than the present house, and had two tier of galleries.

Often heard people speak of Mr. Buckingham; he was an excellent preacher, but it was said that he drank too much; and that was the reason that he was dismissed.

—

THOMAS BENEDICT, aged 82, March 14, 1847. After the burning of Fairfield, the enemy was expected here. They came Saturday, while the people were harvesting. While he was driving the team, John Saunders, one of the tories, came along and said, "O, boys, you are too late to harvest." Saunders had finished his harvest.

The sun was about two hours high, and Saunders was in high spirits at the coming of the enemy : as one of his sons was with the enemy, and he expected his property would be spared. But it was all burnt; and the other son with his negro went off with the enemy.

Our soldiers were collecting fast, and stopped at his father's house, which stood where Mrs. Phillips now lives. A tub of wine and a bowl stood on the stoop ; as they came along, they stopped and drank, and were very merry. His father's family hastily packed up what goods they could ; put them on the cart, which he drove that night up to Belden's Hill, to Thos. St. John's. He and the oxen had worked hard that day, and were very tired. At Mr. St. John's, a party of light-horse came in the night. He fell asleep ; some of them took out his silver brooch, and carried it off. Saw the first smoke of the burning of Norwalk in the morning. Heard the guns "pop, pop, pop, a good while." The first house burned was where George Day now lives. The house where Mr. Benedict now lives was occupied by the British as a hospital for the wounded, and therefore was not burnt at first. When the British retreated, they set it on fire, but our people rallied soon enough to put it out. The house was built by Mr. Benedict's grandfather. On his return to Norwalk, saw a British soldier that had been killed ; Seth Abbott shot him as he was getting over a wall. " Now," says Abbott, before he fired, " if I kill him, it will go right through his heart." He fired, and the soldier fell backward, dead. The British, when they landed on the west side, marched up to near where Capt. Danl. K. Nash now lives. A tall British soldier was shot there.

Mr. Leaming used to preach on the wickedness of resisting the king ; and most of the tories were of his congregation. According to his creed and preaching, we " were only a parcel of rebels." There would not have been so many tories, but for his preaching up such doctrine. He went off with the British.

—

Mrs. Benedict, wife of Thomas, aged 81, Nov., 1846, daughter of Phineas Waterbury ; lived at Roton river, at the head of the pond ;—saw the British fleet when they came from Long Island, to the burning of Norwalk. There were 26 sail, sloops. The enemy used to come every little while to the place where she lived, to drive off cattle. One night she heard the cows low and the dogs bark ; and some one hallooing, " The Tories are after the cattle ;"—" The Tories have got all our cows." Her mother raised the window and called out, " Turn out the Guard—Turn out the Guard !"—so loud, that people a mile distant heard her in two places. One of the tories called to her to be still, or he would shoot her. " I am not afraid of you," she answered ; and called out again, " Turn out the Guard—Turn out the Guard !" The man fired, and Mrs. B. heard the ball whistle ; but the tories ran for their lives ; frightened off by her mother's call for the guard.

A month after this, one night while her brother, aged 20 years, was on guard with others, she heard the dogs bark ; and then a challenge, of " Who comes there ?" The answer was, with an oath, " A friend to King George ;" and immediately guns were fired ; and there was a trampling of steps down the road. One came and said that her brother was wounded ; and presently he was brought in dead—shot through the head. Three were killed, who were all in their 20th year—two wounded.

One night the enemy entered her father's house when they were in bed—seized her father, and carried him a prisoner to New York ; they would not stop to let him dress. ˉThey came into her room ; she told them they were only children there. " D—n her," said one, " lift up the bed." They thrust their bayonets under the bed, and went off.

—

DANIEL NASH, aged 77, son of Daniel, son of Micajah; was told by his grandfather, that *his* grandfather was the first male child born in the town. What his name was, he does not know. [It is among the genealogical records, John Nash.] His sons' names were John and Nathan. From the last John proceeded all the Nash families in this region. Nathan had no children. He was the first Churchman in the family. This account Daniel Nash had from his grandfather, who was brought up by said Nathan. The reason of his change was this : he had been brought up in great abhorrence of religious forms ; and when at a meeting of ministers one of them read a portion of the Bible, Nathan much disliked it ; and so resented it, that he went occasionally to Church, saying that they might just as well read prayers as read the Bible ;—and so turned Churchman.

When the Revolution broke out, Daniel Nash was a boy, about 4 years old, at Patchogue, L. I. Remembers the time when the tea was thrown overboard at Boston. Remembers hearing, before Norwalk was burnt—and afterwards, what was the reason why Gov. Tryon burned it. Some of the Long Island people were refugees on the Connecticut shore ; [Long Island was in possession of the British.] These refugees used to pilot the Americans, when they went in whale-boats to Long

Island for plunder. Gov. Tryon said, if the people on this side did not stop that, he would come over and burn the town ; and he did burn it.

—

NATHANIEL RAYMOND, aged 94, MAY 1, 1847. Has lived near the Old Well wharf all his days ; was a corporal in the guard ; a revolutionary pensioner ; lay often on the rocks at Belden's Point ; was at New York among the Connecticut troops when the British landed at Flatbush ; and in the lines across the island after the British crossed into New York. When the British came to burn the town, they landed at Fitch's Point Saturday night. He carried such of his household effects as he could, down near the pottery called the village, and hid them in a swamp ; then carried his father and mother and some of their effects back some three miles, in a cart ; returned, and with fourteen others, volunteers, under their own command, took arms, and went up to the hill where John Raymond lived. In the night the British fired a ball at them, at random. It struck the ground near them. Sunday morning the harbor was full of boats. They landed at the Old Well : chased the fifteen volunteers over John Raymond's hill, by where Capt. D. K. Nash now lives, and so over to Round hill ; dragging a field-piece, which they fired at the volunteers from the top of Round hill. When the British landed, the volunteers fired at them from John Raymond's hill. Saw Grummon's Hill " all red" with the British : there was " old Tryon and all his tribe." The two parties of the enemy met near Grummon's Hill, and went up to France Street, where was a skirmish. There were about thirty American Regular soldiers in town. Jacob Nash (the grandfather of Capt.

Danl. K. Nash), was killed there. He was a regular soldier at home on a furlough. Our men had an old iron four-pounder at the rocks, which the British took and spiked. The Rev. Mr. Leaming was "as big a tory as ever there could be on earth." He continued praying for the King in public worship, till the inhabitants forbade him. Very many of his congregation were tories ; but the people never molested such as did not commit any hostile act. The violent tories were seized and shut up in Pudding-lane ; some carried to jail. The tories were the informers and pilots of the enemy ; and those who went off, often came back with parties, plundering, driving off cattle, and carrying away such men as they were able to lay their hands on.

MRS. MARY ESTHER ST. JOHN, (widow of WILLIAM), aged 94, in November, 1846. When Fairfield was burnt, her father was harvesting down in the Neck. Expecting the British to come here immediately, they left the harvest ; but when the British crossed to Long Island, her father rallied hands and went down to his harvesting. Saturday, near night, the alarm guns fired. Her husband rode down to the Neck, and returned ; his horse was wet with sweat, as though he had been in the water. She was about putting some bread in the oven. A woman who lived with Mr. Belden (where Gov. Bissell now lives) came running in and asked, " Are you going to stay ?" " No, I am going out of the way." " Well," said the woman, "I shall stay ; I will go to Gov. Tryon, and plead for the house. When he was Governor he stayed with us one night, with his attendants and horses. I will tell him of that, and we are friends to the government." Mrs. St. J. said, " If you are going to stay, take my dough."

She took it, and presently came running for the oven-wood. Mrs. St. J. and her husband and family, with what effects they could carry, went up into the woods, at the East Rocks. They had a bedstead, which they set up ; milked the cows which they drove with them, drank the milk, and stayed there that night. In the morning, the guns were firing; the smoke of the burning houses rose. Her husband said, " The work is begun ; they are burning the town." The woman succeeded in saving Mr. Belden's house. She told Mrs. St. John that she went up to Grummon's Hill, where Gov. Tryon sat, with chairs and a table, writing his orders. She begged for the house ; he wrote her a protection, and sent with her a file of soldiers. When she reached the house, it had already been set on fire in two places, but the soldiers put it out.

The Town House, which stood where the present one stands, was in the Revolution occupied as a guard-house. The troops, on their passage to New York, used to lodge there. She saw many of them, not more than 15 or 16 years old. Mr. Leaming she knew well. She attended his church. He continued to pray for the King as long as he dared to. He went away with the British. It was sad to live in the midst of war ; but what was the most unpleasant of all, was the difference of sentiments among neighbors and kindred. Mrs. St. John lived, in the Revolution, on the old St. John place, nearly opposite Gov. Bissell's. Her house that was burnt in the Revolution, stood between the site of the present house and the widow Buckingham St. John's, at the foot of Grumman's Hill. The latter place was then occupied by a family named Grumman.

Drawn from Nature by B.C.Palmer.

S. E.

· THE GENEALOGICAL REGISTER.

"THE RECORDS OF MARRIAGES AND BIRTHS AND DEATHS."

[The Genealogical Registers are taken almost entirely from the Town Records, and have been transcribed in the same form as they are recorded. A few have been copied from family Bibles; some have been furnished by the families concerned. A large number of families were put on record about the beginning of the present century; and the names of the children born after that record was made, have not been supplied, except in a few instances. I have advertised repeatedly, and in some cases have made personal application for the means of filling out these records; but almost entirely without success. A singular apathy seems to prevail with regard to such matters. Such families must not complain that the records which so nearly concern them are left incomplete. I have used all reasonable diligence to obtain them.]

Thos. Seamer, the Sonne of Rich'd Seamer, of Norwake, tooke to wiffe, Hannaih Marvin, the daughter of Math. Marvin of the same, January, 1653.

[The following items concerning the family of Matthew Marvin, I have received from T. R. Marvin, of Boston, from a record of the names of persons permitted to embark at the port of London after Christmas, 1634, contained in a MS. folio, at the Augmentation office (so called). Under the date of 15th April, 1634, is the following entry: " Theis parties, hereafter expressed, are to be transported to New England, imbarked in the Increase, Robert Lea, Master, having taken the oath of allegiance and supremacy, as also being conformable, &c., whereof they brought testimony per certif. from the justices and ministers where their abodes have lately been. (The following names are included in said list:)

" husbandman, Matthew Marvyn,   Age 35 yrs.
        Uxor, Elizabeth Marvyn, 31
        Elizabeth Marvyn,   31
        Matthew Marvyn,   8
        Marie Marvyn,   6
        Sara Marvyn,   3
        Hanna Marvyn,   ½ "

Reinold Marvin who removed to Saybrook in 1639, and his

9

brother Matthew Marvin were among the original settlers of Hartford, Conn. Matthew represented the town of Norwalk in the General Court in 1654.

The children of Matt. Marvin, sen., were as follows:

1. Matthew, born in Eng. abt. 1627.
2. Mary, born in Eng. abt. 1629, married to Richard Bushnell of Saybrook in 1648.

Sarah, b. in Eng. abt. 1632, married to William Goodridge of Weathersfield, 1648.

4. Hannah, b. in Eng. abt. 1634, m. to Thomas Seymour of Norwalk, Jan. 1653.

5. Abigail, b. at Hartford, Conn. m. John Bouton of Norwalk Jan. 1656.

6. Samuel, b. at Hartford, Feb. 1647—8.

7. Rachel, b. at Hartford, " close of 1649."]

Hannaih Seamer, the Daughter of Thos. Seamer, borne the 12th of Desember, 1654.

Abigall Seamer, the Daughter of Thos. Seamer, borne in January, 1655.

Mary Seamer, and Sarah Seamer, beinge twinns, daughters of Thos. Seamer, borne in the mounth of September, 1658.

Thos. Seamer, the sonne of Thos. Seamer, borne in September, 1660.

John Bowten of Norwake, tooke to wiffe Abigall Marvin, the daughter of Math. Marvin, senr. of the same, January the 1st, 1656.

[The name of JOHN BOUTON appears on p. 17, as among the first settlers of Norwalk. At what time he came to this country the family have no record. He was a French Protestant, and it is said there are many of the same name still living in France and Germany, and that a great similarity exists between the families *there* and *here*. He had five children after his marriage as here recorded, viz. JOHN, Matthew, Rachel, Abigail, and Mary.' He must also have had children by a previous marriage. (See record of marriage of Daniel Kcllogge to Bridget Bowten, in 1665, p. 187.)

His son John had two children, JAKIN and Joseph, and perhaps more, although no others appear on the record.

His grandson JAKIN, had two children by his first wife, Joseph and Sarah; and by his second wife, two sons, Esaias and Moses, and seven or eight daughters.

JOSEPH, his great-grandson, married Susannah Raymond, August 25th, 1748, daughter of Joshua Raymond, and had eleven children, six sons and five daughters. The sons were WILLIAM, Joshua, Joseph, Seth, Ira, and Aaron. The daughters were Rebeckah, Betty, Nancy, Susannah, and Deborah. He was an officer in the expedition sent against the French Provinces in 1758, '9, and kept a journal of the service, which was unfortunately lost in pulling down the old family mansion, a few years since, which stood on the spot where Dea. JOHN BOUTON, his grandson, now resides.

WILLIAM, the son of Joseph, the 5th descendant from the 1st John, was married to Sarah Benedict, February 15th, 1769, by whom he had fourteen children, viz. Isaac (who died), Isaac, William, Betty, ESTHER, Sally, Clara, Seth, Joseph, Susannah, John, Mary, Ann, and Nathaniel.

Joseph, the son of Joseph, was killed at Red Hook in the revolutionary war. Seth, his brother, was killed by falling from a tree. Joshua listed in the army at the age of 14, as a drummer, was taken prisoner, and kept on board a man-of-war till the peace, and arrived home just in time to see his father before he died. He afterwards followed the sea, and was a skilful and able captain.

The descendants of the fourteen children of WILLIAM are very numerous. See Appendix A.]—*Communicated by S. W. Benedict.*

John Bowten, the sonne of John Bowten, borne the last day of September, 1659.

Mathewe Bowten, the sonne of John Bowten, borne the 24th of Desember, 1661.

Mstr Thomas Handforde, pastor to the church of Norwake, tooke to wiffe the widow Mary ―――― married unto his sayed wiffe at Newe Haven, October the 22th, 1661.

Theophilus Handforde, sonne of mstr Tho. Handforde, born in July, the 29th, 1662.

John Haite tooke to wiffe, Mary Lindall, the daughter of Henry Lindall, deacon of the church of Newe Haven, late deceased, the 14th of September, 1666.

John Haite, the sonne of John Haite, borne the 21th of June, 1669.

Ephraim Lockwoode tooke to wiffe Mercie Sention, daughter of Mathias Sention, sen. of Norwake, the 8th of June, 1665.

John Lockwoode, sonne of Ephraim Lockwoode, born the 19th of March, 1665, 66.

Daniell Lockwoode, sonne of Ephraim Lockwoode, born the 13th of August, 1668.

John Raiment, tooke to wiffe Mary Betts, the daughter of Thos. Betts of Norwake, the 10th of Desember, 1664.

John Raiment, sonne of John Raiment, borne the 9th of September, 1665.

Sarah Lockwoode, the daughter of Ephraim Lockwood, borne the 3th of Nouvember, 1670.

John Platt, the sonne of John Platt, borne in June, 1664.

Josiah Platt, the sonne of John Platt, borne the 28th of Desember, 1667.

Samuell Platt, the sonne of John Platt, borne the 26th of January, 1670.

Thos. Taylor tooke to wiffe Rebechah Kettcham, the daughter of Edwd Kettcham late of Strattforde, deceased. The sayed Thos. was married unto the sayed Rebechah the 14th of ffebruary, Anno 1677.

Thomas Taylor, the sonne of Thos. Taylor, borne the 26th of November, Anno 1668.

Thos Benidict's children.

Mary Benidict, the Daughter of Thos. Benidict, Junr., borne the 4th of Desember, Anno 1666.

Tho. Benidict the sonne of Tho. Benidict, Junr., borne the 5th of Desember, Anno 1670.

[Thos. Benedict, sen'r, was born in England in 1617, and came to New England at the age of 21, and settled in the Massachusetts Bay. He afterwards removed to Southhold, L. I.; thence to Huntington, and thence to Jamaica, from whence he removed to Norwalk in 1665. He had nine children, viz., Thomas, John, Samuel, James, Daniel, Betty, Mary, Sarah, and Rebeckah, all of whom removed with him to Norwalk.

His son Thomas had six children; his son John had nine; Samuel had seven, James seven, Daniel four, Betty (married to

John Slauson of Stamford) two, Mary (married to John Olmsted of Norwalk) ten, Sarah (married to James Beebe of Stratford) two; Rebeckah was married to Doctor Samuel Wood, but we have no record of her children; making the number of grand-children of the said Thomas Benedict, senr, 47, exclusive of the children of his daughter Rebeckah. For a full account of his family, and of the descendants of his son John Benedict, see Appendix B.]

Deborah Taylor, the daughter of Thos. Taylor, borne in June, 1671.

Christopher Comestocke tooke to wiffe Hannaih Platt, the daughter of Richard Platt of Milford, and was married October the 6th, 1663.

Christopher Comestocke's children.

Daniell Comestocke, the sonne of Christopher Comestocke, borne the 21th of July, Anno 1664.

Hannaih Comestocke, the daughter of Christopher Comestocke, borne the 15th of July, Anno 1666.

Abigall Comestocke, the daughter of Christopher Comestocke, borne the 27th of January, Anno 1669.

Mary Comestocke, the daughter of Christopher Comestocke, borne the 19th of ffebruary, Anno 1671.

Samuell Haite, the sonne of John Haite, borne the 17th of October, Anno 1670.

. John Benidict, Junior, tooke to wiffe, Phebe Griggorie, the daughter of John Griggorie, and was married the 11th of November, Anno 1670.

Phebe Benidict, the daughter of John Benidict, junior, was borne the 21th of September, Anno 1673.

John Olmested tooke to wiffe Mary Benidict the daughter of Thomas Benidict, and was married the 17th of July, Anno 1673.

James Pickitt, tooke to wiffe Rebecca Keeiler, the daughter of Ralph Keeiler, late of Norwake, and was married the 17th of July, Anno 1673.

James Sention tooke to wiffe Rebecka Pickett, the daughter of John Pickett of Stratford, and was married the last day of Desember, Anno 1673.

Samuell Raimont the sonne of John Raimont born the 7th of July, Anno, 1673.

Rachell Bowten, the daughter of John Bowten, borne the 15th of Desember, Anno 1667.
Abigall Bowten the daughter of John Bowten, borne the first of April, Anno 1670.
Mary Bowten, the daughter of John Bowten, borne the 26th of May, Anno 1671.

John Taylor, the sonne of Thos. Taylor, borne in the mounth desember, Anno 1673.
Joseph Taylor, the sonne of Thos. Taylor, borne in the mounth of Desember.

Mary Griggorie the daughter of Jakin Griggorie, borne the fifth of Desember, Anno 1669. ⁻
John Griggorie the sonne of Jakin Griggorie, borne the twentie fifth of January, Anno 1670.
Thos. Griggorie the sonne of Jakin Griggorie, borne the 17th of January, Anno 1672.

Robert Stewart tooke to wiffe Bethia Rumball the daughter of Thos. Rumball of Stratford, and was married the 12th of June, Anno 1661.
James Stewart the sonne of Robert Stewart, borne the 19th of March, Anno, 1662, 63.
Abigall Stewart, the daughter of Robert Stewart, borne in August, the middle mounth, Anno 1666.
John Stewart, the sonne of Robert Stewart, borne the 18th of March, Anno 1668, 69.
Deborah Stewart the Daughter of Robert Stewart, borne in May, 1669.
Elissabeth Stewart, the daughter of Robert Stewart, borne in the latter ende of September, Anno 1671.
Phebe Stewart, the Daughter of Robert Stewart, borne the middle of ffebruary, Anno 1673.

Joseph Platt the sonne of John Platt borne the Seventeenth of February, Anno 1672.

Elissabeth Griggorie the daughter of John Griggorie, junior, borne in January, Anno 1665.
Sarah Griggorie the daughter of John Griggorie, junior, borne in Desember, Anno 1667.
Jonathan Griggorie the sonne of John Griggorie junior, borne in June, Anno 1671.

Abigall Griggorie, the daughter of John Griggorie, junior, borne in June, Anno 1672.

Mary Handford, the daughter of Mstr Thos. Handford, borne the thirtieth of November, Anno 1663.

Hannah Hanford, the daughter of Mstr Thos. Hanford borne the twentie eighth of June, Anno 1665.

ⁱ Elissabeth Hanford, the daughter of Mstr Thos. Hanford, borne the ninth of January, Anno 1666.

Thos. Hanford, the sonne of Mstr Thos. Hanford, borne the eighteenth of July, Anno 1668.

Eleazer Hanford, the sonne of Mstr Thos. Hanford, borne the fifteenth of September, Anno 1670.

Elnathan Hanford, the sonne of Mstr Thos. Hanford, borne the leaventh of October, Anno 1672.

Samuell Hanford, the sonne of mstr Thos Hanford, borne the

Judah Griggorie tooke to wiffe Hannah Haite, the daughter of Waltar Haite of Norwake, and was married, October the twentieth, Anno 1664.

Hannah Griggorie, the daughter of Judah Griggorie, was borne the twentie fowrth of September, Anno 1665.

John Griggorie, the sonne of Judah Griggorie, was borne the 17th of March, Anno 1668.

Percie Griggorie, the daughter of Judah Griggorie, was borne the eleventh of ffebruary, Anno 1671.

Danniell Kellogge tooke to wiffe Bridgett Bowten, the daughter of John Bowten, and was married at Norwake, Anno 1665.

Sarah Kellogge, the daughter of Danniell Kellogge, was borne in ffebruary, Anno 1665, 6.

Mary Kellogge, the daughter of Danniell Kellogge, was borne in February, Anno 1662.

Rachell Kellogge, the daughter of Danniell Kellogge, was borne in ffebruary, Anno 1663.

Elissabeth Kellogge, the daughter of Danniell Kellogge, was borne in Auguste, Anno 1666.

Thomas Haite, the sonne of John Haite, borne the fifth of January, Anno Domine sixe hundred seaventie foure.

Mary Haite, the daughter of John Haite, borne the first of September, Anno Domine, sixe hundred and seaventie seaven.

James Benidicte tooke to wiffe Sarah Gregorie, the daughter of John Gregorie, Sen., of Norwake, and was married the tennth of May, Anno 1676.

Sarah Benidicte, the daughter of James Benidict, borne the seventh sixe of June, Anno 1677.

Hannaih Benidict, the daughter of Thos. Benidict, Jun., borne the eighth of January, Anno Domi. 1676.

John Benidict, the sonne of John Benidicte, borne the third of March, Anno 1675, 76.

Johannah Benidicte, the daughter of Samuell Benidicte, borne the twentie second day of October, Anno 1673.

Samuell Benidicte, the sonne of Samuell Benidicte, borne the fifth of March, Anno 1674, 75.

Sarah Platt, the daughter of John Platt, borne the one-and-twentieth of May, in Anno one thous'd sixe hundred seaventie eight.

Thomas Hyatt tooke to wiffe Mary Sention, the daughter of Mathias Sention, of Norwake, and was married about the 10th of November, 1677.

Rebeckah Hyatt, the daughter of Thomas Hyatt, borne in the beginninge of October, Anno 1678.

Ffrancis Bushnell tooke to wiffe Hannah Seamer, daughter of Tho. Seamer, of Norwalke, and was married the 12th of October, 1675.

Hannah Bushnell, the daughter of Ffrancis Bushnell, borne the 22th of Augst, Anno Domie. 1676.

Mary Bushnell, the daughter of Ffrancis Bushnell, borne the 21th of Desember, Anno Domi. 1679.

John Crampton tooke to wiffe Sarah Rockewell, the daughter of John Rockewell, of Stamford, and was married the 8th of October, 1676.

Sarah Crampton, the daughter of John Crampton, borne the 10th of September, 1679.

Elissabeth Webb, the widow of Ritchard Webb, formerly of Norwalke, deceased the twenty fowreth of January, 1680.

Benjamin Skrivener tooke to wiffe Hannah Cram the daughter of John Crampton, of Norwalke, and married the 5th of March, 1679, 80.

Thos. Skrivener, the sonne of Benjamin Skrivener, b the thirtie one of March, one thousand sixe hun. eightie one.

Elissabeth Comstocke, borne the 7th of October, one thousand sixe hundred seaventie foure.

Mercie Comstocke, the daughter of Christe. Comstocke, borne the twelfth of November, one thousand sixe hundred seaventie sixe.

Samuell Comstocke, the sonne of Christe. Comstocke, borne the sixe of Ffebruary, one thowsand sixe hundred seaventie-nine.

Ephraim Lockwood, the sonne of Ephraim Lockwood, borne the first of May, one thowsand sixe hundred and seaventie three.

Joseph Lockwood, the sonne of Ephraim Lockwood, borne the first of Aprill, one thowsand sixe hundred eightie.

John ffitch, the sonne of Tho' ffitch, Sen., tooke to wiffe Rebeckah Lindall, the daughter of Deacon Lindall, formerly of Newe Haven, and was married the third of Desember, one thowsand sixe hundred seaventie fower.

John ffitch, the sonne of John ffitch, was borne the twentie nine of September, one thowsand six hundred seaventie seven.

Rebeckah ffitch, the daughter of John ffitch, was borne the fifteenth day of January, 1679.

John Whitney, the sonne of John Whitney, was borne the 12th of March, 1676, 77.

Joseph Whitney, the sonne of John Whitney, was borne the first of March, 1678.

Henry Whitney, the sonne of John Whitney, was borne the 21th of ffebruary, 1680.

John Keeiler, the sonne of Ralph Keeiler, formerly of Norwake, deceased, tooke to wiffe Hittabell Rockewell, the daughter of John Rockewell, formerly of Stamford, and was married the 18th of June, 1679.

,sabeth Keeiler, the daughter of John Keeiler, was
ᴣ the 19th of March, 1678.

ᴣeph Ketchum tooke to wiffe Mercy Lindall, the daugh-
ᵣf Deacon Lindall, formerly of Newe Haven, and was
ᴍᴀrried the 3th of Aprill, 1679.

Sarah Ketchum, the daughter of Joseph Ketchum, was
borne the 19th of ffebruary, 1681.

Nathaniel Ketchum, the sonne of Joseph Ketchum, was
borne the 23th of January, 1679.

Deborah Haite, the daughter of John Haite, was borne
the 28 of Desember, 1679.

Josiah Gregorie, the sonne of Judah Gregorie, was
borne the 13th of July, 1679.

Benjamin Gregorie, the sonne of Judah Gregorie, borne
the 26 of March, 1682.

Abigall Crampton, the daughter of John Crampton,
borne the 9th of August, 1681.

Samuell Sension, of Norwalk, deceased, and dyed the
14th of January, 1684.

Sarah Sension, the daughter of Samuell Sension, deceased and dyed the 5th of January, 1685.

Abigall Comstock, the daughter of Christopher Comstock, deceased and dyed the 9th of ffebruary, in the
yeere 1689.

Sarah Sturdivant, the daughter of William Sturdivant,
Born the 9th of Aprill, 1678.

John Sturdivant, the sonn of William Sturdivant, borne
the 20th of July, 1676.

Daniel Comstock, the son of Christopher Comstock,
tooke to wiffe Elissabeth Wheeler, the daughter of John
Wheeler, of Ffaierfield, at the Black Rock, the 13th of June,
in the yeere 1692.

Jonathan Abbitt, the sonn of Jonathan Abbitt, borne the
6th of Aprill, in the yeere 1697.

Samuell Benydicke tooke to wiffe Rebeckah Andrews,
the daughter of Thos. Andrews, formerly of Faierfeild,
and was married the 7th of July, 1678.

Thos. Benydicke, the sonne of Samuell Benydicke, borne the 27th of March, Anno 1679.

Abraham Benydike, the sonne of Samuell Benydicke, born the twentieth-one of June, Anno 1681.

Thomas Gregorie tooke to wiffe Elissabeth Pardie, the daughter of George Pardie, of Newe Haven, and was married the twenty-five of Desember, Anno 1679.

Martha Gregorie, the daughter of Thos. Gregorie, born the thirtee one day of Aprill, Anno 1680.

Samuell Gregorie, the sonne of Jackin Gregorie, born the 10th of March, one thousand sixe hundred seaventie five, seaventie sixe.

Sarah Gregorie, the daughter of Jackin Gregorie, born the 15th of September, 1678.

Matthew Gregorie, the sonne of Jackin Greogorie, borne the 17th of Desember, 1680.

Jackin Gregorie, the sonne of Jackin Gregorie, borne the 10th of May, 1682.

Sarah Haies, the daughter of Samuell Haies, borne the 19th of September, 1673.

Isake Haies, the sonne of Samuell Haies, was borne the 27 of August, Anno 1682.

James Jupp took to wiffe Anie Hickens, the daughter of Tho. Hickens, formerly of Stamford, deceased, and was married the 2th of January, 1682.

John Keeiler, the sonne of John Keeiler, born the 26th of Desember, 1682.

John Crampton, the sonne of John Crampton, was born the 7th of January, 1682.

Samuell Keeiler, the sonne of Ralph Keeiler, formerly of Norwalke, deceased, tooke to wiffe Sarah Sention, the daughter of Marke Sention, and was married the 10th of March, Anno 1681, 82.

Nathaniell ffitch, the sonne of John ffitch, borne the sixth of Nov., 1682.

Thomas Barnam, the sonne of Thos. Barnam, born the 9th of July, 1663.

John Barnam, the sonne of Thomas Barnam, borne the 24th of ffebruary, 1677.

Hannah Barnam, the daughter of Thos. Barnam, borne the 4th of October, Anno 1680.

Ebbinezer Barnam, the daughter of Thos. Barnam, borne the 29th of May, 1682.

James Beebe tooke to wiffe Sarah Benydicke, the daughter of Ths. Benydicke, Sen., of Norwalke, and was married the 19th of Desember, 1679.

Sarah Beebe, the daughter of James Beebe, was borne the 13th of November, 1680.

Elissabeth Sention, the daughter of Marke Sention, borne the 6th of Desember, 1656.

Sarah Sention, the daughter of Marke Sention, borne the 18th of January, 1659.

Danniell Kellogge, the sonne of Danniell Kellogge, was borne the seaventh of May, Anno 1671.

Samuell Kellogge, the sonne of Danniell Kellogge, was borne the latter end of ffebruary, Anno 1673.

Samuell Sention tooke to wiffe Elissabeth Haite, the daughter of Walter Haite, and was married in September, 1663.

Sarah Sention, the daughter of Samuell Sention, borne in January, Anno 1664.

Thos. Sention, the sonne of Sam'll Sention, borne in October, 1666.

Elissabeth Sention, the daughter of Sam'l Sention, borne in Aprill, Anno 1673.

Joseph Griggorie, the sonne of Judah Griggorie, borne the sixteenth of July, Anno 1674.

James Pickett, the sonne of James Pickett, borne the seaventh of May, Anno 1674.

Hannaih Platt, the daughter of John Platt, borne the 15th of Desember, Anno 1674. I say the fifteenth of Desember, Anno 1674.

John Whitney tooke to wiffe Elissabeth Smith, the daughter of Richard Smith, and was married the 17th of March, Anno 1674, 75.

Eliphalett Lockwoode, the sonne of Ephraim Lockwoode, borne the twentie seaven of ffebruary, 1675.

Abigall Haite, the daughter of Zerrubabell Haite, borne the second day of ffebruary, Anno 1675.

Mercie Seamer, the daughter of Thos. Seamer, borne in November, one thowsand sixe hundr'd sixtie sixe.

Mathewe Seamer, the sonne of Thos. Seamer, borne in May, one thowsande sixe hundred sixtie nine. —

Elissabeth Seamer, the daughter of Thos. Seamer, borne in Desember, 1000 sixe hundrede seaventie three.

Rebecka Seamer, the daughter of Thos. Seamer, borne in January, 1000 sixe hundrede seaventie five.

Liddia Griggorie, the daughter of Judah Griggorie, borne the ninth of January, one thowsand sixe hundred seaventie sixe.

Mary Griggorie, the daughter of John Griggorie, Junr., borne in Desember, 1674.

John Platt, Jun'r., of the towne of Norwalke, tooke to wife and was married unto Sarah Lockwood, the daughter of Ephraim Lockwood, of Norwalk, in May, in the yeare of our Lord one thousand six hundred and ninety five.

Sarah Platt, the daughter of John Platt, Jr., Junior, was borne on the thirtieth day of March, 1697.

Elisabeth Platt, the daughter of John Platt, Jr., was borne on the eleaventh day of June, in the yeare of our Lord one thousand six hundred and ninety nine.

John Platt, the sonn of John, borne the 2d day of Aprill, in the year of our Lord 1702.

Abigail Platt, the daughter of John Platt, born the 12th day of Feb., 1707–8.

Elisabeth Raymond, the daughter of Serjnt. John Raymond, born the two and twentieth day of August, in the yeare of our Lord 1697.

Hannah Raymond, the daughter of the abovesayd Serjnt. John Raymond, was born the two and twentieth day of July, in the yeare of our Lord 1700.

John Raymond, Jr., took to wife and was married unto Elisabeth Sension, the daughter of Samuell Sension, on the 7th day of March, 1690.

John Raymond, son of the above, born May 19, 1693.

James Olmsted, son of James, born March 10, 1676–7.
Samuel, - - " May 13, 1683.
John, - - " Aug. 14, 1692.

Nathan, born April 27, 1678, married Sarah Keeler, daughter of Ralph Keeler, Dec. 7, 1702.

Edmund Wareing took to wife Elizabeth Bouton, ye daughter of Serjeant John Bouton, of Norwalk, Oct. 6, 1698.

Edmund Wareing, son of Edmund Wareing,
     born Sept. 16, 1700.
Isaac Wareing, born Jan. 13, 1702.
John " born Dec. 21, 1704.
Solomon " born April 24, 1707.
Mary " born Dec. 22, 1708.
Nathan " born Feb. 6, 1710–11.
Jacob " born Jan.·15, 1712–13.
Michael " born July 16, 1715.
Eliakim " born July 8, 1717.
Elisabeth " born March 8,1719–20.
Abigail " born April 19, 1723.
(The above) born " in Oyster Bay, in Queen's village."

In Norwalk, Hannah Wareing, ye daugh'r of s'd Edm. Wareing, born Sept. 7, 1725.

John Marven took to wife Mary Beears, ye daughter of Mr. James Beears, of Fairfield, March 22, 1704.

John Marvin, ye first son of John Marvin,
     born July 22, 1705.
Nathan, born March 4, 1707.
Seth,   born July 13, 1709.
David,   born Aug. 24, 1711.
Elisabeth, born Oct. 23, 1713.
Mary,   born Dec. 29, 1716.
Elihu,   born Oct. 10, 1719.

Mrs. Mary Marven, wife of the above John Marven, departed this life, April 17, 1720.

(The above) John Marven, the son of Matthew Marven, born Sept. 2, 1678.

Joseph Lockwood took to wife Mary Wood, ye daughter of Mr. John Wood, of Stamford, Aug. 14, 1707.

Ephraim Lockwood, ye son of Mr. Joseph
Lockwood, born Aug. 23, 1708.
Joseph,   born Nov. 23, 1710.
Ruth,   born July 17, 1714

Daniel,	born Dec.	5, 1716.
Mary,	born March	7, 1719–20.
Elisabeth,	born May	23, 1721.

Richard Whitne, ye son of John Whitne, born April 18, 1687.

Richard Whitne took to wife Hannah Darling, ye daughter of Mr. John Darling, of Fairfield, April 17, 1709.

Elijah Whitne, ye son of s'd Richard,	
	born April 16, 1710.
Samuell,	born Oct. 5, 1711.

Mr. Mark Saint John died or deceased Aug. 12, 1693.

Joseph Saint John took to wife Sarah Betts, ye daughter of Mr. Thomas Betts, March 5, 1695–6.

Sarah Saint John,	born June	13, 1697.
Mary,	born Aug.	22, 1701.
Joseph,	born Nov.	5, 1703.
Elizabeth,	born Feb.	6, 1706–7.

John Raymond, Junr., took to wife Elizabeth Saint John, the daughter of Samuell Sension, alias Saint John, and married her, March 7, 1690.

John Raymond ye son of sd John Raymond,	
	borne May, 19, 1693.
Mary Raymond,	borne March 5, 1694.
Elizabeth,	borne Aug. 22, 1697.
Hannah,	borne July 22, 1700.
Lemuell,	borne Jan. 7, 1702.
Jabez,	borne April 1, 1705.
Asael,	borne Sept. 22, 1707.
Elija,	borne Nov. 7, 1709.
Sarah,	borne Nov. 12, 1711.

Zuriel Raymond says he was born 4 years after his sister Sarah, and the 3d day of December, which make Dec. 3, 1715.

Christopher Comstock, deceased Dec. 28, 1702.

Samuell Comstock, ye son of Christopher Comstock, borne Feb. 6, 1679, 80.

Samuell Comstock took to wife Sarah Hanford, ye

daughter of the Reverend Mr. Thomas Hanford, Dec. 27, 1705.

Sarah Comstock, ye daughter of Samuell, borne March 25, 1707.
Samuell, born Nov. 12, 1708.
Mary,   born Aug. 5, 1710.

James Bennedick, ye son of John Benedict, born Jan. 15, 1685.

James Benedict took to wife Sarah Hyatt, the daughter of Thomas Hyatt, deceased, April 7, 1709.

Sarah Bennedick, ye daughter of ye said James Bennedick, born May 23, 1710.

Jonathan Abbott took to wife Sarah Olmsted, ye daughter of Leftent. John Olmsted of Norwalk, June, 5th, 1696.

Jonathan Abbott, the son of ye said Jonathan Abbott was born April 6, 1697.
Sarah,   born June 16, 1699.
Eunis,   born Jan. 23, 1702.
Mary   born July 8, 1704.
Deborah,   born Dec. 3, 1707.
Keziah,   born April 17, 1711.
Lemuell,   born Mar. 21, 1713–14.
Jane,   born Oct. 5, 1716.
Mindwell,   born Dec. 21, 1718.

Moses Comstock took to wife Abigail Brinsmaid ye daughter of Mr. Daniel Brinsmaid of Hartford, deceased, Feb. 23, 1709–10.

The said Moses Comstock departed this life January 18, 1766, in the 82d year of his age.

Abigail, ye wife of Moses Comstock departed this life Nov. 16, 1766, in the 75th year of her age.

Mercy Wood, daughter of Samuell Wood, born March 30, 1717.
Samuell Wood, son of said Samuell Wood born Aug. 1718.

Mr. Alexander Resseguié took to wife Mrs. Sarah Bontecou, ye daughter of Mr. Peter Bontecou of New York, Oct. 19, 1709.

Alexander, son of Alex. Resseguie,
        born Aug, 27, 1710.
Peter,   born Dec. 19, 1711.
James,   born Nov. 6, 1713.
Abraham, born July 27, 1718.
Isaac,   born May 24, 1717.
Jacob,   born Aug. 14, 1719.
Sarah,   born July 12, 1721.

Joseph Whitne took to wife Hannah Hayt, the daughter of Mr. Zerubbabell Hayt, of Norwalk, July 6, 1704.

Hezekiah Whitne son of said Joseph,
        born April 10, 1705.
Hannah,   born Nov. 5, 1707.
Joseph,   born Dec. 6, 1710.
Thankful, born March 1, 1713–14.
David,   born June 24, 1721.
Abraham, born Feb. 23, 1723–4.

Joseph Plat, ye son of Deacon John Plat, born Feb. 14, 1672-3.

Joseph Platt took to wife Elizabeth Marven, the daughter of Mr. Matthew Marven, Nov. 6, 1700.

Elizabeth, daughter of said Joseph, born Dec. 2, 1761.

Elizabeth Platt, ye wife of said Joseph Platt, departed this life April 9, 1703.

Joseph Platt took to wife Hannah Hanford, the daughter of ye Reverend Thomas Hanford, deceased, Jan. 26, 1703–4.

Hannah Platt, daughter of ye said Joseph Platt, born Oct. 29, 1704.

Joseph Platt, ye son of, &c., born Sept. 9, 1716.

John Keeler, Junr., took to wife Rhoda Hayt, ye daughter of Deacon Zerubbabel Hayt, April 19, 1710.

Abigail Keeler daughter of said Zerubbabel, born March 27, 1711–12.

William Reed, Jun., was born Nov. 16, 1708.

Isaac Brown, ye son of James Brown, born March 1, 1690.

Nathaniel Ketchum took to wife Sarah Wakeling, yᵉ daughter of Mr. Deliverance Wakeling, deceased, late of Stratford, June 12, 1710.

Nathaniel Ketchum, yᵉ son of said Nathaniel, born March 17, 1710–11.

Isaac Hayes took to wife Elizabeth Sherwood, daughter of Mr. Isaac Sherwood, of Fairfield, July 10, 1701.

> Eunice Hayes, daughter of yᵉ said Isaac,
>   born May 2, 1702.
> Jeremiah, born Feb. 1, 1703–4.
> Isaac,   born March 23, 1706.
> Jeremiah, departed this life, April 20, 1707.
> Elizabeth, born May 23, 1708.
> Samuel,   born Oct. 30, 1710.

Isaac Hayes, sen., departed this life Jan. 5, 1711–12.

John Nash took to wife Mary Barley, the daughter of Mr. Thomas Barley, of Fairfield, May 1, 1684.

> John, son of said John, born Dec. 25, 1688.
> Nathan,   born Jan. 26, 1692–3.

Mary, wife of said John Nash, departed this life Sept. 2, 1711.

John Nash, Jr. took to wife Abigail Blakely, yᵉ daughter of Ebenezer Blakely, of New Haven, May 19, 1709.

> Edward Nash, son of said John, born July 21, 1710.
> Mary,   born April 27, 1712.
> John,   born Dec. 23, 1713.

Joseph Blachly took to wife Mehitable Keeler, the daughter of Mr. John Keeler, of Norwalk, Oct. 14, 1703.

Joseph Blachly departed this life Oct. 14, 1704.

Mary Blachly, yᵉ daughter of said Joseph, born Nov. 9, 1704.

Caleb Hayt, took to wife the widow Mehitable Blatchly, Feb. 25, 1707–8.

> Benijah Hayt, yᵉ son of said Caleb, born Dec. 8, 1708.
> David,   "   "   born Dec. 3, 1710.
> The said Mehitable departed this life March 21, 1755.
> The said Caleb Hayt departed this life April 11, 1755.

Ebenezer Gregory took to wife Mary Fitch, the daughter of Mr. John Fitch of Norwalk, Dec. 13, 1711.

Henry Whitney took to wife Elizabeth Olmstead, yᵉ daughter of yᵉ late Lieut. John Olmstead, deceased, June 14, 1710.

Elizabeth Whitney, daughter of said Henry, born Aug. 24, 1711.

Caleb Hayt, Jr., took to wife Ruth, daughter of Mr. Samuel Bouton of Danbury, and was married to her, May 16, 1750.

Sarah Hayt daughter of said Caleb and Ruth
born Dec. 19, 1752.
Ruth, born July 29, 1753.
Ruth, yᵒ wife of said Caleb, departed this life April 9, 1755.

Samuel Kellogg took to wife Sarah Platt, yᵉ daughter of Deacon John Platt, Sept. 6, 1704.

Sarah Kellogg, y daughter of said Samuel Kellogg,
born Sept. 26, 1705.
Samuel, son, born Dec. 23, 1706.
Mary, daughter, born Jan. 29, 1708.
Martin, son, born Mar. 23, 1711.
Abigail, daughter, born Jan. 19; 1712.
Lidiah, " born Oct. 30, 1713.
Gidion, son, born Dec. 5, 1717.
Epenetus, son, born June 26, 1719.

John Bartlett took to wife Elizabeth Haynes the daughter of Mr. Wm. Haynes, Feb. 20, 1706.

Elizabeth Bartlett, yᵉ daughter of said John Bartlett,
born Dec. 4, 1707.
Hannah, daughter, born Oct. 13, 1709.
William, son, born Dec. 10, 1711.
Isabel, daughter, born Aug. 18, 1714.
Mary, daughter, born Apr. 17, 1716.
Sarah, daughter, born Sept. 20, 1718.
John, son, born Apr. 5, 1719.

Elizabeth, yᵉ wife of said John Bartlett, departed this life Feb. 26, 1723–4.

Sr. John Bartlett, departed this life August 5, 1761, in yᵉ 85th year of his age.

Their son, Samuel Bartlett departed this life Nov. 16, 1762.

Thomas Reed took to wife Mary Olmstead, the daughter of St. John Olmstead of Norwalk, May 9, 1694.

Mary Reed ye daughter of ye said Thos. Reed, born May, 2, 1695.

Eunice,   born Feb. 26, 1696–7.
Thomas,   born May   7, 1699.
John,   born Aug.   7, 1701.
Elizabeth,   born Oct.   7, 1703.
Ann,   born July   6, 1706.
Temperance, born Oct. 16, 1708.

Death—Ann Reed departed this life Feb. 9, 1709–10.

Elias, son of said Thos. Reed, born Mar. 10, 1711.

Nathan,   "   "   born Aug. 13, 1713.

Samuel Platt took to wife Rebekak Benndick, daughter of Mr. Samuel Bennedick of Danbury, and was married June 18, 1712.

Rebekah Platt, daughter of ye said Samuel Platt, born April 9, 1713.

The above named Samuel Platt departed this life Dec. 4, 1713.

John Scrivener took to wife Deborah Lees, the daughter of Lt. Wm. Lees, March 9, 1709–10.

Mary Scrivener, the daughter of said John Scrivener, born March, 1711.

Rebekah,   born Oct. 12, 1772.

Nathan Bears, the son of Nathan Bears was born Sept. 8, 1745.

Ebenezer, born Sept. 28, 1747.
Samuel,   born Dec. 6, 1749.
Lydia,   born Oct. 24, 1751.
          Said Lydia died June 3, 1796.
Hannah,   born July 17, 1754.
Abijah,   born April 7, 1756.
          Said Abijah died June 26, 1784.
Ezekiel, born March 9, 1758.
          Said Ezekiel died June 9, 1795.
Sarah,   born March 12, 1760.
          Said Sarah died July 19, 1781.

Abigail, born March 6, 1762.
Mary, born Sept. 2, 1764.
Anna, born Feb. 19, 1767.
Esther, born Feb. 6, 1770.

Eliphalet Lockwood ye son of Ephraim Lockwood took to wife Mary Gold, ye daughter of John Gold of Stanford and was marryed, Oct. 11, 1699.

Hannah Lockwood ye daughter of ye sd Eliphalet born July 28, 1700.
Damaris, born Nov. 7, 1701.
Mary, born Nov. 4, 1704.
Eliphalet, born June 24, 1706.
John, born Jan. 8, 1707-8.
Mercy, born Apr. 11, 1709.
Peter, born Mar. 16, 1710-11.
Hannah, 2d daughter of that name born July 12, 1712.
Abigail, born Oct. 17, 1716.

The third born child of ye above sd Eliphelet Lockwood was a son, and born Nov. 28, 1703 and departed this life, Dec. 20, 1703.

Hannah, the first born of ye sd Eliphelet, departed this life, July 16, 1712.

Mercy Lockwood, daughter, departed this life Oct. 1, 1712.

Hannah Lockwood ye second, departed this life Oct. 27, 1713.

John Lockwood, son to Eliphelet, departed this life Oct. 17, 1734.

Samuel Keeler Jun. took to wife Rebeckah Bennedick, ye daughter of Mr. James Bennedick, of Danbury, and was married Jan. 18, 1704-5.

Samuel Keeler, ye son of said Sam. Keeler was born Jan. 14, 1705-6.
Rebeckah, daughter, born Oct. 28, 1708.
Rebeckah, wife, departed this life, Mar. 20, 1709.
Rebeckah, daughter, born Apr. 7, 1769.

Samuell Keeler took to wife Sarah Betts, the daughter of Mr. Thomas Betts, of Norwalk, and was married Dec. 11, 1712.

Sarah Keeler, daugh ⸱ ⸱   1 Sam. and Sarah, was
   born Jan. 1, 1714.
Matthew, son, born Mar. 14, 1717.
Mary, daughter, born Jan. 29, 1718—19.
Elizabeth, daughter, born Apr. 20, 1722.
Hannah, daughter, born Oct. 18, 1725.
Rebeckah, daughter, born Aug. 27, 1729.
The said Sam. Keeler departed this life Aug. 8, 1763.

Samuell Canfield took to wife Abigail Austin, the daughter of Thomas Austin, of Stanford, Aug. 1, 1709.

  Samuel Canfield, son of said Sam., born June 4, 1710.
  Abigail Canfield, wife, departed this life June 11, 1710.

Samuell Canfield took to wife Abigail Dean, the daughter of John ͺDean, of Stanford, and was married May, 9,
1711.
  Samuel Canfield departed this life Sept. 1712.

James Dickson took to wife Hannah Rumsy, the daughter of Ensigne Benjamin Rumsey, and was married Dec·
8, 1709.'

  John Dickson, the son of yᵉ said Jas. Dickson, was
   born Oct. 22, 1711.
  Benjamin, born Jan. 9, 1713--14.' ᛁ

John Whitne Jun. took to wife Elisabeth Finch, yᵉ
daughter of Mr. Joseph Finch, of Greenwich, and was
married to her Mar. 4, 1709—10.

  John Whitne, son of yᵉ said John Whitne, born
  Mar. 4, 1711—12.
  The above said John Whitne Jun. departed this life
  Feb. 3, 1712—13.

James Hayes took to wife Mary Allen, the daughter of
Mr. Thos. Allen, deceased, late of Burlington, in yᵉ province of New Jersey, and was married Apr. 1, 1703.

  Eunice Hayes, yᵉ daughter of yᵉ s'd James Hayes
   born Jan. 21, 1704—5.
  Mary, born June 1, 1706.
  Nathaniell, born Mar. 20, 1708.
  James, born June 25, 1710.
  Rachell, born Mar. 4, 1711.

Elizabeth,   born Feb. 15, 1712.
Thomas,   born Jan. 31, 1714.
Samuell,   born Oct. 29, 1716.
Allen,   born Aug. 5, 1718.

John Bolt took to wife Elizabeth Clemmons, daughter of Wm. Clemmons, of Stanford, Nov. 20, 1694.

Richard Bolt, ye son of ye said John Bolt,
               born Apr. 30, 1696.
Charles,   born Aug. 30, 1702.
Sarah,   born June 12, 1705.
Abigail,   born Nov. 7, 1707.
John,   born Oct. 7, 1710.
William,   born Nov. 7, 1713.
Benjamin,   born Sept. 26, 1718.

Thomas Rockwell took to wife Sarah Resco, daughter of Mr. John Resco, of Norwalk, and was married Dec. 9, 1703.

Sarah Rockwell, daughter of ye said Thos. Rockwell,
               born Oct. 21, 1704.
Thomas, son, born Dec. 13, 1708.
John, son,   born Jan. 9, 17 .
Jabez, son, born Mar. 18, 1712.

The above said Thomas Rockwell departed this life June, 1712.

James Lockwood took to wife Lidia Smith, the daughter of Mr. Samuel Smith, and was married Oct. 23, 1707.

Lidiah Lockwood, born Dec. 17, 1710.
The said Lidiah departed this life June 18, 1712.
Hannah,   born Oct. 23, 1713.
James,   born Dec. 20, 1714.
Lidiah,   born Jan. 10, 1716–17.
Job,   born July 13, 1718.
John,   born Feb. 8, 1719–20.
Samuel,   born Nov. 30, 1721.

David Tuttle took to wife Mary Reed, the daughter of Mr. John Reed, of Norwalk, Nov. 24, 1698.

Solomon,   born Aug. 26, 1699.
David,   born Mar. 6, 1701.
Mary,   born Nov. 24, 1704.
Nathan,   born Aug. 16, 1707.

Katharine,	born Jan. 2, 1709–10.
Ann,	born Dec. 28, 1713.
Lidia,	born July 11, 1717.

' Samuel Betts took to wife Judith Rennolds, the daughter of Mr. John Rennolds, of Greenwich, and was married to her Dec. 10, 1692.

Mary,	born Sept. 10, 1693.
Samuell,	born Oct. 28, 1695.
Stephen,	born Aug. 1, 1698.
Nathan,	born Nov. 5, 1700.
Hephzibah,	born Oct. 29, 1703.
Judith,	born Aug. 25, 1714.

Samuel Hartshorn, yᵉ son of Mr. Jonathan Hartshorn, late of New London, was born in Norwalk, April 24, 1717.

William Parker took to wife the widow Mary Rockwell, and was married to her Oct 22, 1717.

William,	born Oct. 7, 1720.
John,	born July 6, 1722.
Mary,	born Nov. 5, 1724.

James St. John, yᵉ son of James St. John, born Mar. 30, 1738: said James St. John took to wife Abigail Person, yᵉ daughter of Mr. Stephen Person, of Darby, and was married to her Mar. 30, 1738.

Isaac,	born Apr. 14, 1739.
Ezra,	born Sept. 7, 1741.
Abigail,	born Jan. 1, 1743–4

Joseph Kellogg took to wife Sarah Plum, daughter of Mr. John Plum, of Milford, Nov. 25, 1702.

Elizabeth,	born Oct. 5, 1703.
Sarah,	born Apr. 5, 1706.
Joseph,	born Sept. 26, 1707.
Rachel,	born July 15, 1710.
Hannah,	born Aug. 1, 1712.

Sarah, wife of yᵉ above Joseph Kellogg, departed this life Aug. 17, 1712.

Joseph Kellogg took to wife the widow, Mary Lyon, Aug. 17, 1712.

| David, | born Sept. 28, 1715. |
| Benjamin, | born Sept. 26, 1716. |

William Truesdell, son of Wm. and Martha Truesdell,
born July 21, 1722.
Stephen,   born Aug. 28, 1724.
Sam'l,   born June 18, 1738.
Charles,   born May 10, 1740.
Mary,   born May 27, 1743.
Richard,   born May 20, 1744.

Thomas Benedict took to wife Rachel Smith, the daughter of Mr. Samuel Smith, of Norwalk, and was married to
her May 13, 169—. *Obliterated.*

Mary,   born Dec.   4, 169— *Obliterated.*
Thomas,   born Oct. 29, 170—   "
Samuel,   born Jan. 31, 170—   "
Daniel,   born Apr.   7, 170—   "
Rachel,   born Sept. 27, 171—   "
Nehemiah,   born Dec. 21, 171—   "
Sarah,   born June   6, 17 —   "

Daniel Benedict, the son of the above Thomas B., departed this life June 9, 17—.

Rachel, wife of the above Thomas, departed this life
Dec. 1, 17—.

Thomas Raymond took to wife Sarah Andrews, the
daughter of Abraham Andrews, late of Waterbury, and
was married to her Nov. 15, 170—.

Thomas, son, born Jan. 12, 170— *Obliterated.*
Abraham,   born Oct.   4, 170—   "
Benjamin,   born Jan. 23, 170—   "
Comfort,   born July 15, 17 —   "
James,   born Dec.   5, 171—   "
David,   born Feb.   3, 1715.
Thankful,   born Oct. 24, 1719.
Thomas,   born Nov. 17, 172—   "
David,   born Mar. 27, 172—   "

Sarah Raymond, daughter of said Thomas, aged about
5 mo. died June 3, 170—.

David, aged about 7 weeks, died Sept. 171—.

Thomas, ye first-born son of said Thomas, died Dec. 3,
172—.

David, died May 31, 172—.

Lt. John Belden departed this life Nov. 26, 171—.

10

John Copp took to wife Mrs. Ruth Belden, widow and relict of Lt. John Belden, late of Norwalk, Jan. 4, 171—.

Samuel Grumman, late of Fairfield, took to wife Rebeckah Betts, daughter of Mr. Daniel Betts, of Norwalk, Jan. 10, 1721-2.

Sarah Grumman, daughter, born Oct. 28, 1722.	
Samuel,	born May 8, 1725.
Rebeckah,	born Sept. 24, 1727.
Mary,	born Oct. 20, 1729.
Thomas,	born Aug. 22, 1731.

Sarah Lockwood, ye daughter of Joseph and Mary Lockwood, was born Nov. 28, 1723, and departed this life Feb. 1, 1726-7.

Isaac Lockwood, ye son of ye said Joseph and Mary Lockwood, was born Dec. 24, 1726.

Thomas Fitch,* Jun., of Norwalk, took to wife Hannah

* Thomas Fitch graduated at Yale College in 1721, was Lieut. Gov., Chief Justice, and Governor of the Colony from 1754 to 1766.

The following is the inscription on his tombstone :

THE HONORABLE THOMAS FITCH, ESQ.,

GOV. OF THE COLONY OF CONNECTICUT,

Eminent and distinguished among mortals
for great abilities, large acquirements, and a
virtuous character;
a clear, strong, sedate mind,
and an accurate, extensive acquaintance
with law and civil government;
a happy talent of presiding,
close application and strict fidelity,
in the discharge of important trusts,
no less than
for his employments by the voice of the people
in the chief offices of State,
and at the head of the colony.
Having served his generation by the will of God,
fell asleep July 18, Anno Domini 1774,
in the 78th year of his age.

Hall, yᵉ daughter of Mr. Richard Hall, of New Haven, Sept. 4, 1724.

Thomas,	born Aug. 12, 1725.
Jonathan,	born Apr. 12, 1727.
Ebenezer,	born Feb. 25, 1728-9.
Hannah,	born Apr. 10, 1731.
Mary,	born Sept. 20, 1733.

David Lambert, of Norwalk, took to wife Laurana Bill, daughter of Mr. John Bill, of Lebanon, and was married to her Feb. 1, 1726-7.

Elisabeth, daughter, born Feb. 17, 1727-8.

Elisabeth Hayes, widow of Mr. Samuel Hayes, departed this life Nov. 3, 1729.

Mr. Thomas Fitch, sen., deceased May 10, 1731.

Thomas Reed, jr., took to wife Sarah Bennam, daughter of John Bennam, of West Haven, Oct. 2, 172—.

Thomas, son,	born June 22, 1730.
Ebenezer,	born Apr. 3, 1732.
Jesse,	born July 29, 1734.
Peter,	born Apr. 3, 1737.
Sarah,	born June 19, 1737.
Eli,	born Sept. 24, 1743.

Nathaniel Finch, of Norwalk, took to wife Hannah Raymond, daughter of Capt. John Raymond, Nov. 24, 1725.

| Hannah, | born Nov. 2, 1725. |
| Dann, | born Sept. 29, 1731. |

Thomas Person, Jun., of Darby, took to wife Ruth Holebrook, the daughter of Mr. Abel Holebrook, Feb. 22, 1727-8.

Mehetabel,	born Jan. 13, 1728-9.
Timothy,	born Nov. 7, 1732.
Nathan,	born Nov. 27, 1734.

Ruth, yᵉ wife of sᵈ Thos. Person, died Oct. 14, 1737.

Said Thos. Person took to wife yᵉ widow Elisabeth Thomas, Mar. 7, 1738.

John Betts, yᵉ son of John Betts, took to wife Damaris

Lockwood, daughter of Mr. Eliphelet Lockwood, Apr. 17, 1722.

Thaddeus Betts,*	son of ye s^d	John,	born May 3, 1724.

Thaddeus Betts,* son of ye s^d John, born May 3, 1724.
Mary, " daughter, born May 4, 1727.
Hannah, " " born May 21, 1730.
John, " son, born Aug. 11, 1735.

James Brown took to wife Joanna Whitehead, the daughter of Mr. Sam'l Whitehead, of Elizabethtown, in East New Jersey, Dec. 20, 1714 ; their 1st child was a son, born Oct. 20, 1715, and departed this life Nov. 4th following.

Rebeckah, born Jan. 20, 1716–17.
Joannah, born Aug. 28, 1718.
James, born Dec. 18, 1720.
Mary, born Sept. 19, 1722.
Elisabeth, born Mar. 22, 1723–4.
Samuel, born May 3, 1726.
Ann, born June 1, 1728.

James Picket took to wife Deborah Stewart, daughter of Ensigne James Stewart, Apr. 14, 1726.

Sarah, born Sept. 12, 1728.
Esther, born Nov. 14, 1730.
James, born Apr. 24, 1732.
Deborah, born Oct. 3, 1734.
John, born Sept. 6, 1737.
Ezra, born July 12, 1740.

Josiah Whitne, of Norwalk, took to wife Eunice Hanford, the daughter of Mr. Eleazer Hanford, Oct. 30, 1729. .

Josiah, born Feb. 10, 1730–1.
Stephen, born Feb. 10, 1732–3.
Henry, born Feb. 19, 1735–6.
Eliezer, born Mar. 7, 1737–8.
Isaac, born Mar. 27, 1741.

Ebenezer Smith, of Norwalk, took to wife Elizabeth Bartell, the daughter of Mr. John Barttell, June 2, 1729.

Ephraim, born Mar. 24, 1730.
Jedediah, born Sept. 5, 1732.
Isaac, born Oct. 25, 1734.

* Thaddeus Betts, M.D., graduated at Yale in 1745.

Stephen Buckingham,* Junior, of Norwalk, took to wife Elisabeth Sherwood, daughter to Lt. Issac Sherwood, of Fairfield, and was married to her Feb. 24, 1728–9.

Solomon,	born Feb. 1, 1730–1.
Temperance,	born Jan. 14, 1838–9.
Daniel,	born Aug. 21, 1735.
Ann,	born July 3, 1737.

Esther Prindle, daughter of Sam'l Prindle, born at New Haven, Feb. 1, 1718–19.

Moses, son of said Sam'l, born in Norwalk, Aug. 4, 1725.

Joseph, born July 17, 1730.

William Edwards, of Norwalk, took to wife Abigail Couch, daughter of Mr. Simon Couch, late of Fairfield, deceased, May 4, 1713.

William, their first-born, born Mar. 11, 1713–14. Died Apr. 25, 1716.

Abigail,	born Aug. 18, 1716.
William,	born June 17, 1718.
Mary,	born Sept. 13, 1721.
Hannah,	born Sept. 22, 1724.
Deborah,	born Feb. 12, 1726–7.
John,	born June 14, 1728.
Couch,	born Apr. 22, 1730.
Gershom,	born Jan. 28, 1733.

* Stephen Buckingham, Jr., was not (as might be supposed) the son of Rev. Stephen Buckingham, but of Daniel Buckingham (probably of Saybrook). He probably took the title of Junior to distinguish himself from Rev. Stephen. There is on the Saybrook Records, a deed of Nov. 3, 1726, from " Stephen Buckingham, Junior, of Norwalk, husbandman, conveying to Thomas Lynde, of Saybrook," some land, " being land conveyed by Samuel Marvin to my uncle Mr. Thomas Buckingham, and to my honored father, Mr. Daniel Buckingham." This Stephen Buckingham, Junior, was a grandson of Rev. Thomas Buckingham, of Saybrook, and was born Aug. 4, 1703. (*From Nathaniel Goodwin, of Hartford*).

The old inhabitants of Norwalk say they have always heard that Rev. Stephen Buckingham had no children.

A Record of the children of Lt. John Taylor, and Wait his wife, that were born in Norwalk, viz.

Noah,   born Oct. 5, 1699.
Josiah,   born Oct. 17, 1701.
Reuben,   born Nov. 21, 1703.
Sarah,   born Nov. 22, 1706.
Mary,   born Oct. 2, 1709.

Wait Taylor, the wife of yᵉ Sᵈ Lt. John Taylor, departed this life Jan. 29, 1721–22.

Sᵈ Lt. John Taylor departed this life Nov. 18, 1744.

John Raymond, Jr., took to wife Katharine Hanford, the daughter to Mr. Thomas Hanford, of Norwalk, Dec. 24,1719.

John, .   born Oct. 8, 1720.
Katharine, born Oct. 31, 1721.
Mary,   born June 17, 1723.
Gershom,   born Jan. 18, 1724–5.
Katharine, died Mar. 23, 1726–7.
Jesse,   born July 10, 1729.
Elisabeth, born Mar. 10, 1730–1.
      and died Apr. 18, 1731.
Hannah,   born Aug. 31, 1732.
Elisabeth, born June 28, 1734.
      and died Dec. 19, 1734.

Mrs. Katharine Raymond departed this life about 11 of yᵉ clock a.m. Oct. 2, 1740–1.

Samuel Raymond, Jr., of Norwalk, tooke to wife Elisabeth Hayt, the daugh'r of Joseph Hayt, of S'd Norwalk.

Eliakim,   born Feb. 20, 1720.
Rebeckah, born April 27, 1722.
Samuel,   born Dec. 11, 1734.
Elizabeth, born July   9, 1728.

Moses Fountain, of Norwalk, took to wife the widow Elizabeth Gregory, Aug. 13, 1719.

Moses,   born Sept. 7, 1720.
Joseph,   born Dec.   4, 1723.
Sam'l,   born March 7, 1725–6.
Matthew,   born March 4, 1730–1.

Samuel Richards took to wife Elizabeth Latham, daugh'r of Mr. John Latham, March 4, 1714.

Ruth,   born Jan.   5, 1714–15.

Sam'l,   born Dec. 23, 1716.
Mary,   born April 19, 1719.
John,   born Feb. 16, 1720–21.
James,   born Oct. 29, 1723.
Sarah,   born June 24, 1727.
Elisabeth, born May 25, 1729.'
Thankfull, born June 5, 1731.'
Moses,   born March 6, 1732–3.'
Daniel,   born Mar. 19, 1734–5.'

— Samuel Benedict took to wife Jemima Canfield, relict of Ebenezer Canfield, dec'd, April 18, 1724.

Jemima,   born March 8, 1724–5.
Sam'l,   born Dec. 5, 1726.
Mary,   born June 14, 1728.
Daniel,   born March 8, 1729–30.
Stephen,   born May 20, 1731.
Sarah,   born Jan. 30, 1733–4.
Abigail,   born July 7, 1735.
Esther,   born Sept. 9, 1737.'
Rachel,   born June 24, 1739.

Eliasaph Kellogg took to wife Rachel Benedict, daugh'r of Ensign Thomas Benedict, Anno 1734, June 13th.

Johannah, born May 27, 1735.
Rachel,   born April 25, 1737. }
    And died, Nov. 30, 1738. }
Rachel,   born Dec. 3, 1738.
Lidia,   born Mar. 26, 1740.
Esther,   born Oct. 23, 1741.
Thomas,   born Aug. 1, 1743.
Eliasaph,   born Sept. 8, 1745.
Milisan,   born Mar. 23, 1746–7.
Deborah,   born April 20, 1749.

William Reed took to wife Rachel Kellogg, daugh'r of Mr. Joseph Kellogg, late of Norwalk, Nov. 28, 1729.

Joseph,   born Oct. 30, 1731.
William,   born March 20, 1733–4.

William Jervis took to wife Hannah Forward, daugh'r of Mr. Joseph Forward, of Danbury, March 27, 1723.

Joseph,   born Feb. 17, 1723–4.
Joannah,   born Sept 27, 1725.

Hannah,	born Nov.	23, 1727.
Sarah,	born Dec.	27, 1730.
Sarah,	died, June	6, 1732.

Nehemiah Benedict took to wife Hannah Keeler, the daugh'r of Capt. Sam'l Keeler, Dec. 17, 1751.

Nehemiah,	born Oct. 15, 1752—died June 26, 1776.
William,	born Sept. 14, 1754—died Aug. [3, 1776.
Waters,	born Oct. 27, 1756—died Jan. 12, 1764.
Hannah,	born Dec. 11, 1759.
Thomas,	born Mar. 25, 1764—died July 24, 1787.

Hannah, wife of said Nehemiah,
                                    died Dec. 6, 1783.
Hannah, the daughter,   died Feb. 21, 1786.
Robin, negro man belonging to s'd Nehemiah, died Jan. 20, 1788.

Jemima Dean, daugh'r of Jonathan and Rebecca his wife,   born April 29, 1753.
| Esther, | born July 18, 1755. |
| Joseph, | born Sept. 10, 1757. |

Thos. Betts (born in 1717) took to wife Betty Benedict, daughter of Capt. Thomas Benedict, May 22, 1748.

Betty,	born———— ———died Jan. —, 1769
Thomas,	born March 14, 1753—died Jan. 17, 1813.
Esther,	born———— —, 1749.
Lydia,	born————, 1755.
Susannah,	born———— —, 1757
Hezekiah,	born July 31, 1760—died May 31, 1837.
	Was a soldier in the Revolution.

Mr. Ralph Isaacs took to wife Mrs. Mary Rumsey, daugh. of Mr. Benjamin Rumsey, of Fairfield, March 7, 1725–6.

Samuel,	born Jan. 16, 1726–7.
Mary,	born Sept. 27, 1728.
Esther,	born July 19, 1730.
Isaac,	born July 19, 1732.
Sarah,	born Aug. 31, 1735.
Benjamin,	born Sept. 19, 1737.
Ralph,	born June 4, 1741
Grace,	born June 10, 1743

Rogers Uriah, his Family.

Hannah,	the daughter of Uriah, was	
	born June	7, 1735.
Lydia,	born Dec.	15, 1737.
Uriah,	born Dec.	17, 1739.
James,	born Sept.	5, 1742.
John,	born Nov.	3, 1744.
Esther,	born Oct.	1, 1746.
David,	born Aug.	21, 1748.
Abigail,	born Oct.	14, 1749.

South Carolina.

These are to certify, whom it may concern, that, on the twenty seventh day of July, this present year of our Lord, that Joseph Whitne and Mary Coyt were joyn'd together in marriage, according to the rites and ceremonies of the Church of England, by the Reverend Mr. Alexander Garden, Rector of the Parish of St. Philip, of Charlestown, in the sd. Province, as appears by the Register's book of the sd. parish.

Given under our hand and seal at Charlestown, the second day of August, and year of our Lord one thousand seven hundred and thirty six.

A. GARDEN, Min'r.

JAMES FOWLER, } Church Wardens.
EDWARD HEXT, }

Recorded by me,   ELNATHAN HANFORD, Register.

Ebenezer Abbott took to wife Ann Lion, daughter of ―― Lion, of ――, and was married to her Nov. 3 1730.

Abigail,	born Sept. 13, 1731.
Ruth,	born June 2, 1733.
Abijah,	born Sept. 3, 1735.
Lois,	born Sept. 11, 1737.
Seth,	born Dec. 23, 1739.
Ebenezer,	born Nov. 28, 1741.

Ebenezer Fitch took to wife Lydia Mills, daugh'r of Mr. Samuell Mills, Jr., of Greenwich, Dec. 20, 1750.

Jabez,	born Sept. 11, 1751.
Syrah,	born Aug. 11, 1753.
Ebenezer,	born Sept. 9, 1755.
Hannah,	born Aug. 8, 1758.

10*

Joshua Raymond took to wife Elizabeth Fitch, daughter of Mr. Thomas Fitch, of Norwalk, and was married to her May 17th, 1721.

Elizabeth Raymond, daughter of Josh. Raymond,
		born Mar.	21, 1721–2.
Stephen,	son,	born Jan.	1, 1724–5.
Sarah,	daughter,	born July	6, 1727.
James,	son,	born Oct.	2, 1729.
Susannah,	daughter,	born Aug.	28, 1732.
Martha,	daughter,	born Jan.	5, 1734–5.
Joshua,	son,	born Sept.	12, 1738.

John Brown took to wife Mary Raymond, daughter of Mr. Samuel Raymond—marryed to her May 6, 1729.

John Brown, son to ye said John Brown,
	born March 28, 1731.	
Betty, daughter,	born Jan.	14, 1729–30.
Judith, daughter,	born March 31, 1732.	

John Kellogg took to wife Ann Coley, daughter of Samuel Coley, of Fairfield, and was marryed to her Jan. 1, 1729–30.

Ezra Kellogg, son to John Kellogg,
	born April 3, 1731.	
Mary, daughter,	born Jan'y 22, 1732–3.	
Ann, daughter,	born Mar. 16, 1734–5.	
John,	son,	born May 25, 1737.
Seth,	son,	born Feb'y 8, 1739–40.

John Kellogg departed this life April 17, 1740.

Thomas Benedick, Jr., took to wife Deborah Waters, daughter Mr. Jonath. Waters, of Jamaica, on Long Island, in ye province of New York, and was marryed May 21, 1725.

Thomas Benedick, son of sd Thomas, was
	born Feb. 25, 1725–6.	
Deborah,	daughter,	born June 8, 1728.
Nehemiah,	son,	born Jan. 9, 1729–30.
Rachel,	daughter,	born Feb. 28, 1731–2.
Hannah,	daughter,	born Dec. 13, 1733.
Jonathan,	son,	born June 18, 1736.

Ezra Hayt took to wife Phebe Benedick, daughter of Deacon John Benedick, and was married to her April 4, 1731.

Anna Hayt, daughter of said Ezra Hayt, was
born Febr'y 7, 1732–3.
Ezra,   son,   born March 14, 1734–5.
Thaddeus,   son,   born April 28, 1737.

Ephraim Lockwood took to wife Thankfull Grummon, daughter to John Grummon, of Fairfield, and was marryed to her Oct. 30, 1734.

Sarah Lockwood, daughter of sd. Ephraim Lockwood,
born July 23, 1735.
Nehemiah,   son,   born May 18, 1740.
Mary,   daughter, born Mar. 3, 1741-2.

David Hayt took to wife Ruth Lockwood, daughter of Mr. Joseph Lockwood, of Norwalk, and was married January 5, 1735–6.

Isaac Hayt, son to ye said David Hayt,
born Sept. 28, 1736.
Timothy, son, born May 27, 1739.

John Rockwell took to wife Abigail Belden, daughter of William Belden, of Norwalk, and married to her August 17, 1733.

John Rockwell, son to ye said John Rockwell,
born Sept. 3, 1734.
Thomas,   son, born August 27, 1736.

The above named John Rockwell departed this life, on ye Island of Statia, on ye May 25, 1737.

Abigail Rockwell, widow and relict of ye said John Rockwell, departed this life May 7, 1739.

John Marven took to wife Rachel Saint John, ye daughter of Mr. Matthias Saint John, of Norwalk, and was married to her April 27th, 1721.

Hannah, daughter of ye said John Marven, by ye said Rachel,   born Des. 4, 1722.
Joseph,   son,   born May 29, 1724.
Rachel, daughter, born Dec. 24, } 1725.
The sd. Rachel departed this life, Dec. 26, }

Benjamin Marven, son of ye said
    John Marven, born Mar. 14, } 1727–8.
The sd Benjamin departed this life Mar. 17, }
Rachel Marven, born ye daugh-
    ter of John and Rachel,   Mar. 27,   1728–9.
Sarah,   born May 18, } 1733.
The sd. Sarah departed this life May 21, }
Ann Marven, daughter of ye
    said John & Rachel, born Sept. 7,   1741.

Josiah Hull took to wife Hannah Prindle, daughter to Mr. Eleazor Prindle, late of Milford, deceased, and was married to her July 27, 1729.

    Eleazor, ye son of ye s'd Josiah Hull,
                  was born Dec. 29, 1728.
The s'd Eleazor departed this life Mar. 28, 1729.
    Hannah, ye daughter of ye s'd Josiah Hull,
                  was born April 9, 1730.
    Josiah,   son,   born June 19, 1732.
    Eleazor,   son,   born July 31, 1734.

Jacob Green took to wife Elizabeth Reed, daughter to Mr. John Reed, of Norwalk, and was marryed to her Novem. 12, 1719.

    Elizabeth, daughter of s'd Jacob Green,
                  was born Nov. 6, 1720.
    Elija,   son,   born April 9, 1723.
    Eleazor,   son,   born Feb. 25, 1724–5.
    Ruth,   daughter, born Feb. 25, 1726–7.
    Asahel,   son,   born Oct. 25, 1729.

John Olmsted took to wife Mary Small, daughter to Mr. Robert Small transient sometime of Norwalk, and was marryed to her, ye s'd Mary, February 29, 1717–18.

    Silvanus Olmsted, son to ye s'd John Olmsted,
                  born Nov. 25, 1718.
    Phebe,   daughter, born Aug. 5, 1720.
    Ruben,   son,   born April 5, 1722.
    David,   son,   born Feb'y 6, 1724–5.
    Small,   son,   born Mar. 2, 1727–8.
    John,   son,   born Mar. 29, 1729.
    Ichabod,   son,   born June 14, 1733.

John Parrat took to wife Eunice Stewart, daughter to Ensigne James Stewart, of Norwalk, March 4, 1723-4.

Elisabeth, born Jan,   11, 1724-5.
Hannah,   born Sept.   5, 1726.
John,   born May   20, 1728.
Sarah,   born Sept.   21, 1730.
Abraham, born July   26, 1732.

Eunice, wife of said John, departed this life March 30, 1735-6.

John Little took to wife Sarah Boult, daughter to John Boult, late of Norwalk, dec'd, April 14, 1735.

James, son, born Dec. 22, 1735.

John Belden took to wife Ruhamar Hill, daughter of Capt. John Hill, of Westerly, in ye Government of Road Island, and was married to her May 9, 1728.

John,   born April 26, 1729.
Thomas,   born Mar. 25, 1731.
Hezekiah, born April 25, 1736.
Mary,   born Jan. 22, 1739-40.

Elijah Whitne took to wife Rebeckah Seymer, daughter to Mr. John Seymer, July 6, 1734.

Hannah, born April 22, 1735.
Elijah, born Oct. 13, 1736.

These may certifie that Hezekiah Whitne and Margaret Harris were joyned together in marriage, on or about ye thirde daye of January, 1732-3, pr. me, Moses Dickinson.

Betty, daugh'r of Hezekiah Whitne,
            born Jan. 24, 1733-4.
Abigail, born May 14, 1735-6.
Ruth,   born Jan. 3, 1736-7.
Jeremiah, born Mar. 17, 1739-40.

Josiah Taylar and Thankfull French were joyned together in marriage August ye second, 1729, pr. me, Stephen Buckingham.

Josiah, son of Josiah and Thankfull,
            born July 4, 1730.
Jonathan, born Dec. 7, 1731.

Levi,	born Dec. 17, 1733
Gamaliel,	born Jan. 9, 1735.
Barak,	born Nov. 26, 1737.
Abijah,	born Sep. 22, 1740.
Paul,	born Mar. 12, 1741–2.
Sarah,	born July 16, 1741–2.
Thankfui,	born Oct. 5, 1746.
Eleazar,	born Mar. 2, 1749.
Deborah,	born May 18, 1756.

Daniel Hayt, Jr., took to wife Sarah Benedick, daughr. to Ensigne Thomas Benedick, Senr., of Norwalk, and was married to her April 28, 1735.

Daniel,	son, born May 18, 1736.
Rachel,	born Sept. 3, 1738.
Nehemiah,	born July 25, 1740.
Phineas,	born April 11, 1742.
Elisabeth,	born June 17, 1744.
Sarah,	born April 25, 1749.
Thomas,	born Dec. 24, 1752.
Daniel,	born Feb. 27, 1759.

Peter Lockwood took to wife Mrs. Abigail Hawley, the daughter of the Reverend Thomas Hawley, of Ridgefield, Sept. 8, 1737.

Abigail,	born Oct. 17, 1738.
Eliphelet,	born Oct. 17, 1741.
Hannah,	born Sept. 23, 1743.
Mary,	born Aug. 31, 1745.
Dorothy,	born Dec. 7, 1747.

Abigail, the wife of ye said Peter Lockwood, departed this life June 6, 1749.

Dorothy, daughter, deceased June 23, 1750.

Peter Lockwood abovesaid, took to wife Elisabeth, daughter of Mr. David Lambert, and was married to her Jan. 1, 1750–51.

Lambert, the son of sd. Peter and Elisabeth, born Dec. 14, 1753, died 18 days old.

David Kellogg took to wife Judeth Raymond, daughr. of Mr. Daniel Raymond, Feb. 28, 1733–4.

Mary Kellogg, daughter of sd. David and Judith,
                born Sept. 23, 1734.
Rachel,   born April 17, 1737.
Judith,   born Aug. 23, 1739.
Joseph,   born Mar. 23, 1741-2.

Nathaniel Street took to wife Mary Raymond, daughter
of Capt. John Raymond, of Norwalk, and was married to
her Nov. 25, 1719.

Samuel Street, son of ye sd. Nath'l and Mary Street,
                born Oct. 13, 1720.
Hannah,   born Sept. 8, 1722.
Timothy,   born Dec. 1, 1723.
John,   born July 22, 1728.
Ebenezer,   born Nov. 1, 1735.

James Hays took to wife Rhoda Hayt, daughter to Mr.
Caleb Hayt, of Norwalk, and was married to her Dec. 29
1734.

Samuel Hays, son of sd. James Hays,
                born Mar. 25, 1725-6.
Elijah,   born Feb. 5, 1737-8.
James,   born Feb. 7, 1739-40.
John,   born April 19, 1742.

John Abbot took to wife Eunice Judd, daughter of Mr.
John Judd, of Farmington, dec'd, and was married May 11,
1724.

Jerusha Abbot, daughter of s'd John Abbot,
                born Mar. 25, 1725.
John,   born Mar. 1, 1726-7.
Thaddeus,   born Mar. 17, 1728-9.
Jesse,   born June 11, 1731.
Phebee,   born Feb. 25, 1732-3.

John Darrow, late of New London, took to wife Sarah
Hanford, daughter to Mr. Eleaser Hanford, late of Norwalk,
deceased, and was marryed to her Oct. 30, 1735.

Samuel, ⎱ Twins, son and daughter to ye sd. John
Hannah, ⎰ Darrow, and were
                born Sept. 29, 1736.
John,   born Feb. 22, 1738-9.
Isaac,   born May 17, 1741.
Paul,   born Oct. 9, 1743.

Robert Smith took to wife Judith Fountain, daughter of Mr. James Fountain, late of Greenwich, deceased, and was married to her Mar. 11, 1724.

Fountain Smith, son to ye sd. Robert and Judith,
born Mar. 2, 1725.
James, born Nov. 14, 1726.
Judith, born Aug. 21, 1728.
Febe, born Sep. 21, 1730.
Febe, born Dec. 20, 1731.
Abraham, born May 17, 1734.

Daniel Belden, son of Danl. and Esther Belden,
born Mar. 6, 1744–5.
Elisabeth, daughter, born Nov. 24, 1747.

John Taylar, Junr., took to wife Sarah Lockwood, daughter of Mr. Daniel Lockwood, late of Norwalk, dec'd, and was married to her Nov. 6, 1723.

John Taylor, son to s'd John and Sarah, born Aug. 20, 1724—deceased Nov. 27, 1724.

Sarah Taylor, ye wife of ye above sd. John Taylor, departed this life Jan. 24, 1724–5.

The sd. John Taylor, Junr., took to wife Hannah Steuart, daughter to Lt. James Steuart, of Norwalk, and was married to her Jan. 19, 1726–7.

John Taylor, son to ye sd. John and Hannah,
born Nov. 29, 1727.
James, born July 12, 1729.
Hannah, born June 1, 1731.
Eli, born June 5, 1733.
Seth, born Mar. 30, 1735.
Bette, born Mar. 7, 1736–7.
Asher, born Sep. 11, 1740.

Nathan Betts, took to wife Mary Belden, daughter of Mr. William Belden of Norwalk and was married to her Sept. 20, 1727.

Mary Betts, daughter to ye sd Nathan and Mary,
born Sept. 22, 1728.
and deceased Oct. 5, 1728.
Nathan, born Oct. 13, 1729.
Mary, born Dec. 2, 1731.

Ruth,   born Oct. 6, 1733.
William,   born Apr. 11, 1736.
Judith,   born July 18, 1738.
Azer,   born Sept.13, 1740.

Nathan Read, took to wife Mary Peck yᵉ Daughter of Mr. Samuel Peck, Junr. of Greenwich, Deceased and was married to her Dec. 22, 1737.

Mary Peck yᵉ wife of Nathan Read was Born May 12, 1716.

Mary Read, yᵉ daughter of Nathan Read, was
               born July 17, 1740.
Ann,   born Jan. 18, 1742—3.
Hannah,   born July 16, 1745.
Nathan,   born July 22, 1747.
David,   born Sept. 2, 1750.
Elisabeth,   born June 7, 1753.
Elias,   born Nov. 3, 1756.

Matthew Fitch took to wife Jemime St. John Daughter of Mr. Eber St. John and was married to her ——— ——

Jemimah, Daughter of Sᵈ Matthew and Jemimah Fitch Born Dec. 25, 1735.

Jemimah wife departed this life ——— ——

The said Matthew Fitch, took to wife Lyddia Olmsted the daughter of Nathan Olmstead, Decᵈ and was married to her Dec. 7, 1738.

Nathan Fitch, son of Sᵈ Matthew and Lyddia was
               born Oct. 12, 1739.
Mercy,   born Dec. 29, 1740.
Hannah,   born Aug. 24, 1742.
Matthew,   born June 17, 1744.
Lyddia,   born Apr. 4, 1746.
Rebecca,   born July 9, 1748.
Susanna,   born Aug. 29, 1750.

Abraham Camp was married to Milleson Jarvis, daughr. of Mr. Benajah Jarvis, of Long Island, May 16, 1764.

Sarah,   born June 4, 1765.
Abigail,   born March 8, 1767.
Samuel,   born Aug. 11, 1769.

Joseph Bouton, son of Jakin, married to Susannah Raymond, Aug. 25, 1748.

William,   born Jan. 16, 1749.
Susanna,   born Jan. 27, 1751.
Betty,   born Dec. 29, 1753.
Joseph,   born March 3, 1755.
Rebecca,   born June 3, 1757.
Joshua,   born Oct. 18, 1759.
Seth,   born April 16, 1762.
Ira,   born Feb. 7, 1765.
Nancy,   born June 16, 1767.
Debbe,   born Aug. 27, 1769.
Aaaron,   born April 19, 1772.

Fairchild, Thomas, his Family.

Sarah, daughr. of S^d Thomas, born Nov. 14, 1742.
Jonathan,   born Aug. 29, 1744.
John,   born April 5, 1747.
Mary,   born Jan. 31, 1748—9.

Saml Gregory Jr. son of Saml and Abigail Gregory born Aug. 24, 1749.

John Betts Jr. and Lydia Ketchum married Feb. 17, 1765.

Saml born April 26, 1766.

The S^d Lydia departed this life, the 12th day of June 1766.

The S^d John Betts married to Leah Hickox, Jan. 10, 1773.

Lydia,   b. May   1774.   d. Aug. 1775.
John Goold,   b. Dec. 24, 1775.   d. Dec. 4, 1776.
Sarah,   b. Sept. 9, 1779.
Esther,   b. Jan. 15, 1781.   d. Jan. 2, 1785.
Charles,   b. Nov, 8, 1783.
Esther,   b. Dec. 8, 1785.
John Goold,   b. Dec. 24, 1787.
George,   b. May 7, 1787.

Joseph Lockwood married to Rachel Mallery March 2, 1758.

Josiah, born Dec. 23, 1758.

Seth Mervine took to wife Phebe Lees, the daughter of William Lees.

Seth,   born Dec. 21, 1749.
Ellen,   born Mar. 20, 1752.
Moses,   born Aug. 25, 1754.
Elihu,   born June 8, 1756.

Charles Pope took to wife Judith Smith the daughter of Mr. Robert Smith of Norwalk Dec. 3, 1749.

Sarah,   born May 21, 1751.
Joanna,   born April 24, 1754.

Eliakim Raymond took to wife Hannah Street, the daughter of Mr. Nathl Street Nov. 27, 1740.

Rebeckah,   born Aug. 3, 1741.
Elisabeth,   born Dec. 21, 1743.
Hannah,   born Nov. 2, 1745.
Eliakim,   born Nov. 2, 1747.
Nathaniel,   born Sept. 9, 1749. Died Jan. 9, 1752.
Street,   born June 25, 1751.

Nehemiah St. John took to wife Lois Cornell, daughter of Paul Cornell of N. Haven, Dec. 8, 1743.

Thaddeus,   born Sept. 10, 1744.
Hannah,   born Oct. 7, 1756.
John,   born Jan. 2, 1747-8.
Eben,   born Sept. 16, 1749.
Martha,   born Nov. 14, 1751.
Nehemiah,   born Jan. 16, 1754.
Aaron,   born Nov. 29, 1755.
Elijah,   born Feb. 26, 1758.
Hannah,   born Sept. 4, 1760.
Susannah,   born July 31, 1762.
Seth,   born June 12, 1764.
Cornwall,   born Mar. 2, 1768. Died Aug. 2, 1769.

John Fitch married to ——

Ruth,   born Mar. 29, 1768.
Esek,   born Nov. 26, 1769.

Michael Wairing was married to Elisabeth the daughter of James Scofield of Stamford, by Stephen Buckingham,

Henry,   born Oct. 6, 1744.

Elisabeth Hyat, daughter of Ebenezer and Elisabeth Hyat, born June 6, 1718.

John, son of Ebenezer above, born July 15, 1720.

Sarah,	born June 15, 1722.
Mary,	born Jan. 16, 1724-5.
Ebeneser,	born Feb. 1, 1726.
Thomas,	born May 25, 1729.
Hannah,	born Mar. 7, 1731.
Daniel,	born Jan. 22, 1732-3.
Ann,	born Nov. 1735.
Abigail,	born Oct. 8, 1737.
Deborah,	born Aug. 3, 1739.
Hannah,	died Jan. 28, 1739-40.
Gershom,	born April 27, 1742.
Hannah,	born July 1, 1744. Died Jan.7,1744.

Gershom Raymond married to Abagail Taylor, April 12, 1749.

Paul,	born June 28, 1750.
Katharine,	born July 1, 1752.
Edward,	born Feb. 20, 175-.
Azuba,	born Mar. 25, 1758.
Anna,	born Sept. 2, 1760.
Gershom,	born Nov. 13, 1762.

Daniel Reed, of Norwalk, married to Sally Hawley, of Salem, Oct. 3, 1797.

Nathan Hoyt, married to Elizabeth Lockwood April 9, 1741.

Eunice,	born July 18, 1742.
Asa,	born Aug. 23, 1744.
Sarah,	born Nov. 12, 1746.
Ruth,	born Jan. 17, 1748.
Betty,	born June 16, 1751.
Nathan,	born Aug. 17, 1754.
Mary,	born Oct. 27, 1756.
Hannah,	born April 28, 1759.
Saml,	born Aug. 14, 1761.
Grace,	born Sept. 3, 1763.

Josiah Thacher married to Mary Fitch, Dec. 19, 1751

Mary,	born Sept. 14, 1753.
Hannah,	born May 15, 1760.
Thomas Fitch,	born June 16, 1769.
Esther Ann,	born Jan. 26, 1773.
	Died March 15, 1774.
Esther Ann,	born Apr. 19, 1775.
	Died Sept. 16, 1776.

Mary Thacher, his wife, died Sept. 30, 1776.

The s^d Josiah married to Wait Burwell, Dec. 3, 1785.

Sarah Raymond, daughter of Benj. Raymond and Rebecka his wife, born Sept. 10, 1729.

Rebecka,	born May 24, 1731.
Benjamin,	born Mar. 7, 1733.
Seth,	born Feb. 12, 1738--9.

Mary Dickinson, daughter to the Revd. Mr. Moses Dickinson, and Martha his wife, born Aug. 18, 1721.

Moses,	born Feb. 17, 1722-3.
	died Sept. 16, 1742.
Abigail,	born July 30, 1724.
Hezekiah,	born Aug. 11, 1727.
Samuel,	born Oct. 23, 1728.
John,	born Oct. 6, 1734-5.
Martha,	born Mar. 8, 1734-5.

Isabel Weed, daughter of Nathan Ward of Stamford, born July 23, 1751.

Eliakim Wairing took to wife Ann Reed, the daughter of Mr. John Reed, Dec. 7, 1738.

Zacheus,	born Oct. 19, 1741.
Jesse,	born June 14, 1744.

Ann Hanford, daughter of Elnathan Hanford, born Sept. 22, 1726.

Hannah, daughter of the same, born March 8, 1728--9.

Elnathan,	born Nov. 7, 1731.
Sarah,	born July 29, 1734.
Isaac,	born Oct. 19, 1736.
John,	born Feb. 13, 1739.
James,	born Sept. 10, 1741.
Thomas,	born Dec. 31, 1743.
David,	born May 3, 1746.
Mary,	born April 18, 1748. Died Nov. 27,1750.
Catherine	born July 26, 1750.

Sarah, the wife of s^d Elnathan, departed this life Dec. 17, 1751.

Jeremiah B. Eells married to Lois Benedict, Nov. 28 1754.

John,	born Nov. 16, 1755.
Jeremiah,	born Nov. 22, 1757.

Anna,	born Nov. 12, 1759.
Lois,	born July 12, 1761.
Martha,	born April 14, 1763.
Sarah,	born Jan. 18, 1765.
Dinah,	born Feb. 7, 1767.
Samuel,	born Oct. 3, 1768.
Samuel 2d,	born Apr. 13, 1770.
Nathaniel,	born Jan. 10, 1772.
Beard,	born Nov. 7, 1773.
James T.,	born Nov. 6, 1775.
Betsey,	born May 13, 1780.

Thaddeus Betts married to Mary Goold, Nov. 8, 1752. The said Mary died the 20th day of the same month.

The said Thaddeus married to Elizabeth Maltby, May 15, 1754.

Sarah,	born Mar. 7, 1757.
William Maltby, born Jan. 4, 1759. Died in 1832.	
Mary,	born July 14, 1761.*

Samuel Fairchild married to Sarah Jones Nov. 15, 1654. Said Sarah died May 23, 1655.

The said Samuel married to Hannah Tuttle, Jan. 6, 1757.

Sarah,	born Nov. 9, 1757.
Gilbert,	born Oct. 2, 1759.
Hannah,	born May 1, 1763.
Betty,	born June 19, 1765..

Jabez Saunders married to Abigail Platt, Aug. 1, 1753.

Saml,	born Feb. 22, 1754.
Platt,	born Dec. 14, 1756.
Thomas,	born Dec. 28, 1758.
Aaron,	born Dec. 23, 1790.
Polly,	born Mar. 30, 1762.
Esther,	born June 14, 1764.
Saml,	born May 16, 1767.

* Eleanor Fairchild was the daughter of Jonathan and Eleanor Fairchild. Her first husband was Seth Benedict, son of Thomas and Millisson Benedict, with whom she lived 10 years. After his death, about the year 1768 she had married to Daniel Lyman, Esq., of New Haven. After his death she married Thaddeus Betts, of Norwalk. She died March 23d, 1825, in the 95th year of her age. She was a member of the church 61 years.

Susannah,	born July, 28, 1769.
Sarah,	born Mar. 2, 1783.
Betsey,	born Apr. 17, 1775.

John Nash married to Sarah Jackson, 1736.

Anna,	born Mar. 6, 1737.
Jedediah,	born Dec. 31, 1739.
John,	born Jan. 6, 1741.
Sarah,	born Oct. 5, 1745.
Rhuamah,	born Sept. 8, 1647.
Phila,	born Sept. 28, 1749.
Esther,	born Feb. 10, 1751.
Hannah,	born Feb. 18, 1753.
Moses,	born Feb. 19, 1754.

Abraham Whitney married to Ann Plumb, Dec. 23, 1750.

Saml,	born Sept. 28, 1752.
Stephen,	born Jan. 20, 1756.
Archibald,	born Jan. 23, 1756.
Ann,	born Jan. 27, 1758.
Susa,	born Jan. 2, 1760.
Abraham,	born April 2, 1762.
John,	born May 17, 1764.
Sally,	born July 27, 1766.
Polly,	born Jan. 2, 1769.
Mercy,	born April 4, 1771.

Timothy Keeler married to Hannah Hecox, April 15, 1750.

Uriah,	born Mar. 19, 1760.
Hannah,	born Feb. 24, 1762.
Sarah,	born Sept. 17, 1765.
Benjamin,	born Aug. 1, 1771.
Stephen,	born June 27, 1776.

John Cannon   married to Esther Perry, Dec. 1, 1750.

John,	born July 7, 1752.
Saml,	born July 28, 1754.
James,	born June 19, 1757.
Sarah,	born Mar. 21, 1759.
Le Grand,	born Oct. 26, 1722.
Lewes,	born Nov. 3, 1766.
Willm Aspewall,	born Feb. 23, 1767.
Esther Mary,	born Feb. 17, 1772.

Matthew Betts, married to Mary St. John, April 12, 1750.

| Ruth, | born Oct. 12, 1750. |

Leah Taylor, daughter of Noah and Elizabeth Taylor, born Aug. 26, 1649.

Carter Hickox married to said Leah Jan. 10, 1773.

Abijah and Debeorah Comstock married May 30, 1745 *

Thos.,	born Jan. 26, 1747.
David,	born Sept. 19, 1748.
Enoch,	born July 24, 1750.
Hannah,	born Aug. 6, 1755.
Deborah,	born May 20, 1756.
Ruth,	born May 28, 1758.
Samuel,	born July 15, 1767.

Job Bartram m. to Jerusher Thompson, Nov. 18, 1726. The sd. Jerusher died Nov. 23, 1773.

The sd. Job Bartram m. to Abigail Starr Nov. 7, 1774. The sd. Abigail died Jan. 14, 1776.

The sd. Job Bartram m. to Elizabeth Scudder Aug. 27 1776.

Daniel Starr B.,	born Jan. 2, 1776.
Isaac,	born Mar. 27, 1777—died Mar. 28, 1777.
John,	born Dec. 27, 1778—died Feb. 12, 1779.
Isaac Scudder,	born July 2, 1780—died Feb. 12, 1783.
Guladia,	born Dec. 22, 1782.
Betsey,	born July 10, 1785.

Saml. Hanford and his wife Elizabeth m. March 5, 1761.

Sam'l.,	born April 25, 1765.
Eliphalet,	born June 27, 1769—died Oct. 26, 1796.
Sarah,	born July 2d, 1771.
Stephen,	born Dec. 28, 1773
Elisha,	born Aug. 10, 1778.
Holly,	born Aug. 29, 1782.
Elizabeth,	born May 8, 1786.

George Raymond m. to Anna Hoyt, Nov. 15, 1785.

Alfred,	born July 23, 1786.
Nancey,	born March 13, 1789.
Esther Mary,	born April 21, 1791.
Harriett,	born Sept. 30, 1792.
George Alfred,	born May 31, 1794.
Hannah,	born Sept. 17, 1796.

Jonathan Camp, born May 17, 1735. ⎱ married 1759.
Mary Burwell, born April 17, 1734. ⎰

The following are their children, viz:—

Ann Camp,˙ bo.n Oct. 18, 1761—died Dec. 18, 1761.
Esther,   born Feb. 24, 1763—Mrs. S. Fitch.
Mary,   born Dec. 17, 1764—Mrs. St. John.
Hannah,   born Apr. 24, 1766—Stephen Bouton.
Jonathan,   born Feb. 20, 1768.
Stephen,   born Sept. 22, 1769.
Ann,   born Oct.   7, 1771—Samuel Beardsley,
William,   born May   5, 1773—died Aug. 1775.
Rebecca,   born Dec. 28, 1774—Daniel Nash.

John Hickok, born April 28, 1734. ⎱ married ——
Lydia Kellogg, born April 5, 1740. ⎰

The following are their children:—

Huldah Hickok, born Nov. 1, 1757—wife of Eph.
                           Waring and Rev. Amzi Lewis.
John,   born Sept. 24, 1759—died Sept. 1776.
Lydia,   born Jan. 2, 1762—Jesse Richards.
Seth,   born Jan. 6, 1764—died Mar. 5, 1773.
Eliaseph,   born Jan. 31, 1766—died June 11, 1767.
Jesse,   born Nov. 4, 1769.
Rachel B.,   born July 31, 1771—Stephen Camp.
Seth,   born Sept. 22, 1773.
Eliaseph,   born May 29, 1776—died Oct. 7, 1777.
Peninah,   born Feb. 15, 1778—Ezra Hoyt.
Millisent,   born Sept. 14, 1780—Jona. B. Benedict.

Jonathan Camp, Jr., married to Hannah Bouton May 19, 1792.

Sarah,   bo May 4, 1794.
Mary,   bo.n July 31, 1797.
Willia..i,   born June 27, 1799.
Jonathan,   born Sept. 15, 1801.
Stephen W., born Feb. 8, 1807.
Mary E.   born April 14, 1808.

Stephen Camp,   ⎱ married Sept. 27, 1792.
Rachel B. Hickok,   ⎰

Nathan,   born May 22, 1795.
Harvey,   born Oct.   6, 1798.
Amzi,   born Jan, 21, 1801.
Celina,   born Mar. 19, 1803—John Partrick.
Elizabeth,   born Oct. 28, 1805—Henry W. Smith.

11

Ebenezer Church married to Susannah Fitch, Jan. 1746.

| Daniel, | born Mar. | 1, 1746. |
| Richard, | born Oct. | 1747. |

Said Susannah died Oct. 7, 1747.

Said Ebenezer married to Ruth ——— Nov. 1755.

Sarah,	born Oct.	15, 1756.
Ebenezer,	born July	31, 1758.
Ruth,	born Jan.	29, 1760.
Esther,	born Mar.	23, 1762.
Saml.	born Nov.	25, 1763.
Grace,	born Aug.	7, 1765.
—Josiah,	born Jan.	10, 1767.
John,	born Jan.	12, 1769.
Elizabeth,	born Oct.	10, 1770.
Isaac,	born May	3, 1772.

* Eliakim Raymond married to Hannah Street, daughter of Nathaniel Street, Nov. 27, 1740.

Rebeckah,	born Aug.	3, 1741.
Elizabeth,	born Dec.	20, 1743.
Hannah,	born Nov.	21, 1745.
Eliakim,	born Nov.	2, 1747.
Nathaniel,	born Sept.	9, 1749.—d. Jan. 2, 1751.
Street,	born June	25, 1751.—d. Nov. 26,1776.
Nathaniel,	born May	4, 1753.
Mary,	born May	13, 1755.
Esther,	born Feb.	13, 1757.
George,	born Jan.	1, 1759.
Henry,	born Oct.	26, 1764.
Naphtali,	born Mar.	26, 1776.

Hannah, wife of said Eliakim, died March 19, 1795.

James Fitch, son of James, m. to Ann Hanford,Oct. 1746.

Sarah,	born Dec.	24, 1751.
Susannah,	born Dec.	26, 1756.
James, Nancy,	} born Apr.	11, 1758.
Rulette,	born Aug.	4, 1762.

Ann, wife of said James, died Dec. 1768.

Sam'l Merwine married to Deborah Clark, Nov. 25, 1735.

Esther,	born Aug.	22, 1736.
Rebeckah,	born May,	19, 173-.
Samuel,	born Feb.	7, 173-.
Betty,	born Jan.	12, 1743.

* See record on page 223, which is imperfect.

Joseph Warring married to Elizabeth Byxbee, Nov. 12, 1754.

Joseph,	born June 15, 1755.
James,	born Aug. 2, 1757.
Jesse,	born May 12, 1759.

Peter White married to Elizabeth Jarvis, —— 1739.

Samuel,	born July 13, 1740.
Sarah,	born —— 1742.
Deborah,	born July 1, 1744.
Betty,	born Feb. 1750.
James,	born Nov. 5, 1752.
John,	born Feb. 1755.

Caleb St. John married to Mercy Seely, March 10, 1757.

Mary,	born Jan. 17, 1761.
Caleb,	born Nov. 11, 1764.
Sarah,	born Nov. 18, 1767.
Eliphalet,	born Apr. 22, 1770.
Elizabeth,	born Dec. 6, 1774.

William Bolt and Lydia Fitch married Dec. 8, 1748.

Lydia,	born Mar. 23, 1750.
Elizabeth,	born May 25, 1752.
William,	born Mar. 24, 1755.
John,	born Jan. 18, 1758.
Charles,	born Nov. 26, 1761.

Stephen Betts, married to Mary Burwell, April 14, 1747.

Betty,	born Mar. 5, 1757.
Susa,	born Feb. 23, 1761.
Burral,	born Jan. 30, 1763.
Lewis,	born June 16, 1766.
Samuel,	born Apr. 14, 1768.
Philo,	born Nov. 29, 1769.
Molly,	born Aug. 8, 1770.
Hiram,	born July 21, 1777.

John Hickox, married to Lydia Kellogg, March 29, 1757.

Huldah,	born Nov. 1, 1757.
John,	born Sept. 24, 1759.
Lydia,	born Jan. 2, 1762.
Seth,	born Jan. 6, 1764.—d. Mar. 6, 1773.
Eliaseph,	born Jan. 31, 1767.—d. June 11,1768.
Jesse,	born Nove. 4, 1769.

Rachel,	born July 31, 1771.
Seth,	born Sept. 22, 1773.
Eliaseph,	born May 30, 1777.
Peninah,	born Feb. 15, 1778.
Millison,	born Sept. 4, 1780.

Esaias Bouton married to Phebe Byxbee, May 30, 1753.

Phebe,	born Mar. 5, 1754.
Nathan,	born Sept. 30, 1756.
Lydia,	born Jan. 21, 1759.
Stephen,	born July 4, 1760.
Samuel,	born July 14, 1762.
Hannah,	born May 16, 176–.
Josiah,	born June 26, 1768.

Seth Betts married to Mary Gregory, Dec. 7, 1752.

Silas,	born Oct. 27, 1753.
Molly,	born Mar. 19, 1757.
Esther,	born Feb. 17, 1763.
Seth,	born Dec. 12, 1765.

David Whitney married to Elizabeth Hyatt, May 11, 1741.

Ebenezer,	born Aug. 8, 1742.
Timothy,	born July 13, 1744.
Betty,	born Apr. 5, 1746.
David,	born Feb. 17, 1748.
Ann,	born Feb. 14, 1749.
Esther,	born Feb. 3, 1751.
Abigail,	born April 3, 1754.
Ann,	born April 10, 1756.
Deborah,	born July 20, 1758.
David,	born Aug. 25, 1761.

Revd. Wm. Gaylord, married to Elizabeth Bishop, March 25, 1753.

Aaron,	born Oct. 22, 1754.
Elizabeth,	born Oct. 24, 1756.
Samuel,	born Oct. 28, 1758.
Sarah,	born June 18, 1759.
Deodate,	born July 20, 1760.
Moses,	born May 4, 1762.

Abraham Scribner, son of Abraham and Sarah,
born June 28, 1745.
Sarah, daughter of Abraham and Sarah,
born Oct. 15, 1746.

Rhoda,	born Oct. 18, 1748.
Ann,	born April 7, 1751.
Levi,	born June 28, 1753.
Rachel,	born Aug. 28, 1755.
Moses,	born June 30, 1757.
Jonathan,	born Sept. 5, 1759.
Ezra,	born June 19, 1761.
Esther,	born Aug. 3, 1763.
Silas,	born Sept. 15, 1765.

Samuel Fitch married to Elizabeth Platt, July 2, 1750.

Susanna,	born Dec. 6, 1750.
Joseph,	born Jan. 4, 1753.
Samuel,	born April 21, 1761.
Elizabeth,	born Jan. 14, 1763.
Anna, Sarah,	born Nov. 23, 1766.

Zechariah Whitman, born Dec. 25, 1771.

| Esther, | born Sept. 29, 1773. |

Elijah Fitch married to Phebe Smith, Oct. 25, 1752.

Phebe,	born Sept. 3, 1753.
Hannah,	born Sept. 20, 1755.
Stephen,	born Oct. 25, 1757.
Molly,	born Nov. 14, 1759.
Elizabeth,	born Mar. 25, 1762.
William,	born Aug. 23, 1764.
Lydia,	born July 23, 1766.
Buckingham,	born Aug. 23, 17—.
Lydia,	born May 2, 1771.
Elijah,	born Sept. 3, 1773.

Matthew Scribner married to Martha Smith, Nov. 10, 1742.

Nathaniel,	born Dec. 23, 1743.
Matthew,	born Feb. 7, 1746.
Martha,	born Feb. 20, 1748.
Enoch,	born Aug. 29, 1750.
Elijah,	born June 25, 1753.
Jeremiah,	born Dec. 15, 1755.
Kezia,	born Jan. 20, 1758.
Abigail,	born Nov. 9, 1760.
Elizabeth,	born Dec. 10, 1763.

Micajah Nash married to Mary Scribner, Oct. 9, 1744.

Jesse,	born July 21, 1745.
Daniel,	born Dec. 2, 1747.
Samuel,	born Feb. 5, 1750.

Nathan Jarvis married to Ann Kellogg. Jan. 1757.

Ann,	born Oct. 5, 1758.
Betty,	born Sept. 10, 1761.
Mary,	born June 11, 1765.
Samuel,	born Sept. 16, 1768.
William,	born June 12, 1771.
Nathan,	born June 19, 1773.
Esther,	born Aug. 27, 1775.
Hannah,	born Feb. 25, 1780.

Nathan Gregory married to Sarah St. John, July 3, 1754

Ebenezer,	born Jan. 10, 1755.
Anna,	born Mar. 14, 1758.
Noah,	born Feb. 20, 1760.
Sally,	born Mar. 9, 1763.
Polly,	born Nov. 28, 1772.

John Carter married to Hannah Benedict, Oct. 1753.

Hannah,	born July 9, 1754.
Rachel,	born Nov. 19, 1756.
Deborah,	born Dec. 29, 1757.
Sarah,	born Jan. 1760.
Mercy,	born Oct. 5, 1761.
Elizabeth,	born Oct. 5, 1763.
Ebenezer,	born Aug. 3, 1765.
Samuel,	born Apr. 22, 1768.
Mary,	born Nov. 20, 1771.
John,	born ——— 1774.

[SAMUEL CARTER, settled in Norwalk in 1705. He was born in London, and when about 12 years old, was enticed away by the captain of a vessel coming to this country, and brought to Boston. In 1690 he married Mercy Brook, who died in 1700. Their children were—

Samuel,	born 1692.
Mercy,	born 1694.
Ebenezer,	born 1697.
Thomas,	born 1699.
Mary,	born 1700.

In 1701, he married Hannah Weller.
By his second wife, his children were—

Joseph,   born 1702.
Hannah,   born 1703.

He lived in Deerfield, Mass. When Deerfield was taken and burnt, February 29, 1704, he was absent from the town. His whole family were captured Joseph had died before. Thomas were slain by the Indians on the meadows. The ˙mother, and Mary, and Hannah, were slain on the journey. The four eldest arrived in Canada. The three eldest married there. Ebenezer was stolen away by merchants trading between Albany and Montreal, and restored to his father. The rest died in Canada. Ebenezer married Hannah, daughter of Matthias St. John, of Norwalk. In 1731, he removed to the Parish of Canaan, now New Canaan. His father lived on the place now owned and occupied by Jonathan Camp, Jr. His wife died February, 1774, aged 74, and he died in the following summer, aged 77. Their children were—

Mary, married to Jonathan Husted, Dec. 3, 1744.˙ She had no children.

Hannah married Jonathan Burrall, April 7, 1746.

Her children were—

Theophilus,   born 1784—died 1772.
Samuel, ,   born 1785—died 1821.
Charles,
Jonathan,
Susannah,

Elizabeth, married Levi Hanford,

Her children were Ebenezer, Levi, Elizabeth, and John.

John born February 22, 1730, married Hannah Benedict, daughter of Thomas Benedict. She was the mother of all his children, and died in 1780. The children were—

Hannah,   born 1754—married John Benedict.
Rachel,   born 1756—married Nathan Kellogg.
Deborah,   married Gabriel North.
Sally,   born 1769—married Andrew Powers, and
                        after his decease, Enoch St.
                        John, and died March 14, 1808.
Elizabeth,   born 1763—married Robert North.
Ebenezer,   born 1765—married Susannah Benedict,
                        Sept. 24, 1788; and Rhoda
                        Weed, April 1, 1795.
Samuel,   born 1768—married Sarah Hanford. -died
                        Dec. 1831.
Polly,   born 1771- married Stephen Hoyt May 20,
                        1794

Thomas Gregory married to Mary Betts, May 18, 1747.

Naomi,	born April 13, 1748.
Josiah,	born May 12, 1750.
Mary,	born Oct. 8, 1752.
Jehiel,	born Nov. 17, 1754.
Abigail,	born Dec. 13, 1762.

John Sanders married to Elizabeth Cane, Nov. 23, 1747.

Billy,	born Feb. 16, 1749.
John,	born Apr. 19, 1751.
Phebe,	born Mar. 22, 1756.
Hannah,	born Aug. 27, 1756.
Esther,	born Apr. 18, 1761.
Holmes,	born Aug. 23, 1763.
Susannah,	born Jan. 29, 1766.
Sarah,	born Apr. 18, 1768.

John Lockwood married to Mary Keeler, April 27, 1746.

Mary	born, Dec. 18, 1748.
Lydia,	born May 22, 1751.
Sarah,	born Oct. 5, 175 .
Hannah,	born June 23, 1757.

Benjamin Whitney married to Lois Kellogg, Jan. 3, 1757.

Hannah,	born June 4, 1757.
Martha,	born Mar. 5, 1759.
Saml Kellogg,	born Feb. 2, 1761.
Henry,	born May 26, 1763.
Anna,	born July 29, 1765.
Polly,	born May 1, 1769.
Benjamin,	born Mar. 4, 1771.

Timothy Whitney married to Annah Wood, Feb. 25, 1770,

Lewis,	born Mar. 19, 1771.—d. Feb. 11, 1772.
Suky,	born Mar. 17, 1773.
Esther,	born June 25, 1775.
Timothy,	born Nov. 8, 1777.
Sally,	born Sept. 12, 1782.

The s^d Annah, wife to s^d Timothy, died Aug. 7, 1785.

The s^d Timothy m. to Abigail Wood, Apr. 23, 1786.

Lewis,	born Aug. 29, 1787.
Nancy,	born Dec. 26, 1788.
Elizabeth,	born Jan. 4, 1796.

Ebenezer Phillips, m. to Mary Benedict, Jan. 17, 1782.

Esther,	born Mar. 5, 1787.—d. Feb. 12, 1788.
Esther,	born Apr. 17, 1788.
Sally,	born Dec. 11, 1790.
Elizabeth,	born July 9, 1798.

PHILLIPS' FAMILY RECORD.

[Rev. George Phillips was born in Raymond, in Norfolk, England, and arrived in this country, in company with Gov. Winthrop, 2d July, 1630. Settled in Watertown, Mass., and died July 1st, 1644. His son, Samuel Phillips, born in Boxford, England, died in Rowley, Mass., April 22d, 1696, aged 71. His children were Sarah, Samuel, George,[1] Elizabeth, Dorcas, Mary, and John.

[1] Rev. George Philips, son of Samuel, was born in 1664. Settled in Brook Haven, L. I., in 1697, died in 1739, aged 75. His children were, George, who lived and died in Smithtown, L. I.; John, who lived and died in Boston; and William, who lived in Smithtown, L. I., and died January 1st, 1778. Sybil, his wife, died October 31st, 1767, aged 74. Their children were,

John, born Sept. 3d, 1737; died in Milford, Ct., March 12th, 1780.

William, born May 27th, 1741; died in Brook Haven, L. I., March 27th, 1799.

Zebulon, born April 14th, 1746; died in Peekskill, N.Y., January 13th, 1815.

James, born March 13th, 1751; died in Coventry, N. Y., January 25th, 1841.

Ebenezer, born July 15th, 1753; died in Norwalk, Ct., August 5th, 1829.

Sarah, born October 24th, 1756; died in North Salem, N. Y., February 12th, 1827.

Philetus, born November 24th, 1759; died in Greenville, N. Y., May 17, 1818.

Elizabeth, born November 9th, 1762, died in Brook Haven, L. I., February 4th, 1844.]

Asahel Raymond m. to Mary Veal, Apr. 22, 1784.

Medad,	born Mar. 12, 1786.
Polly,	born Oct. 30, 1788.
Charles,	born Jan. 26, 1791.
Philetus,	born Aug. 22, 1792.
Hiram,	born Apr. 2, 1794.
Almena,	born Apr. 29, 1797.

11*

Melzer Carver married to Phebe Wicks, Jan. 29, 1777.

Amos,	born Dec. 11, 1778.
Charles,	born July 19, 1781.
Hannah,	born Dec. 11, 1783.
Nancy,	born Sept. 17, 1785.
Joseph,	born July 24, 1786.
Ebenezer,	born July 22, 1787.
Stephen,	born Sept. 28, 1791.
William,	born Oct. 22, 1793.
George,	born Dec. 23, 1795.
John,	born Aug. 28, 1797.

Paul Raymond married to Elizabeth Reed, Jan, 11, 1776.

Elizabeth,	born April 18, 1777.
Elias,	born June 16, 1779.
John,	born June 15, 1781.
Abigail,	born May 31, 1783.
Nancy,	born Oct. 9, 1787.
John Taylor,	born Dec. 7, 1791.
Mary,	born April 17, 1794.

Joseph Lockwood married to Isabel Hyatt, Oct. 31, 1774.

Joseph,	born Oct. 2, 1778.
William,	born July 23, 1780.
Fanny,	born June 29, 1784.

John Peck married to Esther Raymond, Aug. 6, 1797.

David Bolt, Jr., married to Sarah Taylor, March 17, 1790.

Sarah,	born Nov. 11, 1790.
Fred. Anson,	born Aug. 18, 1793.
Rhua,	born Aug. 22, 1797.

Saml. Keeler married to widow Ann Thatcher, March, 3, 1785.

Joseph,	born Oct. 18, 1786.
Charles,	born Apr. 6, 1789.
Samuel,	born Mar. 17, 1792

Margaret N. Belknap, daughter of Abel and Hannah Belknap, born May 16, 1791.

Edwin Starr,	born Dec. 11, 1794.
Julia Ann,	born Aug. 27, 1799.

Asa Hayt married to Ruth Kellogg, Oct. 26, 1766.

Henry,	born May		1, 1767.
Esther,	born Nov.	9, 1769.
Asa,	born Feb.	28, 1772.
Francis,	born July	19, 1774.
Ruth,	born Feb.	21, 1777.
James,	born Dec.	5, 1779.
Lewis,	born June	24, 1782.
Anna,	born Oct.	26, 1784.
Eli,	born April	30, 1787.

Caleb Comstock married to Lucy Mead, Nov. 10, 1786.

Moses,	born Nov.	3, 1787.
Matthew,	born May	21, 1789.
Molly,	born May	29, 1791.
Caleb,	born Jan.	5, 1793.
Joshua,	born Sept.	6, 1795.
Abigail,	born Oct.	30, 1797.
Betty,	born Sept.	13, 1799.
Xenophon,	born Sept.	28, 1801.
Anna,	born Jan.	5, 1804.
Eli,	born Nov.	27, 1805.

Thomas Hayt, Jr., married to Elizabeth Phillips, Jan. 5, 1793.

Matthew Reed, died December 4, 1797.

Charles Robert Sherman, son of Tayler and Eliz.
Sherman, born Sept. 26, 1788.

| Daniel, | born Mar. | 28, 1790. |
| Betsey, | born Dec. | 7, 1791. |

Roger Minot Sherman* married to Betsey Gould, Dec. 19, 1796.

William. Gould, } born Oct. 18, 1799.
James Minot, }

Samuel Burrall m. to Deborah Benedict Jan. 1, 1782.

Samuel	born Sept. 11, 1783—died June 26, 1793.
John,	born Dec. 7, 1785.
Charles,	born Oct. 1, 1791.

* The late Judge Sherman, of Fairfield. He began his pro‑
fessional career in Norwalk.

William Benedict m. to Nancy Fitch, Feb. 20, 1782.

Anna,	born July 31, 1783. m. N.Lockwood.	
Charlotte,	born Sept. 29, 1795. m. Jer. Camp.	
Charles,	born Sept. 29, 1785.	
Suky,	born Jan. 30, 1788. m. James I. Hoyt.	
Sally,	born Nov. 17, 1790. m. Daniel Smith.	
Esther,	born May 10, 1793. m. Edw. Smith.	
Mary,	born Apr. 4, 1796. m. Geo. Brown.	
Fanny Roe,	born Dec. 30, 1798. m. S.W.Benedict.	
.Deborah,	born Dec, 30, 1798. m. Geo. Scribner.	

Nathaniel Raymond married to Rebeckah Benedict, Feb. 17, 1762.

Sarah,	born Mar.	10, 1763.
Susannah,	born May	13, 1765.
Anah,	born Nov.	8, 1767.
Hannah,	born June	6, 1770.
Rebeckah,	born Aug.	11, 1773.
Nehemiah,	born Jan.	5, 1776.
Nathaniel,	born March 9, 1778.	

The said Rebeckah, wife to said Nathaniel, died Feb. 19, 1781. The said Nathaniel married to Widow Seymore, Aug. 17, 1781.

Aaron Gregory m. to Betty Keeler, June 25, 1772.

Esther,	born July	4, 1773.
Ebenezer,	born Mar.	7, 1775.

The said Betty, wife to sᵈ Aaron, died 1778.

The said Aaron Gregory m. Bridget Belden, Feb. 15, 1780.

Betty,	born Apr.	21, 1784.

Isaac Scudder Isaacs married to Susannah St. John, June 6, 1777.

Benjamin,	born July	17, 1778.
William,	born Nov.	5, 1788.
Charles,	born June	7, 1795.
John,	born Sept.	21, 1799.

Alethea, daughter of Peter and Mercy James, born Feb. 15, 1765.

Peter,	born Jan.	12, 1767.
Sarah,	born Dec.	7, 1768.
Jemmey,	born Mar.	23, 1771.
Daniel,	born Sept.	10, 1773.
William,	born Feb.	17, 1777.
Edward,	born Mar.	9, 1779.

Children of Theophilus Fitch, the son of John Fitch.

Comfort,	born Jan.	30, 1737.
Ruth,	born April	1, 1739.
John,	born Aug.	24, 1740.
Sarah,	born Sept.	10, 1742.
Mary,	born July	11, 1744.
Samuel,	born Jan.	26, 1746–7.
Sarah,	born Jan.	9, 1748–9.
Theophilus,	born Sept.	1, 1751.
Ann,	born July	29, 1756.
Joseph,	born Oct.	21, 1758.

Theophilus Fitch married Anna Gregory, Feb. 7, 1781.

Samuel,	born Dec.	17, 1781.
Betsey,	born July	2, 1784.
Nathan,	born April	14, 1787.

Job. Hayt married to Anah Raymond, Aug. 4, 1785.

Lemuel,	born Mar.	23, 1786.
Nathan,	born Mar.	2, 1788.
Lucretia,	born April	24, 1790.
Geo. Anson,	born Oct.	19, 1793.
Esther,	born Aug,	21, 1796.
Nelson,	born Jan.	6, 1797.

Joseph Waring, jr., married to Anna Bates, Oct. 17, 1776.

Samuel Bates,	born April	28, 1777.
Betty,	born July	3, 1778.
Jane,	born Sept.	2, 1779.

Avery Brown married to Betty Waring, Sept. 6, 1795.

| Avery, | born Feb. 2, 1797. |

John Stuart, married to Sarah Hurlburt, Dec. 1, 1779.

Lois,	born Sept. 13, 1780.
Gilbert,	born Aug. 19, 1783.
William, } Henry, }	born July 24, 1785.
William, 2d.	born May 23, 1789.
Sarah,	born Feb. 28, 1791.

Edmond Tuttle married Salome Phillips, Nov. 18, 1788.

Edmond,	born April	12, 1789.
Polly,	born April	12, 1791.
Arete,	born Oct.	19, 1793.
Lewis,	born July	31, 1796.

Holmes Sanders married to —————— Dec. 25, 1788.

Charles,	born Nov.	29, 1789.
William,	born July	24, 1791.
Geo. Ogilvie,	born July	26, 1793.
Sally,	born June	8, 179–.
Harvey,	born Jan.	9, 1798.

Gershom Richards married to Elizabeth Richards, March 14, 1773.

Elizabeth,	born Aug.	21, 1773.
Hannah,	born Sept.	14, 1774.
Saml. Fitch,	born Oct.	1, 1777.
Rufus,	born April	25, 1781.
Polly,	born July	9, 1788.

Barnabas Mervine married to Hannah Richards, April 27, 1797.

*George,	born Feb.	23, 1798.
Charles R.	born Sept.	30, 1811.
Mary,	born Nov.	19, 1816.

[Matthew Marvin was born October, 1703, and died December 6, 1745. From him descended, by Elizabeth Clark, of Ripton, (now Huntington,) Fairfield, Co.

Hannah,	born Sept. 3, 1732—died Dec.	1806.
Matthew,	born Oct. 21, 1734—died Oct.	1791.
Ozias,	born Jan. 29, 1737—died April	1806.
Barnabas,	born Dec. 25, 1739.	1810.
Silas,	born Feb. 4, 1742.	
Uriah,	born Feb. 17, 1744—died about 1830.	
Ichabod,	born Dec. 15, 1745—died Feb.	1792.]

Ozias Merwine married to Sarah Lockwood, Nov. 26, 1761.

Ozias,	born Feb.	10, 1763.
Hannah,	born Oct.	7, 1764.
Elizabeth,	born Nov.	24, 1766.
Sarah,	born June	21, 1768.
Esther,	born June	12, 1770.
Joseph L.,	born Dec.	11, 1774.
Clark,	born Oct.	13, 1776.
Asa,	born Oct.	13, 1778.
Polly,	born June	9, 1781.
Silas,	born March	1, 1784.
Charles,	born Feb,	21, 1786.

* Graduated at New Haven, 1817.

Darius Olmsted married to Esther Gregory, Sept. 10, 1775.

Aaron,	born Mar.	3, 1776.
David,	born Feb.	2, 1779.
Silas,	born Dec.	5, 1780.
Mary,	born Jan.	12, 1783.
Esther,	born June	19, 1785.
Charles,	born Nov.	6, 1791.

Theodore Husted married to Abigail Seymore, Jan. 24, 1782.

Polly,	born Jan.	15, 1783.
Thomas Seymore,	born Mar.	6, 1784.
Nancy,	born Jan.	12, 1786.
Thos. Seymore, 2d.	born Feb.	6, 1788.
Thaddeus,	born Jan.	29, 1790.
Samuel,	born April	26, 1798.
Morris,	born Feb.	13, 1795.
Morris, 2d.,	born June	2, 1797.

Joseph Hurlbutt married to Sally Lewis, Aug. 9, 1772.

Lewis,	born Oct.	24, 1773
Sally,	born Aug.	26, 1775.
Foster,	born Oct.	12, 1777.
Anna,	born Feb.	17, 1780.
Orasha,	born May	13, 1782.
Anna, 2d.,	born July	23, 1784.
Clara, ⎱ Joel, ⎰	born Feb.	7, 1787.
Lette,	born May	3, 1789.
Walter,	born May	17, 1791.
Polly,	born May	1, 1793.
Sukey,	born Mar.	24, 1795.
Dudley,	born May	16, 1797.

Thomas Fitch Thatcher married to Susannah Lockwood, March 28, 1790.

Ephraim Curtis married Abigail Cromwell, Oct. 27, 1796. John Bailey, born Oct. 13, 1797.

Daniel Hanford married to Susannah Platt, Jan. 9, 1773.

Edward.	born March 3, 1774.
Andrew,	born Aug. 18, 1775—d. Oct. 16, 1776.
Joseph Platt,	born Aug. 23, 1777—d. Sept 18, 1778.
Andrew,	born Dec. 9, 1779.
Joseph Platt,	born April 17, 1782.
Debby,	born April 19, 1784.

William Bouton married to Sarah Benedict, Feb. 15, 1769.

Isaac,	born Sept.	19, 1769.—d. July 24, 1779.
Isaac, 2d.,	born Nov.	20, 1771.
William,	born Mar.	14, 1774.
Betty,	born Aug.	12, 1776.
Esther,	born May	20, 1779.
Sarah,	born June	7, 1781.
Clara,	born July	6, 1783.
Seth,	born Sept.	8, 1785.
Joseph,	born Oct.	22, 1787.
Susanna,	born Dec.	12, 1789.
John,	born Feb.	18, 1792.
Mary,	born Nov.	28, 1793.
Anna,	born June	21, 1796.
*Nathaniel,	born June	22, 1799.

Abijah Betts married to Mary Betts, Jan. 3, 1771.

Lydia,	born Dec.	17, 1771.
Mary,	born Sept.	10, 1776.
Sarah,	born May	28, 1781.

John Grumman married to Sarah Nash, Jan. 15, 1767.

| John, | born Oct. | 22, 1772. |
| Sarah, | born Feb. | 19, 1777. |

Lewis Mallory (born Oct. 1, 1768), married to Anna Seymour (born Jan. 12, 1772), Feb. 20, 1793.

Charles,	born Dec.	2, 1793—died.
Alfred,	born Nov.	8, 1796.
James,	born July	10, 1799.
Charles,	born Nov.	2, 1801.
Mary Esther,	born June	26, 1804—married to A. E. Beard.
Harriet,	born Oct.	6, 1810—married to Rev. Geo. H. Hulin—died April 1, 1836.

Nathaniel Fitch married to Anna Smith, Nov. 11, 1790.

Polly,	born Dec.	27, 1792.
Anna,	born Jan.	15, 1795.
Nathaniel,	born June	1, 1797.

* Rev. Nathaniel Bouton, of Concord, N. H., graduated at Yale, 1821.

Daniel Richards married to Abigail Waring, Dec. 31, 1761.

Daniel,	born Oct.	7, 1762.
Stephen,	born Jan.	29, 1765.
Paul,	born Mar.	26, 1767.
William,	born Dec.	10, 1769.
Anna,	born July	10, 1772.
Sarah,	born Mar.	21, 1774.
Anna,	born Aug.	20, 1776.
William,	born June	26, 1779.
Abigail,	born Mar.	6, 1782.

Abijah St. John married to Hannah Hendrick, Oct. 2, 1793.

| Polly, | born Dec. | 11, 1794. |
| Hiram, | born Mar. | 25, 1797. |

Peter St. John, Jr., married to Rachel Jones, July 8, 1793.

Chauncey,	born April	12, 1794.
Smith,	born Oct.	8, 1795.
Cyrus,	born Sept.	30, 1799.

Cook St. John married to Polly Seymour, Dec. 22, 1796.

Thaddeus,	born Nov.	25, 1797.
Betty,	born Mar.	31, 1800.
William,	born June	4, 1802.

Betsey Mills, daughter of Joseph and Amelia Mills, born Nov. 3, 1794.

Stephen St. John, the 4th, (born Oct. 9, 1792), married to Sarah Betts, (born Dec. 22, 1777)—Jan. 4, 1797.

Caroline,	born June	8, 1800.
Edward Betts,	born Dec.	4, 1801.
Alanson Platt,	born Aug.	20, 1803.
Jesup Raymond,	born Sept.	7, 1805.
Sally Ann,	born Oct.	31, 1807.
Moses Betts,	born Dec.	19, 1809.
Cha's Grandison,	born Dec.	2, 1811.
Harriet Henrietta,	born Sept.	28, 1813.
Hiram,	born Dec.	22, 1814.
Catherine,	born July	1, 1816.
Harriet Emeline,	born Sept.	20, 1818.

Phinehas St. John married to Esther Whitney, Oct. 27, 1773.

Esther,	born Nov.	2, 1774.
Betty,	born Dec.	23, 1776.
Phinehas,	born Nov.	30, 1778.
Nathan,	born May	5, 1781.
Esther,	born Sept.	21, 1783.

Job Lockwood married to Sarah Hickox, June 12, 1791.

Abigail,	born Oct.	13, 1791.
Hannah,	born July	1, 1793.
Polly,	born Sept.	28, 1795.

Lemuel Deforest married to Phebe Keeler, Dec. 26, 1751.

The said Phebe died Jan. 10, 1790.

David Comstock married to Sarah Leeds, Dec. 29, 1774.

Elisha,	born April	23, 1776.
Abijah,	born Feb.	1, 1778.
Sarah,	born Aug.	31, 1780.
David,	born July	31, 1784.
Elizabeth,	born Oct.	28, 1797.

Sarah, wife of said David, died May 8, 1790.

The said David Comstock married to Deborah Weed, Feb. 5, 1795.

John,	born May	23, 1797.
Samuel,	born Nov.	26, 1798.
Mary,	born Sept.	10, 1800.

Elias Gregory married to Elizabeth Gregory, Dec. 29, 1776.

Sarah,	born March	5, 1777.
Matthew Fitch,	born Aug.	2, 1778.
James,	born June	24, 1788.

Isaiah Gregory married to Sarah Comstock, Feb, 18, 1767.

Mabel,	born April	18, 1773.
Jerrol,	born March	3, 1776.
Grace, Matthew, }	born April	20, 1779.
Sherman,	born Aug.	20, 1782.
Zillah,	born Mar.	30, 1786.
Anna,	born Feb.	10, 1789.

Samuel C. Silliman, Esq., married to Dinah Comstock.

The said Samuel died Feb. 14, 1798.

Rebeckah Dikeman, daughter of Levi Dikeman, born Sept. 9, 1782.

Levi,	born Oct. 6, 1784.
Esther,	born July 18, 1789.
Polly,	born Feb. 10, 1792.
Aaron,	born Jan. 3, 1796.

Alick Knapp, daughter of Nathan and Sarah Knapp, born May 3, 1792.

Sarah,	born Nov. 6, 1794.
Mary,	born July 3, 1800.
Anna,	born Oct. 15, 1802.

Ebenezer Hayt married to Mary St. John, Nov. 25, 1771.

Stephen,	born Sept. 17, 1786.
Ebenezer,	born Oct. 18, 1788.
Ansel,	born Feb. 28, 1791.
Elsey,	born July 19, 1794.
Lewis S.,	born Aug. 21, 1798.

James Fitch, Jr., married to Esther Camp, Oct. 9, 1783.

Esther,	born July 18, 1784.
Burwell,	born June 5, 1789.
Stephen,	born May 7, 1793.
John H.	born Oct. 6, 1795.

Hanford Fairweather married to Mary Whitney, March 26, 1775.

Anna,	born Aug. 22, 1775.
Jedidiah,	born Feb. 1, 1779.
James,	born Mar. 29, 1781.
Thos. Cort,	born May, 17, 1783.
Thomas,	born Feb. 10, 1786.
Maria,	born Sept. 10, 1788.
Betsey,	born Sept. 27, 1792.

The said Hanford Fairweather died Aug. 27, 1795.

William Hill married to Esther Wasson, April 30, 1779.

Rebeckah, born April 3, 1780.

Jesse St. John married to Anna Weed, Sept. 28, 1790.

Nathan,	born March 8, 1793.
Thomas,	born March 2, 1795.
Albert,	born Aug. 20, 1797.

Aaron Keeler and Mercy James married May 20, 1781.

Nathan,	born May	20, 1782.
John,	born June	29, 1784.
James,	born April	30, 1787.
Mariah,	born Mar.	23, 1792.
Seth,	born May	17, 1795.

Ann Burnet, daughter of Rev. Matthias Burnet, Pastor of the First Church in Norwalk, and of Ann his wife, born in Norwalk, April 11, 1786.

James, son of said Matthias and Ann, born on Long Island, Jan. 6, 1779.

Mrs. Ann Burnet died July 7, 1789.

The said Matthias Burnet, married to his 2d. wife, Miss Fanny Roe, daughter of Rev. Azel Roe, in Wood-bridge, New Jersey, June 30, 1793.

| John, | born Dec. | 10, 1781. |

David Lambert, Jr., married to Susannah Rogers, Dec. 17, 1769.

Elizabeth,	born Feb.	3, 1771.
David R.,	born Dec.	8, 1772.
Lurany,	born Jan.	22, 1778.
Henry Bill,	born March 8, 1777.
Esther,	born April	14, 1780.
Sarah S,	born June	26, 1782.
Samuel F.,	born Dec.	25, 1784.
John James,	born June	18, 1787.
Julia Maria,	born April	5, 1792.

Olney Stone married to Betty Reed, March 8, 1785.

John,	born Aug.	22, 1785.
Phebe,	born Sept.	25, 1791.
Isaac,	born June	28, 1794.

Hugh Knox, son of the Rev. Dr. Hugh Knox, born on the Island of St. Croix, Dec. 19, 1781.

Goold Hayt married to Elizabeth Dimon, June 13, 1765.

Thomas,	born Feb.	26, 1767.
Goold,	born Nov.	16, 1769.
Esther,	born Oct.	14, 1773.
Ebenezer D,	born Aug.	¦3, 1776.
Munson,	born Mar.	17, 1781.

Jedediah Brown married to Mary Lockwood, Nov. 13, 768.

Sukey,	born July	4, 1769.
Samuel,	born June	26, 1771.
Sally,	born Jan,¹	15, 1774.
Violette,	born March	2, 1776.
Jedediah,	born July	31, 1778.
Polly,	born April	1, 1781.
Katharine,	born June	5, 1783—d. Feb. 19, 1785.
Katharine, 2d.,	born Feb.	15, 1787.
Nancy,	born May	22, 1789.
Samuel,	born Dec.	1, 1791.

John Kellogg married to Sarah Smith, May 29, 1764.

Jeremiah,	born April	30, 1765.
Josiah,	born June	6, 1769.

Sarah, wife to said John, died Sept. 8, 1773,
The said John Kellogg was married to Sarah Bishop, ιpril 16, 1774.

Sarah,	born May	27, 1775.
Rhoda,	born Dec.	6, 1777.

Eliakim Waring married Phebe Bouton, Jan. 17, 1771.

Elias,	born Oct.	16, 1771.
Hannah,	born Aug.	30, 1775.
Nathan,	born May	1, 1777.
Stephen,	born March	9, 1783.
Hannah,	born July	19, 1793.

Nathaniel Selleck married to Azubah Raymond, March 6, 1778.

Raymond,	born July	11, 1779.
Ann,	born Aug.	14, 1783.
Polly,	born May	10, 1787.
Charlotte,	born Feb.	28, 1789.
Lewis,	born April	13, 1798.

John Platt married to Charrity Morehouse, Sept. 3, 1758.

Sarah,	born Sept.	4, 1759.
Hannah,	born April	30, 1761.
Anna,	born Feb.	12, 176-.
Sukey,	born June	17, 1770.
Esther,	born Nov.	12, 1772.
Jonathan,	born April	14, 1775.

John Hayt married to Ruth Gregory, June 5, 1783.

Aaron,	born Sept.	2, 1784.
Esther,	born May	10, 1787.
Betsey,	born Feb.	8, 1789.
Sally,	born April	25, 1791.
Sukey,	born Feb.	7, 1795.
Nathaniel,	born May	1, 1797.
Ruth,	born June	16, 1799.

Eliakim Smith married to Katherine Hanford, March, 1759.

Enoch,	born Dec,	29, 1759.
Katherine,	born Mar.	12, 1762.
Eliakim,	born Feb.	19, 1765.
Josiah,	born May	1, 1775.

Katherine, wife of Eliakim Smith, died: the said Eliakim married to Lydia Middlebrooks, May 5, 1777.

Nathan,	born Feb.	18, 1778.
Samuel,	born May	1, 1780.
Lewis,	born Oct.	30, 1784.
Francis,	born Apr.	25, 1792.

Isaac Betts married to Polly Hanford, Nov. 23, 1783.

Eliakim Smith, Jr., married to Hannah Middlebrooks, Jan. 14, 1790.

Hannah,	born Nov.	13, 1790.
Lucretia,	born April	8, 1793.
Clarissa,	born March	6, 1795.
Fanny,	born Oct,	12, 1797.

Theophilus B. Hanford married to Polly Whillock, Sept. 27, 1796.

Edwin Van Antwerp, son of Nicholas and Ann Van Antwerp, born Nov. 6, 1800.

Moses Byxbee married to Elizabeth Hayt, Jan. 26, 1764.

| Phebe, | born Aug. | 26, 1774. |

Walter Hayt married to Grace Hayt, Aug. 16, 1786.

Walter,	born June	10, 1787.
Ezra,	born July	17, 1789.
Cornelia,	born Nov.	5, 1791.
Nancy,	born July	25, 1794.
Grace,	born June	25, 1797.

Jonathan Hayt married to Sarah Middlebrook, April 14, 1793.

Elnathan, born Sept. 5, 1794.
Squire Middlebrook, born Dec. 11, 1796.

Seth Keeler married to Hannah Rogers, Nov. 7, 1773.

Samuel Platt married to Ann Raymond, March 2, 1757.

Justus, born Dec. 4, 1757—d. Aug. 22, 1764.
Jabez, born Nov. 22, 1761.
Esther, born Aug. 11, 1763.
Joseph, born June 25, 1765.
Justus, born Sept. 10, 1768.
Hannah, born May 24, 1771.
Betty, born Nov. 27, 1773.
John, born Dec. 17, 1777.
Ann, born Feb. 6, 1781.

The said Ann Platt, wife to said Samuel, died Feb. 20, 1781.

John Chapman, married to Susan Fitch, March 26, 789.

Ann, } born Aug. 25, 1792.
Jas. Fitch, }
John, born Sept. 15, 1794.
Clark Marvin, born Oct. 26, 1796.

Adonijah St. John married to Abigail Weed, 13, 1780.

Molly Cook, born Feb. 11, 1782.
Gideon, born Aug. 31, 1783.
Stephen, born Feb. 23, 1785.

Abigail, wife of said Adonijah, died Feb. 26, 1786.

Thomas Saunders jr., married to Mary Finch, Sept. 24, 1799.

Thomas, born March 3, 1776.
Stephen, born Dec. 16, 1778.
Elizabeth, born May 20, 1781.
Polly, born April 9, 1787.
Stephen, born Aug. 30, 1789.

Lewis Raymond married to Jane Warren, July 5, 1796.

Samuel Warren, born March 8, 1797.

Isaac Richards married to Hannah Benedict, Oct. 14, 1779.

Hannah B.,	born July 18, 1780.
Isaac,	born Oct. 25, 1782.
Waters,	born Feb. 8, 1786.

The said Hannah, wife to said Isaac, died Feb. 21, 1786.

The said Isaac Richards, married to Eunice Taylor, Dec· 7, 1786.

Aaron Raymond married to Harriet Wilks, Oct. 27, 1784.

Olive,	born Oct. 19, 1785.
Mary,	born Sept.19, 1787.
Betsey,	born Jan. 13, 1790.
Orange,	born Feb. 7, 1792.
Lucina,	born Aug. 25, 1793.
Hannah,	born Oct. 28, 1795.

Matthew Merwine married to Nancy St. John, April 7, 1792.

Julia,	born Sept. 27, 1795.
Nancy,	born Sept. 11, 1797.

William Downs married to Hannah Bulkeley, Feb. 14, 1769.

Thomas,	born Oct. 4, 1769.
Isaac,	born March 14, 1772.
Sarah,	born Aug. 19, 1773.
Joseph,	born Dec. 13, 1777.
Ellen,	born April 12, 1780.
Rhoda,	born Aug. 12, 1782.
William,	born Jan. 12, 1789.

Hannah, wife of the said William, died Feb. 10, 1789.

The said William Downs married to Elizabeth Waterbury, March 12, 1791.

Haynes Fitch, married to Ann Cook, Sept. 23, 1770.

Hannah Tousey, born	July	4, 1771.
William Haynes, born	Aug.	21, 1772.
Josiah H.	born Sept.	23, 1773.
Jedediah,	born July	17, 1775.
Cook,	born Feb.	5, 1777.
Daniel,	born June	12, 1779.
David,	born March	29, 1781.
Doct.Grant Fitch,born	Dec.	2, 1782.
Zalmon,	born April	1, 1784.

John Benedict, Jr., married Jane Raymond, April 4, 1792.

Alfred,	born Dec.	27, 1793.
*Henry,	born Jan.	22, 1796.
Betsey,	born Aug.	17, 1799—d. March, 1838.
Anson,	born Nov.	21, 1801.
John,	born April	14, 1804.
Jane Ann,	born Dec.	27, 1806.
Samuel R.,	born Aug.	25, 1809.
Harriet,	born Feb.	2, 1812.
Amanda,	born Aug.	30, 1818.

Evert Quintard married Hannah Raymond, Nov. 10, 1790.

Susannah,	born Nov.	18, 1791.
Susan,	born Jan.	2, 1795.
Caroline.		

Asa Smith married Jerusha Knapp, Jan. 16, 1792.

Noah,	born May	17, 1794.
Stephen,	born Mar.	16, 1796.
Asa E.,	born Oct.	1, 1798.
Rufus R.,	born Mar.	12, 1801—d. June 28, 1838.
Henry W.,	born Aug.	4, 1803.
Doctor S.,	born May	22, 1805.
George E.,	born Feb.	20, 1807.
Ward B.,	born Aug.	20, 1809.
Eliza Jane,	born July	8, 1812.

Levi Hanford married Polly Mead, Aug., 1782.

Polly,	born Feb.	5, 1783.
Elizabeth,	born Jan.	26, 1785.
John Mead,	born Jan.	29, 1787.
Ebenezer,	born Nov.	8, 1789.
Levi,	born Feb.	15, 1792.
Anna,	born Aug.	27, 1794.
Betty,	born March	27, 1797.

Ebenezer Hanford 2d, married Lucretia Hanford, April, 2, 1780.

Thaddeus,	born Nov.	21, 1780.
William,	born Oct.	18, 1782.
Henry,	born Dec.	22, 1784.
Lucretia,	born May	20, 1790.
Deborah,	born Nov.	21, 1793.
Mary Hyatt,	born Jan.	12, 1794.

* Rev. Henry Benedict graduated at Yale College in 1822.
12

Currence Hays, daughter of Silas and Rhuama Hays, born Jan. 21, 1798.

John Finch, son of Ichabod and Sarah Finch,

	born June	15, 1786.
Budd,	born June	13, 1789.
Polly,	born July	26, 1793.
Billy,	born May	29, 1796.

Jeremiah Grumman married Sabra Stewart, March 4,1772.

Lewis,	born Nov.	4, 1772.
Jeremiah,	born Oct.	21, 1774.
Uri,	born May	16, 1778.
Joel Keeler,	born July	23, 1780.
Lucretia,	born Aug.	22, 1782.

The said Sabra, wife to said Jeremiah, d. April 14, 1785.

The said Jeremiah married Hannah Fitch, Oct. 27, 1785.

Lucy,	born July	23, 1791.

Stephen Merwine married Lois Disbrow, Feb. 26, 1770.

Hannah,	born May	7, 1778.
Phebe,	born Aug.	29, 1780.
Abigail,	born Feb.	29, 1784.
Betsey,	born Dec.	24, 1785.

The said Lois, wife to said Stephen, died Aug. 8, 1795.

Stephen Merwine married RachelMerwine,Dec.19,1795.

Joseph Jesup married to Susa Betts, Oct. 19, 1780.

Charles,	born Oct.	26, 1781.

Susa, wife of said Joseph, died Jan. 4, 1790.

The said Joseph married to Eunice Hanford, Oct.18,1790.

John,	born April	6, 1794.
Sarah Stebbins,	born Feb.	3, 1797.

Polly Mott, daughter of William and Lettice Mott,

	born Dec.	28, 1777.
William,	born Feb.	28, 1780.
Lettice,	born Feb.	14, 1784.
Clarissa,	born May	1, 1788.

Bethia Knapp, daughter of Epenetus and Mary Kellogg, born Jan. 9, 1777.

Charles,	born March 27,	1779.
Hannah,	born March 21,	1781.

David Morehouse married Sarah Hanford, April 23, 1761.

Samuel,	born March 29, 1762.
Sarah,	born July 26, 1763.
David,	born Nov. 28, 1764.
Anna,	born July 17, 1766.
Esther,	born Feb. 15, 1768.
Rhoda,	born Dec. 23, 1769,
Hanford,	born Nov. 4, 1773.
Noah,	born May 5, 1775.
Lydia,	born Dec. 28, 1776.
Isaac,	born Aug. 1, 1778.
Hannah,	born Oct. 27, 1781.
Aaron,	born May 2, 1783.
Lettee,	born Dec. 14, 1784.
Polly,	born April 26, 1787.

Enoch Betts married Mary Coley, June 27, 1775.

Elias,	born May 10, 1776.
Mary,	born May 19, 1780.
David Coley,	born Feb. 18, 1782.
Enoch,	born June 5, 1785.
Calvin,	born Nov. 28, 1788.
Isaiah,	born March 6, 1791.

Lorinda Sturges, daughter of Ezekiel and Hannah Sturges, born April 29, 1794.

Gilbert Hyatt married to Polly Crofoot, July 10, 1794.

| Hannah, | born July 19, 1795. |
| Anson, | born Aug. 5, 1797. |

Nathan Williams married to Sarah Gregory, April 1761.

Molly,	born April 27, 1761.
Elizabeth,	born April 17, 1763.
Jeremiah,	born Feb. 20, 1766.
Samuel,	born Dec. 3, 1767.
Clark,	born March 18, 1769.
Ruth,	born Jan. 16, 1771.
James,	born July 12, 1773.
Moses,	born Feb. 12, 1778.

Gershom Raymond married Mary Whiting, Jan. 4, 1787.

Polly,	born Sept. 28, 1787.
Whiting,	born Feb. 25, 1789.
Gershom,	born Jan. 29, 1791.
Anson,	born April 11, 1794.
Lewis,	born June 4, 1796.

Daniel Church married to Sarah Pickit, Oct. 16, 1768.

Fitch,   born Mar. 31, 1770.
Susanna,   born Oct. 23, 1771.
Daniel,   born Nov. 28, 1775.
Jas.White,   born Nov. 25, 1777.
Sarah,   born Mar. 23, 1780.
Samuel,   born Aug. 18, 1783.
Hannah,   born May 24, 1785.

Edward Raymond, married to Deborah Whiting, Dec. 9, 1783.

Socrates,   born Aug.   4, 1784.
Sally,   born June 18, 1786.
Lotte,   born Sept. 18, 1790.

Hopkins Byxbee married Anne Raymond, Jan, 19, 1786.

Moses,   born Nov.   9, 1786.
Anne,   born Feb.   8, 1789.
Raymond,   born Nov.   7, 1790.
Henry,   born Oct.   4, 1792.
Ruth,   born Dec. 15, 1794.
William,   born Jan.. 17, 1797.

William St. John married Esther Belden, Jan. 19, 1777.
William,   born Aug. 28, 1777.
Steph. Buckingham born Oct.   3, 1779.
Polly Esther, born Mar. 10, 1783.
Frederick,   born Sept. 13, 1785.
Sally,   born Aug. 12, 1788.
Hooker,   born Jan. 30, 1792.

Samuel Bouton married Eunice Smith, March 1, 1787.

Phebe   born Mar. 14, 1788.
Abbe,   born July 24, 1790.
Hannah,   born Dec.   4, 1792.
Esaias,   born July 18, 1796.

Isaac Bouton married Almira Seymore, Sept. 24, 1794.

Lewis,   born Feb. 26, 1795.
Charles,   born Jan. 30, 1801.
Henry,   born Sept. 19, 1803.
Harriet,   born July 25, 1812.
Julia Ann,   born Mar. 23, 1815.
Esther Mary, born Feb. 26, 1818.

Joseph Byxbee married to Nancy Slawson, Jan. 7, 1787,
John,   born Aug. 10, 1787.
Betty,   born April 15, 1790.

Benjamin P. Reed married Betty Bouton, Jan. 12, 1793.

Wilbur,	born April 20, 1794.	
Stephen,	born Feb. 18, 1796.	
Benjamin,	born	
James M.	born	

Absalom Day married to Betty Smith, Feb. 14, 1792.

Susanna,	born Dec. 1, 1793.	
Absalom George,	born Sept. 16, 1796.	
Noah Smith,	born Sept. 27, 1798.	
Amanda,	born Mar. 29, 1801.	
Eliza,	born Nov. 25, 1803.—d. July 22, 1831.	
Mary,	born Feb. 11, 1806.—d Nov. 1, 1829.	
Jane,	born Oct. 10, 1808.—d. Dec. 3, 1808.	
Charles.	born April 22, 1810.	
Ward Smith,	born May 12, 1812.—d. Aug. 19, 1835.	
Jane, 2d.	born April 6, 1815.—d. Feb. 23, 1835.	
Caroline,	born July 5, 1818.	

Naphtali Raymond married to Rebeckah Stephens, June 11, 1788.

Anna,	born Oct. 20, 1789.	
Amelia,	born Oct. 21, 1790.	
Polly,	born July 31, 1792.	
Clarissa,	born July 14, 1794.	
Lucetta,	born June 7, 1796.	

Samuel Hoyt married to Mary Weed, Oct. 20, 1790.

Huldah,	born April 13, 1792.	
Netus,	born Nov. 20, 1794.	
Henry,	born Dec. 29, 1796.	
Clarinda,	born Feb. 3, 1798.	

Melancton B. Jervis married Polly Smith, Sept. 24, 1797.

Hannah,	born Oct. 9, 1798.	
Sally,	born Feb. 25, 1800.	

Josiah St. John married to Mary Fitch, Dec. 27, 1768

Joseph,	born Sept. 22, 1769.	
Esther,	born Sept. 21, 1772.	
Jesse,	born Nov. 7, 1774.	
Polly,	born Jan. 4, 1777.	
Nancy,	born Feb. 15, 1779.	
Polly,	born July 9, 1782.	
Sally,	born June 4, 1787.	

Polly Nash, daughter of James and Huldah Nash, born Oct. 7, 1805.

John Cannon married to Sarah St. John, in July, 1777.

John,	born May	16, 1778
Sarah,	born Oct.	22, 1780.
George,	born May	7, 1784.
Harriet,	born Oct.	31, 1786.
Antoinette,	born April	20, 1789.
Charles Ogilvie,	born Oct.	13, 1791.
Esther Mary,	born Dec.	7, 1793.
James Le Grand,	born Oct.	12, 1796.

Doctor Jonathan Knight married Ann Fitch, Oct.11, 1781.

*Jonathan,	born Sept.	4, 1789.
James Gale,	born June	3, 1800.
Abigail Ann,	born July	24, 1805.

Hezekiah Raymond married to Lydia Lockwood, Oct. 19, 1769.

John Lockwood,	born July	22, 1770.
Lewis,	born Sept.	8, 1772.
Hezekiah,	born Feb.	13, 1775.
James,	born April	19, 1777.
Waters,	born Sept.	29, 1779.
Lydia,	born Sept.	9, 1781.
Asa,	born Dec.	20, 1783.
Francis,	born Sept.	13, 1786.
Benjamin,	born April	27, 1789.
Sally,	born Sept.	17, 1794,

Jonathan Riggs married to Esther Keeler, Jan. 1, 1792.

Julia,	born Jan.	3, 1793.
James,	born April	13, 1794.
John W.,	born Jan.	29, 1796.
Esther,	born Feb.	4, 1798.

William Keeler married Betty Raymond, Nov. 30, 1796.

Lemuel Brooks married Hannah Raymond, Sept. 19, 1764.

Hannah,	born Feb.	13, 1765.
Lemuel,	born Jan.	22, 1767.
Henry,	born March	5, 1769.
Benjamin,	born Sept.	22, 1772.
Anne,	born Sept.	6, 1775.
Esther,	born June	14, 1778.
George,	born March	18, 1781.
Eli,	born July	23, 1783.
Charles,	born Sept.	14, 1785.
Mary B.,	born May	16, 1790.

* Graduated at Yale, 1808. Prof. Surgery Yale College.

Abraham St. John married to Anna Hoyt, Sept. 23, 1779.

Anner,	born July	8, 1781.
Polly,	born Dec.	9, 1782.
Betsey,	born Jan.	,20, 1790.
Naomi,	born Jan.	28, 1792.

Robert Wasson married to Sarah Kellogg, Nov. 4, 1770.

Robert,	born April	30, 1771.
Samuel,	born Dec.	4, 1772.
Sarah,	born July	13, 1775.
Esther,	born Nov.	5, 1777.
Ann,	born Nov.	27, 1779.
Lucretia,	born Jan.	24, 1782.
Jas. Jackson,	born Oct.	15, 1784.
Hannah,	born Feb.	26, 1787.
Anne,	born Oct.	12, 1789.
Charles, Charlotte,	born May	22, 1792.
John,	born Jan.	4, 1796.

Robert Wasson, jun., married to Rebeckah Raymond, April 30, 1797.

Robert,	born Sept.	1, 1798.

Stephen Betts, 2d, married to Ruth Church, Jan. 4, 1784.

Charles,	born Oct.	29, 1784.
Harriet,	born Dec.	7, 1786.
Esther,	born Aug.	29, 1790.
Lewis,	born Oct.	24, 1796.
Harriet,	born March	14, 1798.

David Bolt married to Sarah Mott.

Elizabeth,	born May	4, 1765.
David,	born Dec.	25, 1766.
Jacob,	born Mar.	26, 1771—d. June 9, 1772.
Jacob,	born Feb.	7, 1773.
John,	born Feb.	9, 1775.
Charles,	born Jan.	3, 1777.
Ebenezer,	born Aug.	¦4, 1780.

Samuel Richards married Mary Webb, March 10, 1791.

Samuel,	born Nov.	14, 1791.
Anson,	born June	2, 1794.

John Reed married to Abby Whitney, July 6, 1775.

John,	born Jan.	8, 1776—died Nov. 1777
John,	born Nov.	1, 1778.
Moses,	born Dec.	14, 1787.
Roswell,	born June	8, 1795.

Jabez Gregory married Mercy St. John, January 20, 1762.

| Lucretia, | born April | 10, 1763. |
| Moses, | born Feb. | 13, 1766. |

Moses Gregory married to Esther Hayt, Feb. 22, 1789.

*Francis H.	born Oct.	9, 1789.
Edmond,	born Dec.	5, 1791--d. May 20, 1792.
Esther Antinetta,	born Oct.	5, 1795.
Augusta,	born	

William Maltby Betts married Lucretia Gregory June 26, 1785.

William,	born June	3, 1787.
†Thaddeus,	born Feb.	4, 1789.
Angelina,	born May	18, 1794.

Ebenezer Lockwood married Mary Godfrey, May 23, 1776.

Benjamin,	born Sept.	18, 1777.
Mary,	born Nov.	12, 1779.
Charles,	born Jan.	24, 1782.
Ebenezer,	born Nov.	3, 1783.
Nathan,	born Sept.	12, 1785.
Asa,	born May	24, 1788.
James,	born April	26, 1791.
Joseph,	born Dec.	22, 1792.
Polly,	born Aug.	18, 1795.
Alfred, ?	born May	6, 1797.

Joshua Bouton married Margaret McLean, Nov. 17, 1784.

Sarah Sears,	born Aug.	25, 1785.
Cornelia,	born Mar.	15, 1787.
George,	born Oct.	23, 1789.
Alexander,	born June	29, 1791.
Harriet,	born Feb.	6, 1793.
Charles,	born May	25, 1795.

John Byxbee, jun., married Rhoda Selleck, Aug. 2, 1782

Andrew,	born May	26, 1783.
James,	born June	13, 1785.
Elizabeth,	born July	26, 1787.
Henry,	born Dec.	27, 1790.
Harvey,	born Feb.	24, 1796.

* Capt. Francis H. Gregory, of the U. S. Navy.

† Graduated at Yale in 1807, Lieutenant Gov. of Connecticut, U. S. Senator, died at Washington, 1840.

William Benedict, jun., married to Betty St. John, Dec. 31, 1795.

Jemima,	born May	14, 1796.
William,	born Dec.	21, 1797.
Charles,	born Feb.	17, 1802.
MaryEsther,	born June	11, 1808.
Frances A.,	born Aug.	23, 1809.
Betsey,	born Jan.	12, 1811.

Benjamin Reed married to Bethiah Weed, April 25, 1765.

Bethia,	born May	22, 1766.
Sarah,	born
Benjamin,	born March 31, 1770.
Elizabeth,	born June	3, 1776.
Daniel,	born Dec.	11, 1778.
Enos,	born Oct.	30, 1787.

Daniel Reed married Sally Hawley of Salem, Oct. 4, 1797.

William Seymore married Lydia St. John, Jan. 6, 1757.

Polly,	born Jan.	1, 1758.
William,	born March 18, 1760.
Lydia,	born May,	28, 1766.
Mercy,	born Feb.	27, 1769.
Belden,	born Nov.	14, 1771.
Benjamin,	born May	28, 1774.

John Hyatt married to Jane White, Oct. 9, 1794.

| Jane, | born June | 26, 1795. |
| John W., | born June | 29, 1797. |

Josiah Thatcher, jun., married Anna Reed, Oct. 12, 1782.

Polly Street,	born Aug.	5, 1786.
George,	born Oct.	6, 1788.
Esther,	born April	20, 1791.
Harriet,	born Dec.	23, 1792.
Nancy,	born April	28, 1798.

Benjamin Whitney married to Lois Kellogg, Jan. 3, 1757.

Hannah,	born June	4, 1757.
Martha,	born March 5, 1759.
Saml. Kellogg,	born Feb.	2, 1761.
Henry,	born May	26, 1763.
Anna,	born July	29, 1765.
Polly,	born May	1, 1769.
Benjamin,	born March 4, 1771.

12*

Samuel Belden married to Ann Lambson, March 9, 1774.

Thomas,	born Jan.	17, 1775.
Samuel,	born Oct.	27, 1777.
William,	born Sept.	15, 1780.
Hezekiah,	born Jan.	27, 1783.

Thomas Belden married to Betsey Ogilvie, Dec. 24, 1798.

George O.   born March 28, 1797.

Stephen Keeler married Hannah Mervine, June 15, 1773.

Sarah,	born April	26, 1774.
John,	born Dec.	29, 1776.
Lockwood,	born Sept.	9, 1778.
Nancy,	born Aug.	11, 1780.
Lucy,	born April	27, 1782.
Mary,	born July	22, 1787.
Jenny, Esther,	born Dec.	9, 1789.
Roxy,	born April	1, 1794.

Stephen Keeler, married Sarah Burchard, Nov. 25, 1765.

Isaac,	born Oct.	12, 1766.
John,	born Aug.	8, 1768.
Esther,	born Dec.	25, 1771.

Benjamin Ayres married to Sarah Keeler, April 15, 1776.

Stephen,	born Jan.	24, 1777.
Moses,	born June	7, 1782.

Jeremiah Keeler married Molly Wescoat, January 5, 1785.

Isaac Camp, Jr., married Elizabeth Nash, Dec. 21, 1788.

David,	born Dec.	19, 1789.
Susanna,	born July	28, 1791.
Jacob,	born June	10, 1793.
Cyrus,	born May	16, 1795.
Aner Eliz.,	born May	21, 1797.

James Cannon married Rebeckah Goold, June 3, 1779.

Sarah,	born March	9, 1780.
Esther,	born April	27, 1783.
Amelia,	born Feb.	6, 1788.
Mary,	born Feb.	6, 1792.
James,	born Sept.	20, 1796.

Abijah Mead married Lydia Jennings, July 20, 1788.

Lydia,	born April	10, 1789.
George.	born Jan.	30,-1791.
Charlotte,	born Dec.	13, 1794.

Isaac Adams, son of Isaac Adams, born August 9, 1795.
Aaron,   born Dec.   9. 1796.

James St. John and Mary St. John married March 16, 1797.
Martha,   born Nov. 2, 1797.

Isaac St. John married Deborah Guernsey, Jan. 15, 1761.

Jonathan,	born Jan.	26, 1762.
Silas,	born Feb.	14, 1763.
Isaac,	born Dec.	1, 1764.
Henry,	born Oct.	26, 1766.
Polly,	born Aug.	21, 1768.
Deborah,	born Aug.	12, 1770.
James,	born Mar.	11, 1772.
Samuel,	born April	7, 1775.

Deborah, the wife of said Isaac, died Sept. 14, 1792.

The said Isaac St. John married Eunice Smith, March 13, 1796.

Eunice Matilda, born Mar. 12, 1797.

Ezra St. John married Phebe Whitlock, Jan. 20, 1787.

Silas St. John married Sarah Nash, May 1, 1782.

Clarissa,	born Nov.	7, 1785.
Sarah,	born Sept.	8, 1786.
Horatio,	born Dec.	23, 1787.
Nancy,	born July	20, 1789.
Jared	born July	27, 1791.
Lewis,	born June	5, 1793.
Polly,	born April,	5, 1796.

Daniel Weed married Hannah Raymond, March 12, 1787.

Daniel,	born Dec.	12, 1787.
Sarah,	born July	18, 1789.
Harvey,	born Nov.	22, 1791.

The said Hannah, wife to Daniel, died May 17, 1792.

The said Daniel Weed married Martha Benedict, November 12, 1793.

Dorcas B.,	born Sept.	24, 1794.
Hannah,	born Jan.	14, 1797.
Polly,	born April	17, 1799.
John A.,	born April	14, 1801.
Martha,	born July	24, 1803.
Eliza A.,	born June	5, 1806.
*William B.,	born Mar.	22, 1811.

* Rev. William B. Weed, of Stratford, graduated at Yale College in Class of 1830.

Thomas Benedict, Jr., married Mary Waterbury, October 8, 1795.

Thomas,;	born Oct.	7, 1797.
Edwin,	born Aug.	11, 1801.
Catharine,	born Dec.	25, 1806.

Isaac Waring married Eunice Fowler, Nov. 26, 1778.

Isaac,	born Dec.	14, 1780.
Solomon,	born Dec.	15, 1783.
David,	born July	27, 1785.
Eunice,	born May	20, 1788.

Josiah Raymond married Molly Merwine, Nov. 5, 1765.

Polly,	born Sept.	9, 1766.
Hannah,	born Sept.	12, 1767.
Clara,	born Jan.	10, ——.
Thomas,	born Mar.	13, ——.
Jabez,	born June	28, ——.
Clara, 2d,	born Jan.	10, ——.
Rebeckah,	born Aug.	29, 1773.
Platt,	born Dec.	3, 1775.
Merwine, ;	born Nov.	8, 1776.
Josiah,	born March	7, 1778.
Jabez,	born May	11, 1779.
Geo. Anson,	born Aug.	25, 1785.

Noah Nash married Anne Keeler, March 10, 1791.

Keeler,	born Aug.	22, 1791.
Lucinda,	born Feb.	6, 1793.
Polly,	born June	10, 1795.
Clark,	born Oct.	19, 1796.

James Arnold married Betsey Brown, January 24, 1797.

Epenetus Kellogg married Rebeckah Richards, September 16, 1773.

Epenetus,	born April	12, 1774.
Joseph,	born Dec.	5, 1775.
Sarah,	born May	30, 1777.
Anna,	born Nov.	28, 1778.
Epenetus 2d	born Oct.	1, 1780.
Betsey,	born April	26, 1782.
John,	born April	24, 1784.
Rhoda,	born Jan.	16, 1786.
Phebe,	born Dec.	1, 1787.
Ezra,	born Oct.	15, 1789.
Polly,	born March	4, 1792.

William Lockwood married Hannah Selleck, December 31, 1796.

William, born Oct. - 1, 1797.
Hooker, born April 2, 1801—d. July 5, 1801.
Susannah, born May 31, 1803—married Geo. St.
John—died September 23, 1832.
Charlotte S., born Dec. 29, 1805—married Leonard Bradley.

William Lockwood, Sen., died January 17, 1843.

Daniel James married Anna Kellogg, Jan. 18, 1798.
Sally, born Aug. 27, 1798.
William K., born Sept. 15, 1800.

James Selleck, Jr., married Sally Gilbert, Nov. 17, 1791.
Daniel, born Nov. 13, 1767.
Mary, born Feb. 22, 1769.
Thomas, born Feb. 23, 1771.
Nathan, born May 17, 1773.
James, born July 30, 1775.
Samuel, born Sept. 26, 1777.
Joseph, born Mar. 21, 1780.
Hannah, born May 5, 1783.
William, born June 10, 1786.
John M. born Sept. 10, 1787.

John Hanford, Jr., married Sarah Weed, Dec.28, 1790.
Maria, born Oct. 2, 1793.

Aaron Benedict married Sally Mallory.
Polly, born Dec. 19, 1796.
Deborah A., born June 1, 1797.

Jemmy James married Elizabeth Camp, Jan. 21, 1798.
Nelson, born Oct. 19, 1798.

Richard Youngs married Rebeckah Whitmore, December 12, 1776.
Eunice, born Dec. 9, 1779.
William, born Jan. 16, 1783.

The said Rebeckah died August 30, 1783.

The said Richard married Martha Webb, August 1,1784.
Rebeckah, born Oct. 24, 1785.
Hannah, born Aug. 8, 1787.
Daniel, born Feb. 1, 1789.
Susannah, born Dec. 7, 1791.

James Mead married Sarah Gregory, November 7, 1792.

| Lucinda, | born Fcb. | 28, 1793. |
| Orinda, | born Feb. | 28, 1797. |

John Bolt was married to Ruth Lockwood.

James Lockwood married Phebe Lockwood, Decemcember 30, 1767.

Job,	born Sept.	13, 1768.
James,	born May	1, 1770.
Asa,	born Feb.	10, 1772.

The said Phebe, wife of James, died March 5, 1773.

The said James, married Abigail De Forest, Nov. 9, 1774.

Lemuel,	born April	11, 1779.
David,	born Jan.	31, 1782.
Samuel,	born April	30, 1786.

The said Abigail, wife of James, died May 8, 1786.

The said James, married Elizabeth Richards, daughter of Nathan Waring.

| Phebe, | born Jan. | 29, 1791. |
| Sarah, | born Oct. | 28, 1793. |

Jacob Jennings married Grace Parke, January, 14, 1762.

Lydia,	born Nov.	26, 1762.
Isaac P.,	born Aug.	26, 1764.
Grace,	born Nov.	20, 1765.
Seth,	born July	8, 1768.
Clarissa,	born Oct.	16, 1770.
Isaac,	born June	20, 1773.
Anna,	born April	15, 1776.
Jacob,	born April	22, 1779.
Charlotte,	born Aug.	31, 1781.
Sally,	born Feb.	8, 1784.
Lurana,	born Oct.	11, 1786.

Ebenezer Gregory married Olive Smith, March 10, 1757.
Joseph Olmsted married Eunice Stuart, June, 1769.

Hezekiah,	born April	5, 1770.
Hezekiah 2d	born April	13, 1771.
Elizabeth,	born Nov.	5, 1773.
Nancy.	born April	10, 1777.
Esther,	born July	30, 1782.
Elias,	born June	7, 1784.

Thomas Raymond married Eunice Meeker, March 1, 1797.

John Willson married Betty Shute, August 26, 1792.
Alfred Braidy, born May 20, 1795.

Hezekiah Olmsted married Hannah ——, Dec. 17, 1793.

| Seymour, | born Oct. | 21, 1796. |
| Nancy, | born Nov. | 2, 1797. |

John Mead married Elizabeth Olmsted, March 17, 1789.

Stephen,	born Aug.	1, 1791.
Thomas R.,	born Mar.	22, 1794.
Jos. Elmer,	born June	12, 1796.

Gregory Thomas married Mary Ogden, May 8, 1788.

Eunice,	born Dec.	14, 1788.
Charles,	born Nov.	6, 1791.
Anna,	born April	13, 1795.

Enoch Tuttle married Jane Williams, May 5, 1785.

Hannah,	born Feb.	23, 1786.
Betsey,	born May	4, 1790.
Harriet,	born Aug.	23, 1793.
Charles,	born Jan.	1, 1796.
Sally,	born Feb.	6, 1799.

Joseph Everett, married Esther Lockwood, Nov. 1773.

| Sarah, | born Jan. | 13, 1775. |

The said Esther died November 16, 1786.

The said Joseph Everett married Hannah St. John, May 3, 1787.

Esther,	born Aug.	24, 1789.
Abigail,	born March	9, 1793.
Susannah,	born April	19, 1795.
Polly,	born Dec.	6, 1797.
Thomas,	born Oct.	24, 1800.
Hannah,	born Sept.	7, 1801.

Isaac Keeler married Deborah Whitney, Sept. 26, 1781.

William,	born Oct.	27, 1782.
David,	born Aug.	9, 1786.
Launcelot,	born Oct.	2, 1788.
Henrietta,	born June	25, 1792.
Edwin,	born Sept.	22, 1795.

Richard Camp married Anna Coe, November 15, 1771.

Susanna,	born Sept.	16, 1772.
Richard,	born Nov.	30, 1774.
Thomas L.,	born Oct.	10, 1777.
Jeremiah,	born Sept.	16, 1781.
Susanna,	born April	10, 1791.
Lemuel,	born April	16, 1793.

Nathan Hendrick married Abigail Elwood, Nov. 4, 1778.

Samuel,	born Dec.	13, 1779.
Betsey,	born June	9, 1782.
Hezekiah,	born Oct.	21, 1786.
William,	born April	9, 1789.
Andrew,	born July	3. 1793.
Nancy,	born June	9, 1795
Charles,	born Dec.	4, 1797.

Jonathan Nash married Ann Raymond, Dec. 8, 1792.

Ann,	born July	25, 1793.
Amelia,	born Feb.	3, 1794.
Hannah,	born Aug.	29, 1796.
Sukey,	born Dec.	9, 1797.

William Scott and Abigail Belden married Jan. 1, 1757.

William,	born Dec.	25, 1757.
Daniel,	born Mar.	24, 1759.
Moses,	born Jan.	26, 1761.
Ira, -	born Oct.	3, 1762.
John,	born Aug.	26, 1764.
Abigail,	born June	8, 1766.
Aaron,	born April	22, 1768.
Jared,	born April	29, 1772.
Belden,	born Dec.	22, 1773.
James,	born Aug.	22, 1775.
Thomas,	born Nov.	19, 1778.

Nehemiah Benedict married Hannah Benedict, October 26, 1786.

| Nehemiah, | born July | 28, 1787. |
| Hannah, | born Oct. | 18, 1790. |

Ebenezer Ayres (born July 21, 1772), married to Thankful Lockwood (born Nov. 1775,) Nov. 6, 1784.

Alvah,	born May	8, 1795.
William,	born Mar.	31, 1797.
Matilda,	born Jan.	4, 1799.
Hezron L.,	born May	10, 1801.
George,	born April	3, 1803.
Amzi,	born April	21, 1805.
Samuel,	born May	17, 1809.
Eliza Jane,	born Oct.	17, 1811.
Julia Ann,	born Jan.	17, 1814.
Ebenezer,	born Feb.	24, 1816.

Thankful, wife of Ebenezer Ayres, died March 3, 1817

Hezekiah Jarvis married to Mary Nash, Oct. 9, 1767.

Noah,	born July	22, 1768.
Abraham,	born Mar.	26, 1770.
Elijah,	born Mar.	18, 1772.
Stephen,	born Nov.	13, 1774.
James,	born Sept.	16, 1776.

The said Mary, wife to Hezekiah, died March 25, 1778.
The said Hezekiah married Sarah Nash, Dec. 13, 1778.

Samuel,	born Oct.	˙9, 1779.
Abraham,	born Aug.	23, 1781.
Sarah,	born April	18, 1783.
Charles,	born Mar.	28, 1785.
Lovina,	born Oct.	3, 1788.
Amelia,	born Nov.	27, 1790.
Mary,	born May	13, 1793.
William,	born Feb.	29, 1796.

Matthias St. John married Esther Raymond April 4, 1784.

Mary, Sarah,	born Nov.	14, 1785.
Lewis,	born Mar.	25, 1787.
Linus,	born April	20, 1790.
Esther,	born Feb.	5, 1792.

The said Esther, wife to Matthias, died March 12, 1792.
The said Matthias married Esther Abbott, Nov. 2, 1792.

| Jesse, | born Jan. | 6, 1794. |
| Nancy, | born June | 2, 1797. |

David Tuttle married Sally Richards, Dec. 6, 1789.

Maria,	born Aug.	10, 1790.
Ralph,	born Dec.	19, 1792.
Catherine,	born Dec.	25, 1794.
Hiram,	born July	4, 1797.

Enoch St. John, married Sybil Seymore, Nov. 17, 1788.
The said Sybil died July 30, 1789.

The said Enoch married Sally Downs, March 9, 1790.

Enoch C.,	born March	7, 1791.
Samuel,	born Aug.	25, 1793.
Hannah,	born Nov.	12, 1796.

Billy Finch married Susanna Fitch, Nov. 24, 1785.

Nancy,	born Feb.	11, 1787.
Billy,	born March	7, 1790.
John,	born Dec.	7, 1792.

Daniel Smith married Eunice Green, Oct. 13, 1778.

Betty,	born July	12, 1779.
Sally,	born May	31, 1782.
Roxom,	born July	17, 1785.
Maria,	born April	8, 1788.

Nathaniel Benedict, Jr., married Anah Raymond, June 6, 1768.

Mary,	born Mar.	23, 1770.
Andrew,	born June	21, 1772.
Nathaniel,	born July	17, 1774.
Simeon,	born Sept.	2, 1776.
Raymond,	born April	2, 1779.
Asa,	born July	7, 1781.
Uriah,	born Sept.	7, 1782.
Anah,	born Dec.	24, 1785.
Hannah,	born July	4, 1789.
Alfred,	born May	7, 1791.

Anah wife to said Nathaniel, died February 26, 1792.

The said Nathaniel married Hannah Selleck, Apr. 2, 1794.

Nathan Jarvis married Ann Kellogg, January, 1757.

Ann,	born Oct.	5, 1758.
Betty,	born Sept.	10, 1761.
Mary,	born June	11, 1765.
Samuel,	born Sept.	16, 1768.
William,	born June	12, 1771.
Nathan,	born June	19, 1773.
Esther,	born Aug.	27, 1775.
Hannah,	born Feb.	25, 1780.

Sarah Merwine, born Mar. 26, 1748.

Lucy Merwine, born Sept. 26, 1750.

Nathan Nash married Hannah Hitchcock, March 1, 1767.

Gilbert,	born Nov.	9, 1792.
Hezekiah,	born Sept.	13, 1795.
Sarah,	born April	8, 1799.
Mary,	born Feb.	28, 1803.
Hannah,	born Oct.	5, 1805.
James,	born Nov.	19. 1808.

David Nash married Susanna Kellogg, April 23, 1767.

| Elizabeth, | born Feb. | 23, 1768. |
| Jacob, | born June | 30, 1770—d. Nov. 19, 1791. |

The said Susanna died December 10, 1771.

The said David Nash married Rachel Bates, July 19, 1772.

James Seymour married Rebeckah Keeler, Feb. 13, 1774.

James,   born Mar.   16, 1775.
Hannah,   born Feb.   27, 1777.
Hannah 2d,   born April 11, 1779.
Rebeckah,   born June   7, 1781.
Lucretia,   born Jan.   29, 1784.
Ruth,   born April   2, 1787.
Samuel,   born July   30, 1789.
Polly,   born Dec.   31, 1792.
John,   born Feb.   24, 1796.

Ezekiel Morgan married Sarah Whitlock,, May 2, 1793.

Harriet,   born Aug.   22, 1794.
Chloe,   born Nov.   26, 1798.

Stephen Batterson married Sarah Wardwell, Oct. 20, 1784.

Abigail,   born July   31, 1785.
William,   born July   10, 1787.
Isaac,   born June   10, 1791.
Stephen,   born July   12, 1796.

Jos. Hawkins married Rhuama Rockwell, Oct. 18, 1789.

Jos. Brewster born April   1, 1791.
Matilda,   born Sept. 26, 1792.
Sally,   born Sept. 18, 1794.
Zechariah,   born Sept. 25, 1796.
John Wesley   born Mar.   29, 1798.
Ruth Ann,   born Jan.   4, 1799.
Electa,   born Aug.   15, 1801.

Jesse Benedict married Esther St. John, March 22, 1764.

Hannah,   born May   18, 1766.
Jesse,   born Mar.   19, 1767.
Mary,   born Jan.   31, 1770.
David,   born Nov.   24, 1771.
William,   born Feb.   9, 1774.
Esther,   born Dec.   26, 1776.
Elijah,   born June   16, 1782.
Betsey,   born Oct.   27, 1786.

Noah Hickox married Betsey Hurlbutt, Sept. 1 1785.

Lucretia,   born Mar.   19, 1786.
Carter,   born Jan.   9, 1788.
Sally,   born Aug.   16, 1790.
Esther,   born Sept. 30, 1792.
Harriet,   born Nov.   15, 1795.

Aaron Bouton married Polly Mallory, Jan. 18, 1794.

Justus Hayt, married Elizabeth Fitch, May 29, 1765.

Goold,	born May	28, 1766.
Luke,	born June	23, 1768.
Stephen,	born April	22, 1770.
Israel,	born May	22, 1772.
Elizabeth,	born Aug.	24, 1774.
Moses,	born July	15, 1776.
Fitch,	born Jan.	26, 1779.
Polly,	born July	1, 1781.
Hannah,	born May	2, 1784.
Justus,	born Mar.	10, 1788.
Betsey,	born June	26, 1791.
Nancy,	born July	26, 1793.

Goold Hayt married Sarah Reed, May 15, 1786.

Wm. Henry,	born Dec.	18, 1788.
Harriet,	born April	16, 1790.
Jerry,	born June	28, 1792.
Maria,	born Aug.	5, 1794.
Almira,	born Sept.	4, 1796.

Stephen Hayt, married Polly Carter, May 20, 1794.

| Polly, | born May | 4, 1795. |
| Hannah. | born Dec. | 28, 1796. |

Isaac Grumman married Betsey Selleck, Dec. 16, 1784.

Polly,	born Nov.	21, 1785.
Sabra,	born Feb.	13, 1788.
Henry,	born May	4, 1790.
Achsah,	born Jan.	24, 1793.
William,	born July	28, 1795.

Nathaniel Hendrick married Anna Godfrey, June 15, 1781.

Jared Patchen married Nancy Nash, August 31, 1797.

Aaron Adams married Rhoda Hanford March 4, 1784.

Jabez,	born Jan.	28, 1785.
Sally,	born Sept.	28, 1787.
Aaron,	born April	9, 1789.
Isaac,	born June	11, 1792.
Polly,	born April	17, 1794.
Betsey,	born March	7, 1796.

Phinehas Smith married Abiah Keeler, Nov. 2, 1786.

Peter,	born Nov.	10, 1788.
Harriet,	born June	8, 1795.
Peter,	born July	15, 1800.

Elijah Fitch, Jr., married to Mary Olmsted, May 30, 1793.

Lydia,	born Dec.	20, 1793.
Sarah,	born Aug.	2. 1795.
Maria,	born April	8, 1797.
Amarylla T., born Nov.		16, 1798.

William Fitch married to Mary Guire, May 6, 1784.

Smith,	born Dec.	2, 1785.
Abraham,	born Feb.	24, 1788.
Luke,	born July	18, 1792.
Betsey,	born Sept.	30, 1794.
Ursula,	born Feb.	25, 1797.

Samuel Burwell married Sarah Merwine, Nov. 27, 1785.

Hannah J.,	born March	5, 1786.
Betsey,	born Aug.	5, 1787.
Sukey,	born June	22, 1789.
William,	born Sept.	29, 1794.

Reuben Betts married Ellen Hawley, March 25, 1788.

Eunice,	born May	11, 1779.
Daniel L.,	born Sept.	29, 1780.
Polly,	born Nov.	15. 1783.
Ellen,	born Feb.	8, 1785.
Ben. Platt,	born Aug.	5, 1787.
Amelia,	born Dec.	14, 1789.
Charles G.,	born Dec.	1, 1792.

Daniel Nash married Freelove Wright, April 24, 1768.

| Sarah, | born Aug. | 20, 1787. |

Stephen St. John married Deborah Finch, May 3, 1787.

Stephen,	born Dec.	25, 1787.
Deborah,	born Nov.	8, 1789.
Esther,	born Nov.	20, 1791.
Nancy,	born Feb.	17, 1794.
Hannah,	born Feb.	11, 1797.

Stephen Kellogg married Lydia Bouton, Nov. 24, 1778.

Josiah,	born May	20, 1780.
Lydia,	born Nov.	19, 1782.
Andrew,	born Sept.	29, 1784.
Esek,	born Nov.	21, 1786.
Mariah,	born Oct.	21, 1788.
Nathan,	born Dec.	26, 1790.
Jemima,	born Mar.	21, 1793.
Elizabeth,	born Feb.	19, 1795.
Stephen,	born April	27, 1797.

Thomas Betts married Elizabeth Smith, Smithtown, L.
I., March 19, 1782.

Thomas S.,	born April	8, 1786.
Betsey,	born March	7, 1788.
Hannah,	born Oct.	31, 1789.
Polly,	born Dec.	5, 1790.
William,	born June	9, 1792.
Solomon,	born Oct.	3, 1793.
Sally,	born Oct.	13, 1795.
Charles J.,	born Sept.	13, 1797.
George W.	born June	6, 1800.

[Mr. George W. Betts has in his possession a quarto Bible, which
was brought from England, (the tradition is from Smithfield), by
Thomas Betts, the ancestor of the family. The title page to the Old
Testament is wanting; but the title page to the New Testament
shows that it was " translated out of Greek by Theodore Beza ;"
" Englished by L. Tomson ;" " imprinted at London by the depu-
ties of Christopher Barker, Printer to the Queen's most excellent
Majestie."

" Anno Dom. 1591."

In that Bible I find the following record :—
Thomas Betts was born January 17th, in the year 1681-2.

John,	born July	7, 1684.
Sarah,	born Jan.	21, 1686.
Matthew,	born Jan.	10, 1691-2.
Mary,	born Mar.	31, 1694.
Elizabeth,	born Oct.	23, 1699.

John Betts, son of John Betts above said, was born July 27, 1711.

| Ruah, | born April | 17, 1716. |
| Joseph, | born Mar. | 29, 1717. |

The children of Sarah (Betts) Keeler, above named—

Sarah Keeler,	born Jan.	1, 1714.
Matthew,	born Mar.	14, 1716.
Mary,	born Jan.	29, 1718.
Elizabeth,	born April	20, 1722.
Hannah,	born Oct.	18, 1726.

The children of Matthew Betts, who was born Jan. 10, 1691-2.

Mary,	born April	28, 1725.
Matthew,	born Nov.	9, 1726.
Ann,	born Mar.	29, 1729.
Seth,	born June	9, 1734.
Josiah,	born Feb.	5, 1735.]

From the Records of the Town of Guilford, Con.

Thomas Betts and his wife, Mary, removed to Norwalk, (from Guilford, Con)., in 1667; their children were as follows :—

Thomas,   born June   3, 1650.
Hannah,   born Nov. 22, 1652.
*John,   born May 10, 1655.
Stephen,   born Oct.   4, 1657.

[*John was admitted a planter in Guilford, in 1673, and soon after removed to Norwalk, from him descended Doctor Thaddeus Betts, a highly respectable Physician of Norwalk, and the father of William M. Betts, Esq., for many years Post Master and Judge of Probate of Norwalk, a most worthy and excellent man. He was the father of Hon. Thaddeus Betts, who represented his native State in the Senate of the United States, and died at Washington in 1840, at the age of 52 years. His remains repose in the old graveyard in Norwalk, with a suitable monument erected to his memory by his family.]

Wolcott Downs married Hannah Benedict, July 15, 1786.

Betsey,   born Mar. 22, 1787.
Polly,   born Dec.   3, 1788.
William,   born May   3, 1781.

Samuel Carter* married Sarah Hanford, July 14, 1789.

Hanford,   born July 17, 1790.
Hannah,   born Oct. 19, 1791.
Elizabeth,   born March 8, 1793.
Samuel,   born May   4, 1797.

Ebenezer Carter* married Sukey Benedict, Sept. 24, 1788.

John,   born March 8, 1789.

The said Sukey, wife to Ebenezer, died July 8, 1791.

The said Ebenezer married Rhoda Weed June 11, 1795.

Chaunagh,   born Mar. 23, 1796.
Ebenezer,   born Mar. 19, 1797.

David Smith married Mary Blatchley, Nov. 23, 1783.

Henry,   born Dec.   4, 1785.
Cynthia,   born Dec. 13, 1788.
David,   born Sept. 3, 1792.
Polly,   born June 23, 1794.
Eliza,   born July 22, 1797.

* See page 235.

Isaac Hayt married Mary Raymond, June 30 1776.

James,	born Jan.	11, 1777.
Sally,	born Mar.	11, 1778.
Isaac,	born Dec.	20, 1782.
Nancy,	born April	24, 1785.
Mary,	born Dec.	28, 1787.
Hannah,	born Jan.	16, 1789.
Charles,	born June	9, 1791.
Richard,	born July	26, 1793.

James Morgan married Mary Osborne, Jan. 13, 1770.

Zalmon,	born June	27, 1770.
Ezekial,	born Feb.	4, 1772.
William,	born Aug.	20, 1774.
Joel,	born June	7, 1776.
Mary,	born Mar.	10, 1779.
Stephen,	born July	8, 1781.
Dolly,	born Sept,	14, 1784.

Thomas Cole married Mary Resseguie, Nov. 28, 1779.

Thomas,	born Oct.	22, 1780.
Ira,	born Feb.	10, 1783.
Timothy,	born Aug.	11, 1785.
Sally,	born Feb.	9, 1788.
Curtis,	born May	10, 1790.
Samuel,	born Oct.	22, 1792.

Strong Comstock married Abigail Westcoat, July 20, 1773.

Jabez,	born Feb.	22, 1774.
Catherine,	born Sept.	19, 1776.
Philip,	born Oct.	3, 1778.
Samuel,	born Oct.	14, 1780.

The said Abigail, wife of Strong Comstock, died November 28, 1782.

The said Strong Comstock married Betty Betts, November 2, 1783.

Catharine,	born Aug.	2, 1784.
Edward,	born Dec.	28, 1785.
William,	born June	10, 1788.
Susanna,	born June	12, 1791.
Mary,	born May	1, 1793.
Nathan,	born Aug.	8, 1795.
Julia,	born Oct.	21, 1797.

John Abbott, Jr., married Leah Whiting, Nov. 27, 1792.

Lewis Betts married Sarah Andrews, July 11, 1790.

Suky,	born Feb.	14, 1792.
Stephen A.,	born May	4, 1795.

Zadock Hubbell married Mary Hubbell, Oct. 23, 1778.

Sukey,	born Oct.	22, 1779.
Charlotte,	born Jan.	13, 1782.
Urania,	born Feb.	17, 1784.
Abraham,	born Jan.	8, 1784.
Sarah,	born Jan.	26, 1788.
Ruth,	born Nov.	20, 1791.
George,	born Mar.	30, 1794.
Sukey,	born Jan.	5, 1797.

Philo Betts married Hannah Raymond, Oct. 12, 1797.

Seth Hickox married Kezia Hayt, April 1, 1795.

Pamiah,	born Oct.	23, 1795.
Barzillai,	born Sept.	29, 1797.
Phebe,	born Oct.	23, 1799.

Lewis Hurlbutt married Molly Scribner, Dec. 14, 1776.

Lewis,	born Feb.	7, 1777.

Seth Taylor married Martha Gaylord, daughter of Rev. William Gaylord, Wilton, March 7, 1765.

Martha,	born April	28, 1767.
Hannah,	born Jan.	15, 1769.
Seth,	born Feb.	4, 1771.
William,	born April	10, 1773.
Elizabeth,	born May	5, 1775.
John,	born June	15, 1777.
Moses,	born March	7, 1779.
Sally,	born June	10, 1782.
James,	born Jan.	28, 1784.

Joseph Crofoot married Esther St. John, May 15, 1776.

Ebenezer,	born May	10, 1777.

Ebenezer Crofoot, Jr., married Sarah Gregory, Sept. 3, 1795.

Esther,	born Aug.	20, 1796.

Asa Cole married Thankful Fancher, July 11, 1781.

William,	born April	18, 1782.
Mary,	born May	14, 1783.
Lydia,	born April	8, 1788.
Betsey,	born Sept.	30, 1791.

13

Hezekiah Hanford, Jr., married Sarah Fitch, Nov. 6, 1774.

Samuel,	born Mar. 31, 1775.
Elizabeth,	born Aug. 31, 1780.
Elnathan,	born Aug. 15, 1785.
David,	born Aug. 31, 1788.

Samuel Olmsted, 2d, married Anne Dunning, Nov. 25, 1773.

Samuel,	born Dec. 17, 1774.
Sarah,	born July 27, 1776.
Hannah,	born Feb. 12, 1779.
Stephen,	born Dec. 7, 1780.
Noah,	born Oct. 3, 1786.

Samuel Olmsted, 4th, married Rachel St. John, March 16, 1797.

| Marillus, | born Oct. 15, 1797. |

Samuel Middlebrook married Mary Midldebrook, November 16, 1769.

Elizabeth,	born April 2, 1771.
Nathan,	born Sept. 14, 1773.
Saul,	born Nov, 3, 1776.
Daniel,	born Nov. 24, 1778.
Aaron,	born Aug. 12, 1781.
Polly,	born Jan. 24, 1784.
Lewis,	born April 10, 1786.
Sally,	born Sept. 1, 1788.
Henrietta,	born June 21, 1791.
Charles,	born Mar. 20, 1794.

Nathan Middlebrook married Ruth Whitlock, May 21, 1797.

Blackleach Jesup married Abigail Raymond Feb. 27, 1790.

Mary,	born April 18, 1791.
Lydia,	born Oct. 11, 1792.
William,	born July 26, 1794.
Orilla,	born June 1, 1796.
Elizabeth,	born July 26, 1797.

Phinehas Hanford married Betty Adams, Sept., 1775.

Nathan,	born Feb. 18, 1776.
Jabez,	born May 12, 1782.
Betsey,	born Mar. 18, 1785.
Esther,	born Mar. 29, 1787.

Charles Smith married Eunice Green, Jan, 22, 1793.

Lucretia Harriet, born March 4, 1795.
Rhoda E.   born June 28, 1797.

Samuel White married Huldah Sanford, Nov., 1769.

Elizabeth,	born Dec.	12, 1770.
Samuel,	born Feb.	6, 1772.
Stephen,	born May	13, 1775.

The said Huldah, wife of Saml. White, died June 1, 1778.

The said Saml. White married Rebeckah Picket Jan., 1781.

Sarah,	born Jan.	27, 1784.
Huldah,	born July	6, 1785.
James,	born Jan. .	31, 1790.

Samuel White, Jr., married Esther Jarvis, June 21, 1795.

Charles S.,	born Feb.	4, 1796.

Thaddeus Waterbury married Polly Gregory, Mar. 24, 1787.

Annis,	born June	18, 1787.
Elizabeth,	born July	12, 1790.
Rhoda,	born April	4, 1793.
Pamelia,	born May	6, 1797.

Israel Nash married Katherine Rider, Feb. 11, 1796.

Maria,	born March	7, 1797.
Anson,	born June	22, 1798.

Stephen Dikeman, son of John and Sarah Dikeman, born March 5, 1781.

William,	born Mar.	16, 1789.

Abraham Chichester married Mary Arnold, May 30, 1782.

Abijah,	born Aug.	6, 1783.
Abraham,	born Feb.	6, 1786.
Samuel,	born Feb.	1, 1787.
Polly,	born Nov.	28, 1788.
Phebe,	born Dec.	27, 1790.
Aaron,	born June	15, 1792.
Hezekiah,	born Oct.	22, 1794.
Betsey,	born Sept.	26, 1797.

Samuel Turrel married Rachel Burnet, July 30, 1797.

Simeon Stuart married Jemima Dean, Nov. 24, 1773.

Nancy,	born Aug.	14, 1776.
Simeon,	born Sept.	20, 1781.
Jonathan D.,	born Nov.	26, 1783.
Sabra,	born April	25, 1786.
Samuel,	born Aug.	29, 1789.
Seth,	born Dec.	6, 1791.

John Hanford, married Mahitabel Comstock, Oct. 28, 1762.

Eunice,	born Dec.	13, 1763.
Elnathan,	born Jan.	8, 1766.
Uriah,	born July	4, 1768.
Sarah,	born May	9, 1770.
Samuel St. J.	born July	1, 1772.
Huldah,	born March	7, 1776.
John,	born Feb.	16, 1778.
Isaac,	born May	2, 1780.
Mary,	born June	8, 1782.
Charles,	born Dec.	3, 1785.
William,	born Nov.	11, 1787.
Julia,	born Sept.	7, 1790.

Stephen White married Esther Wasson, June 4, 1797.

Huldah S., born Jan. 27, 1798.

Thomas Comstock married Rebeckah Rockwell, February 22, 1771.

| Abijah, | born Feb. | 27, 1772. |
| Stephen, | born Oct. | 22, 1773. |

The said Rebeckah Comstock died July 3, 1774.

The said Thomas Comstock married Phebe Selleck, February 1, 1776.

Nathan,	born May	5, 1779.
Abijah,	born Sept.	2, 1781.
Catherine,	born Jan.	6, 1784.
Phebe,	born Jan.	23, 1789.
Hannah,	born April	27, 1793.
Deborah,	born July	10, 1799.

Stephen Bouton married Hannah Camp, May 26, 1792.

| Hannah, | born March | 8, 1793. |
| Stephen, | born Mar. | 18, 1797. |

Charles Selleck married to Hannah Mather, June 2, 1796.

David,	born April	9, 1797.
Hannah,	born Aug.	8, 1799.
*Chas. Grandison,	born Feb.	26, 1802.
Polly,	born Aug.	11, 1804.
Moses M.	born March	8, 1807.
Emilia,	born Dec.	13, 1809.

* Rev. Charles G. Selleck, graduated at Yale College in 1827,

Abraham Hurlbutt married Martha Morehouse, November 9, 1796.

Sally,   born July   14, 1797.

Daniel Hurlbutt married Naomi Stuart, March 9, 1758.

Ruth,   born Dec.   18, 1758.
Hannah,   born July   25, 1761.

The said Naomi, died July, 1764.

The said Daniel married Esther Patrick, March 20, 1765.

Anna,   born March 8, 1766.
Betsey,   born June   27, 1769.
Daniel,   born Feb.   11, 1772.
Anna,   born April   6, 1774.
Esther,   born April   3, 1776.
John,   born Oct.   14, 1778.
Mary,   born Mar.   27, 1781.
Belden,   born Nov.   14, 1783.
Jenny,   born Mar.   27, 1786.
Sarah,   born Dec.   30, 1788.
Bethia,   born June   15, 1791.

Seth Finch married Adah Hayt, October 23, 1765.

Jacob Selleck married Sarah Fitch, May 2, 1776.

Hannah,   born Jan.   23, 1778.
Jacob,   born Oct.   5, 1780.
Anna,   'born Oct.   7, 1782.
Lydia,   born April 14, 1785.
Polly,   born April   6, 1787.
Samuel,   born May   24, 1791.

Jesse Raymond married Hannah Mather, Dec. 28, 1777.
Hannah,   born July   21, 1778.

Nathan Tuttle married Mercy Greenslit, Jan. 6, 1761.

Enoch,   born April 11, 1762.
John,   born Sept. 24, 1763.

John Tuttle married Isabel Garner, Nov. 26, 1795.

Sarah,   born Sept. 13, 1796.

Saml. Jarvis Camp married Esther Clinton, Oct. 28, 1790.

Esther,   born March 7, 1794.
Betsey M.,   born July   12, 1796.
Mary Ann,   born Sept.   1, 1798.

Joseph Clinton married Abigail Camp, March 13, 1784.

Sarah Jervis, born Oct.   5, 1784.
Ellen C.,   born Nov.   6, 1786.

Benj. St. John married Elizabeth Burchard, Nov. 8, 1781.

James,	born Sept. 16, 1782.
Burchard,	born Jan. 1, 1784.
Lewis,	born Aug. 7, 1785.
Mary,	born Nov. 27, 1788.
Philo,	born Dec. 7, 1791.
Moses,	born Sept. 26, 1793.
Elizabeth,	born Aug, 1, 1796.
Aaron,	born June 23, 1797.

Nehemiah Hanford married Sarah Smith, May 5, 1781.

Rebeckah,	born Jan. 17, 1782.
Sarah,	born Nov. 18, 1783.
Thomas,	born Jan. 26, 1786.
Maria,	born April .3, 1788.
Nancy,	born June 23, 1790.
George O.,	born Mar. 26, 1792.
Henry,	born Mar. 22, 1794.
Elizabeth,	born July 10, 1796.

Jarvis Kellogg married Elizabeth Smith, June 10, 1760.

| Sarah, | born Mar. 15, 1766. |
| Jarvis, | born April 20, 1768. |

The said Elizabeth Kellogg, wife to Jarvis, died November 15, 1778.

The said Jarvis married Hannah Meeker, Nov. 28, 1781.

| Olivia, | born Jan. 30, 1782. |
| Elizabeth, | born Feb. 25, 1785. |

Jerry Smith married Anna Kellogg, October 23, 1791.

Seth,	born Sept. 28, 1792.
Ezra,	born June 24, 1794.
Robert,	born Mar. 20, 1796.
Mary,	born Dec. 16, 1797.

Hezekiah Lockwood married Cate Seymour, January 25, 1776.

Hannah,	born Jan. 12, 1777.
Lewis,	born Feb. 25, 1780.
Betsey,	born Feb. 15, 1781.
Sally,	born July 27, 1784.

Daniel Betts, jr. married Elizabeth Taylor, June, 1771.

Sherman,	born Feb. 6, 1785.
Asahel,	born March 2, 1788.
Aumida,	born Feb. 18, 1794.

Samuel Patrick married Mabel Baker, Feb. 5. 1795.

John,	born Nov. 14, 1796.

Thaddeus Betts, jr. married Deborah Mead, May 10,1763.

Nehemiah,	born Sept. 25, 1765.
Hannah,	born Sept. 27, 1768.
Deborah,	born Feb. 16, 17—.
Anner,	born June 2, 1773.
Sarah,	born Oct. 9, 1777.
Zadock,	born May 10, 1780.
Lydia,	born Nov. 9, 1781.
Rebeckah,	born Dec. 20, 1784.

Rev. Justus Mitchell married Polly Sherman, Sept. 7,1780.

Betsey,	born Aug. 28, 1781.
Sherman,	born July 2, 1782.
Minot,	born Sept. 24, 1784.
Chauncey,	born June 55, 1786.

Thomas Hayt married —— April 9, 1778.

Samuel,	born Nov, 11, 1778.
Mary,	born June 30, 1784.
Elizabeth,	born Aug. 4, 1787.
Ira,	born Feb. 21, 1790.
Anson,	born Jan. 4, 1793.
Sarah,	born Jan. 23, 1797.

Joseph Chapman married Elizabeth Taylor, June, 1771.

Betsey,	born Mar. 11, 1772.
Joseph,	born Aug. 29, 1774.
Lydia,	born Feb. 21, 1776.
William,	born May, 7, 1778.
Polly,	born Aug, 29, 1780.
Sally,	born Oct. 10, 1782.
Lucretia,	born Dec. 13, 1784.
Lucretia, 2d.	born Feb. 16, 1787.
Esther,	born June 9, 175-.
Juliana,	born Nov. 7, 1793.

John Eversley married Abigail Hyatt.

John,	born Aug. 23, 1766.
Molly,	born Mar. 27, 1769.
Betty,	born Jan. 3, 1773.

John Eversley, jr. married Mary Benedict, Nov. 19,1792.

Anah,	born July 30, 1794.
John,	born Aug. 21, 1797.
Charles,	born
Esther M.,	born
Eliza Ann	born

Moses Raymond married Esther Benedict, Nov. 20, 1776.

| Nancy, | born Aug. 28, 1776. |

The said Esther, wife of Moses, died June 2, 177-.
The said Moses married Rebeckah Bouton, Dec. 29, 1778.

Esther,	born Oct. 19, 1779.
Rebeckah,	born Sept. 25, 1781.
Deborah,	born May 22, 1783.
Peggy,	born April 24, 1785.
Peggy, 2d.	born July 3, 1787.
Isaac,	born Sept. 5, 1789.
Susanna,	born Aug. 14 1791.
Anah,	born July 1, 1793.
Anna,	born Aug. 28, 1795.

Isaac Hayt married Phebe Mott, Dec. 25, 1760.

Stephen,	born Oct. 25, 1761.
Esther,	born Sept. 19, 1765.
Phebe,	born Aug. 29, 1769.
Lockwood,	born Aug. 18, 1771.
Lydia,	born Nov. 7, 1774.
Eunice,	born Dec. 27, 1775,

John Hurlburt, married Anna Adams, Nov. 21, 1791.

William,	born Eeb. 22, 1793.
Sally,	born Mar. 25, 1794.
Harriet,	born July 23, 1795,
Rebeckah,	born July 24, 1797.

Moses Gregory married Abigail Gregory, Mar. 22, 1789.

Polly,	born Feb. 24, 1790.
Lewis,	born Sept. 3, 1794.
Henry,	born April, 1, 1796.
Abbe,	born April 26, 1797.

Ephraim Lockwood married Sarah Slawson, Mar. 7, 1770.

Nehemiah,	born Jan. 3, 1771.
Elias,	born May 15, 1773.
Nathan,	born May 9, 1775.
Elias,	born Oct. 15, 1778.
Sarah,	born Mar. 18, 1783.
Esther,	born March 1, 1788.

Sarah Lockwood, wife of Ephraim, died March 1, 1788.
The said Ephraim married Sarah Waring, Oct, 26, 1788.

| Alfred, | born May 1, 1795. |

Nehemiah Lockwood, married Mary Waring, Dec. 17, 1795.

| Elizabeth, | born Jan. 24, 1797. |

Barnabas Mervine, married Molly Adams, Mar. 21, 1764.

Barnabas,	born Dec.	4, 1764.
Molly,	born Dec.	25, 1765.
Nathan,	born May	23, 1767.
Rebeckah,	born Mar.	18, 1769.

The said Molly, wife of Barnabas, died April 5, 1771.
The said Barnabas married Mabel Tuttle, Jan. 16, 1773.

Sally,	born Aug.	7, 1774.
Betsey,	born Dec.	1, 1779.
Samuel,	born Oct.	27, 1783.

James Smith, married Hannah Lockwood, Sept. 14, 1780.

| ` James, | born July | 5, 1785. |
| John, | born Nov. | 5, 1787. |

David Price, married Rachel Smith, March 2, 1778.

| Justus, | born Nov. | 14, 1778. |
| Eunice, | born Dec. | 29, 1782. |

The said Rachel, wife to said David, died Nov. 17, 1784.
The said David married Susanna Saunders, Mar. 30, 1785.

| David, | born July, | 22, 1793. |

William Jelliff, married Huldah ———, Dec. 7, 1771.

William,	born Oct.	29, 1772.
Aaron,	born May	15, 1775.
Sturges,	born Sept.	12, 1777.
Hezekiah,	born July	'8, 1780.
Zalmon,	born Mar.	10, 1783.
Polly,	born Oct.	14, 1785.
David,	born April	8, 1788.
Goold,	born Sept.	27, 1790.
Rachel,	born Jan.	4, 1793.
Hiram,	born Oct.	13, 1796.

Hezekiah Whitlock, married Molly Betts, Oct. 21, 1780.

Thaddeus,	born Mar.	15, 1784.
Nancy,	born Mar.	17, 1787.
Charles,	born Dec.	29, 1790.
Nancy,	born Dec.	27, 1793.
Lewis,	born Oct.	24, 1795.
Burwell,	born Aug.	4, 1797.

Samuel Merwine, jr. married to Ann Burr, June, 1792

| Polly, | born July | 24, 1793. |
| Samuel Sturges, | born June | 24, 1797. |

13*

Daniel Butler married Dinah Ells, Nov. 18, 1792.

James,	born April	8, 1793.
Sarah,	born Dec.	2. 1794.
Lois,	born Sept.	5, 1796.
Ann,	born	

Eliphalet St. John married to Sarah Knapp, Oct. 2, 1793.

| Abigail, | born July 16, 1794, |
| Caleb Lorenzo, | born Jan. 30, 1796. |

William Long married to Esther Lawrence, Feb. 9, 1792.

Sally,	born Sept.	2, 1793.
Betsey,	born Jan.	9, 1796.
Hiram,	born Sept.	3, 1898.

John Finch married Widow Mary Ogden, Dec. 3, 1778.

| Ruamy, | born Sept. 1, 1779. |

Arete, daughter of John Finch, jr. born March 31, 1794.

| Samuel, | born Oct. 14, 1795. |

Samuel Betts, married to Mary Webb, Jan. 3, 1798.

| Samuel, | born, Dec. 9, 1798. |

Samuel Cannon, married to Sarah Belden, Dec. 26, 1781.

Henrietta,	born June 24, 1784.
Le Grand,	born Mar. 20, 1787.
Esther Mary,	born Oct. 3, 1793.

Waters Pellett married Eliz. Middlebrook, Feb. 6, 1792.

Sally,	born Jan.	19, 1794.
Mary,	born Mar.	10, 1796.
Charlotte,	born Jan.	2, 1798.

Daniel Whitlock married Ruth Scribner, Nov. 21, 1771.

Sarah,	born June	8, 1775.
Ruth,	born April	16, 1777.
Phebe,	born Sept.	26, 1780.
Hannah,	born Oct.	19, 1784.
Elizabeth,	born Jan.	31, 1788.
Harvey,	born April	20. 1792.
William,	born Jan.	11, 1796.

John Raymond married Sally Hoyt, Feb. 13, 1791.

Amelia	born April	17, 1796.
Antoinette,	born July	11, 1799.
Charles Edwin,	born Dec.	3d, 1800.
Henry,	born Sept.	2, 1804.

Aaron Comstock married Anne Hanford, Nov. 1774.

Thaddeus,	born Aug.	6, 1775.
Aaron,	born Mar.	25, 1777.
Thaddeus,	born Sept.	10, 1779.
Lucretia,	born Sept.	7, 1782.
Hannah,	born Sept.	8, 1785.
Daniel,	born Aug.	4, 1789.
Anne,	born Feb.	12, 17—.

Silas Betts married Hannah Smith, June 22, 1780.

Hannah,	born April	13, 1782.
Polly,	born Jan	9, 1784.
Sukey,	born Mar.	29, 1786.
Catherine,	born Mar.	16, 1788.
Martha,	born Sept.	19, 1791.
David,	born Jan.	17, 1794.
Ellis A. } Abigail E. }	born Sept.	13. 1796.

Nath. Raymond, Jr., married Dolly Wood, Aug. 3, 1772.

Hannah,	born Oct.	26, 1773.
Nathaniel,	born Feb.	10, 1775.
Rebeckah,	born April	11, 1777.
Street,	born Jan.	8, 1780.
Eliakim,	born May	29, 1782.
Charles,	born Nov.	20, 1784.
Henry,	born Jan.	29, 1787.
Elnathan,	born April	23, 1789.
Alanson,	born Nov.	23, 1791.
Delia,	born Dec.	9, 1793.

Ebenezer Whitney married Ruth Raymond, Dec. 19, 1771.

Betty,	born Feb.	1, 1773.
Asa,	born May	12, 1774,
Abby,	born June	8, 1775.
Asa 2d,	born Aug.	17, 1776.
Lucretia,	born July	19, 1778.
Clarissa,	born Feb.	21, 1780.
Ebenezer,	born Nov.	19, 1783.
Lecretia 2d,	born June	27, 1786.
Roxana,	born Oct.	26, 1789.
Maria,	born June	27, 1792.
George,	born July	26, 1794.
Henry Hayt,	born Feb.	4, 1796.

Steph. Wicks married Susannah Dunning, Sept 27, 1786.

James,	born Oct.	14, 1787.
William,	born March	5, 1789.
Sally,	born Feb.	1, 1791.
Joseph,	born March 15, 1793.	
Benjamin,	born Jan.	13, 1795.
Harriet,	born Jan.	17, 1797.

David Whitney, Jr. married Nancy Raymond, May 12, 1796.

Esther,	born Feb.	18, 1797.
Rebecca,	born Aug.	2, 1798.
Charlotte,	born Feb.	18, 1800.
Nancy,	born Mar.	24, 1802.
Harriet,	born Jan.	28, 1804.
Eliza Hyatt,	born Jan.	1, 1806.
Thaddeus S.	born Feb.	14, 1808.
Moses R,	born Oct.	5, 1811.
Cordelia,	born July	6, 1813.
Selina,	born Oct.	10, 1816.
Minett,	born July	29, 1818.

Thomas Keeler married Anna Squires, October 18, 1767.

Lewis,	born Aug.	14, 1768.
Henry,	born Sept.	2, 1770.
James,	born Feb.	18, 1773.
Isaac,	born Nov.	15, 1775.
Thomas,	born Oct.	4, 1778.
Jasper Sears,	born May	8, 1778.
Anna,	born Jan.	5, 1784.
Erastus,	born Mar.	27, 1787.
Caroline,	born Mar.	20, 1789.
George,	born Feb.	1, 1791.
Polly Sears,	born Oct.	21, 1793.

Ezra Picket married Elizabeth Benedict, March 30, 1761.

Ezra,	born June	27, 1761.
Stephen,	born Feb.	27, 1763.
Esther,	born Mar.	1, 1765.
John,	born Feb.	5, 1769.
Anne,	born Dec.	4, 1771.
Ebenezer, Deborah,	born June	15, 1773.
Hannah,	born Aug.	13, 1775.
Henry,	born Nov.	30, 1777.

John Hays married Hannah Beers, April 2, 1766.

Jesse,	born May	29, 1767.
Rhoda,	born Jan.	21, 1770,

Isaac Arnold, 2d, married Phebe Hayden, Nov. 9, 1786.

Lucretia, born Nov. 3, 1787.
Isaac, born Jan. 16, 1788.
Betsey, born July 9, 1791.
Lewis, born Sept. 24, 1793.
George, born Sept. 9, 1795.

Matthew Mead married Phebe Whelpley, Feb. 7, 1760.

Molly, born Nov. 23, 1760.
Thaddeus, born Oct. 11, 1762.
Elizabeth, born Aug. 7, 1764.
James, born July 5, 1766.
Susa, born June 6, 1768.
David, · born Sept. 3, 1770.
Matthew, born Jan. 27, 1773.
Aaron, born Sept. 6, 1776.
Xenophon, born June 12, 1779.
Roswell, born July 15, 1784.

Jehiel Gregory married Phebe Arnold, March 13, 1775.

Stephen Wood married Hannah Benedict, April 3, 1782.

Hannah, born Jan. 7, 1783.
Stephen, born Dec. 12, 1784.
William, born Jan. 31, 1787.
Nancy, born Aug. 21, 1789.
Esther, born Oct. 9, 1792.
Harriet, born Sept. 21, 1794.
Benning W., born May 24, 1797.

[Their other Children were Charles, Alfred and Edwin.]

James Benedict married Thankful Lockwood, May 25, 1763.

Nehemiah, born April 16, 1764.
Nehemiah 2d born Dec. 29, 1765.
James, born Nov. 24, 1767.
Ruth, born May 28, 1769.
Matthew, born Oct. 29, 1770.
David, born Sept. 22, 1772.
David 2d, born April 7, 1774.
Billy, born March 7, 1777.
Lockwood, born Mar. 29, 1779.
Caleb, born July 6, 1783.
Ruth, born May 17, 1785.

Noah Smith married Rhoda Hays, January 11, 1790.

Hannah, born July 5, 1791.

Selleck Tuttle married Nancy Bessey, Oct. 14, 1792.

Selleck,	born April	18, 1793.
Charles.	born June	3, 1794.
Sally,	born Jan.	4, 1796.

Gilbert Fairchild married Hannah Bennett, June 24, 1779.

Hezekiah,	born Feb.	2, 1780.
Ebenezer,	born Oct.	3, 1783.
Samuel G.,	born Aug.	2, 1792.
Betsey,	born Feb.	7, 1796.

Isaac Benedict married Jane Raymond Oct. 13, 1773.

Isaac,	born July	13, 1774.
Goold,	born Feb.	4, 1776.
Samuel R.,	born Aug.	22, 1779.
Abigail,	born July	24, 1781.
Obadiah,	born Aug.	19, 1783.
Lewis,	born Sept.	27, 1785.
Lorana,	born Sept.	7, 1787.
Amzi,	born May	19, 1791.

The said Jane, wife of Isaac died January 26, 1794.

The said Isaac married Mary Davenport, Aug. 19, 1794.

| Lorana 2d, | born Dec. | 7, 1795. |

Jesse Hickox married Betsey Hayt, November 24, 1791.

| John, | born Nov. | 27, 1792. |
| Albert, | born July | 23, 1797. |

James Trumbull married Phebe Clinton, Jan. 9, 1798.

Peter Adams married Millison Hurlbut, March 17, 1784.

| Nancy, | born Oct. | 15, 1794. |
| Julia Ann, | born Jan. | 19, 1796. |

Zacharia Whitman Fitch married Sarah Gregory, February 20, 1796.

| Elizabeth, | born July | 7, 1796. |

Alvin Hyatt married Abigail Grumman, Sept. 16, 1779.

Aaron,	born July	30, 1780.
Polly,	born Jan.	24, 1782.
Jesse,	born June	5, 1784.
George,	born Oct.	29, 1793.
Sally,	born Sept.	4, 1795.

John Byxbee married Elizabeth Waring, Feb. 17, 1758.

Joseph,	born Aug.	13, 1758.
John,	born April	26, 1761.
Elizabeth,	born May	7, 1763.
Hopkins,	born Feb.	1, 1766.

Stephen Lockwood married Sarah Betts, April 14, 1782.

Sarah,	born Dec.	9, 1782.
Ralph,	born July	9, 1787.
*Stephen,	born June	1, 1789.
Elizabeth,	born Mar.	24, 1791.
George,	born July	29, 1793.
Henry,	born May	11, 1795.
Esther,	born July	13, 1797.
Mary Betts,	born April	17, 1799.

Reuben Olmsted born July 22, 1763.) Married Novem-
Hannah Bass, his wife born in April } ber 18, 1784.
23, 1762.)

Charles,	born May	24, 1785.
Betsey,	born Jan.	20, 1788.
Stephen,	born June	10, 1790.
Seth,	born July	23, 1792.
Esther,	born Feb.	28, 1795.

Jacob Fairweather married Catherine Jarvis, —— 1782.

Hanford,	born June	17, 1782.
Fanny,	born Nov.	10, 1783.
Leander,	born Dec.	9, 1785.
Stephen,	born June	15, 1788.

Isaac Stuart, married Olive Morehouse, Dec. 25, 1771.

Betty,	born July	9, 1772.
Martha,	born Dec.	24, 1777.
†Moses,	born Mar.	26, 1780.
Sarah,	born Aug.	25, 1781.

Joseph St. John married Betsey Nash, Nov. 15, 1792.

Esther,	born Jan.	5, 1794.
Charles,	born Nov.	1, 1795.
Joseph L.,	born Dec.	14, 1797.

Stephen Abbott married Ruth James, March 7, 1780.

Betty,	born Feb.	14, 1781.
Betty 2d,	born July	3, 1785.
Cynthea,	born July	2, 1788.
Stephen J.,	born Nov.	19, 1792.
Charles,	born Mar.	19, 1797.

* Graduated at Yale in 1807.

† Graduated at Yale, 1799. Professor in Andover Theological Seminary.

Elijah Hayt married Mary Raymond, June 13, 1757.

William,	born April	12, 1758.
James,	born Nov.	22, 1759.
Dinah,	born Jan.	7, 1762.
Rachel,	born Aug.	6, 1764.
Elijah,	born Mar.	12, 1766.

The said Mary, wife to said Elijah, died June 12, 1766.

The said Elijah married Abigail Bishop, Feb. 18, 1768.

Andrew	born Dec.	4, 1768.
Mary,	born April	6, 1770.
Samuel,	born June	14, 1772.
Eunice,	born May	1, 1774.
Abigail,	born Oct.	1, 1776.
Hannah,	born July	13, 1778.
Banajah,	born May	28, 1780.

Hezekiah Rogers married Esther Raymond, March 9, 1781.

Sally,	born July	13, 1781.
William,	born Mar.	16, 1783.
Delia,	born Jan.	29, 1785.
Charles,	born Sept.	12, 1787.

Uriah Raymond married Esther Benedict, Jan. 20, 1766.

Mary,	born Dec.	14, 1766.
Esther,	born Jan.	28, 1770.
Esther 2d,	born April	8, 1771.
Betty,	born Dec.	19, 1773.
Sally,	born Feb.	22, 1776.
Uriah,	born Sept.	1, 1778.
Mary, Grace,	born April	12, 1781.
Mary 2d,	born July	17, 1782.
Simeon,	born May	21, 1785.
Eli,	born Jan.	18, 1788.
Harriet,	born July	29, 1790.

Ebenezer Abbott married Esther Middlebrook, February 11, 1768.

Esther,	born Nov.	8, 1770.
Ebenezer,	born Oct.	13, 1772.
Michael,	born Jan.	28, 1775.
Nathan,	born Oct.	22, 1777.
Isaac,	born Oct.	22, 1778.
Sarah,	born Jan.	12, 1780.
Nathan,	born Jan.	23, 1782.
Samuel,	born Oct.	3, 1784.
Elizabeth,	born Feb.	26, 1787.

Enos Kellogg, married Lydia Fitch, March 10, 1774.

Aaron,	born Feb.	10, 1775.
Esther,	born Jan.	12, 1778.
Esther 2d,	born Oct.	30, 1779.
Hannah,	born May	29, 1784.
Rebeckah,	born Mar.	16, 1787.

Chauncey Johnson married Polly Gregory, March 13, 1794.

| George J., | born Feb. | 14, 1795. |
| Sally, | born Jan. | 8, 1797. |

Betsey Mc Nab, daughter of Alexander Mc Nab, born 1776.

John,	born Sept.	—, 1781.
Christiana,	born Mar.	—, 1788.
Anne,	born July	—, 1779.

Joseph Burgess married Amelia Ogden, Nov. 28, 1790.

Samuel,	born May	31, 1791.
Anna,	born Mar.	22, 1795.
Charlotte,	born Dec.	4, 1799.

Seth Seymour married Polly Reed, April 3, 1789.

Maria,	born Nov.	27, 1789.
Alfred,	born April	5, 1792.
Uriah,	born	
Stephen,	born	.

Ezra Seymour married Abigail Waterbury, Nov. 23, 1769.

Hannah,	born April	8, 1770.
Ezra,	born Dec.	16, 1771.
Henry,	born Dec.	25, 1773.
Betty,	born May	25, 1776.
Abigail,	born Sept.	23, 1778.
Nancy,	born Mar.	10, 1781.
Rebeckah,	born Feb.	24, 1783.
Levina,	born April	30, 1785.
Hawley,	born May	22, 1787.
Sybil,	born Nov.	18, 1790.

Henry Chichester married Deborah Hoyt, June 1, 1784.

Walter,	born Jan.	31, 1785.
Sally,	born Feb.	12, 1787.
Amelia,	born Mar.	27, 1795.
Henry,	born April	18, 1799.
Alfred,	born April	4, 1801.
Ward,	born Nov.	28, 1803.
Eliza,	born April	8, 1808.
Emeline,	born Nov.	1, 1810.

Asa Whitney and Catherine Leget married Oct. 7, 1797.

Edwin,	born June	30, 1798.
William R.,	born Oct.	5, 1799.
Catherine,	born Aug.	12, 1801.
Edwin,	born July	15, 1803.
Henry,	born July	25, 1805.
Thomas,	born April	20, 1807.
Simeon R.,	born Aug.	2, 1809.
Asa, H.,	born Feb. 28,	1811.

Joseph Fitch married Hannah Sperry, Oct. 12, 1784.

Hannah,	born April	23, 1786.
Joseph,	born June	15, 1788.
Mabel,	born Nov.	23, 1793.
Philo,	born April	6, 1896

Hezekiah Jennings married Hannah Hoyt, November 27, 1795.

Zalmon,	born Sept.	26, 1796.

Joseph Silliman married Martha Leeds, Nov. 23, 1785.

Joseph,	born Aug.	13, 1786.
William, ᵃ	born Jan.	17, 1788.
Elizabeth L.	born Oct.	22, 1789.
Saml. Cook,	born Jan.	11, 1792.
Elisha,	born Dec.	22, 1793.
Anne,	born Oct.	23, 1795.

Jonathan Hayt, married Hannah ——, Feb. 17, 1770.

Anna,	born Oct.	9, 1771.
Jonathan,	born May	7, 1775.
Eliza,	born Aug.	12, 1777.
Sarah,	born July	25, 1779.
Polly,	born July	26, 1782.
Seth,	born Nov.	11, 1784.
Harvey,	born Aug.	21, 1787.

John Raymond 3d, married Ruth Waring, Dec. 17, 1794.

Polly,	born Oct.	14, 1795.
Abigail,	born July	30, 1797.
Harriet,	born Jan.	29, 1799.

Powel Batterson married Betsey Wilson Jan. 30, 1788.

Clara,	born Oct.	23, 1788.
Lewis M.,	born March	8, 1790.
Powel,	born Aug.	28, 1792.
Betsey,	born Sept.	14, 1796.

Hezekiah Betts married Grace Hanford, Oct. 1, 1785.

* Alfred,	born Sept.	2,	1786.
Amaryllis.	born June	28,	1788.
Robert W.,	born Aug.	23,	1790.
Mehitable,	born Nov,	25,	1792.
Henry,	born Nov,	26,	1794.
Eliza Susan,	born July	8,	1797.
* Xenophon,	born Sept.	22,	1799.
Eulalia,	born Oct.	13,	1802.
Juliette,	born March	3,	1805.
Harriet,	born May	8,	1807.
Solomon E.	born Dec.	23,	1809.

Moses C. Ells, married to Abigail Reed, Nov. 4, 1769.

William,	born Oct.	16,	1772.
Abigail,	born Feb.	2,	1774.
Mary,	born Oct.	5,	1775.
Stephen,	born July,	2,	1777.
Anna,	born Dec.	22,	1778.
Moses,	born Feb.	12,	1784.
Jacob,	born Sept.	5,	1785.
Rhuamah,	born July	5.	1787.
Betsey,	born Nov.	9,	1790.

Benjamin St. John, married Dorcas Bouton, June 20, 1792.

Benjamin M.	born Nov.	7,	1794.
Abraham W.	born Feb.	2,	1799.

Timothy Fitch married Esther Platt, June 8, 1764.

Timothy,	born Dec.	22,	1765.
Hannah,	born Sept.	15,	1766.
William,	born Feb.	13,	1768.
Timothy, 2d.	born Oct.	29,	1769.
Edward,	born May	1,	1772.
Esther E.	born Oct.	30,	1773.
Nancy,	born Dec.	8,	1775.
Joseph,	born Oct.	14,	1777.
Nancy, 2d,	born Aug.	29,	1781.
Sally,	born Feb.	13,	1784.
Thomas,	born Sept.	7.	1785,
Charles,	born Sept.	10,	1790.

Henry Brooks, married to Phebe Youngs, Dec. 8, 1791.

Sally,	born Oct.	17,	1792.
Julia,	born April	6,	1794.

* Rev. Alfred and Xenophon Betts, of Ohio.

Samuel Kellogg married Elizabeth Waring, May 30, 1771.

Samuel,   born June 21, 1772.
Seth,   born Dec. 29, 1773.
Mary,   born Dec. 31, 1776.
Abigail,   born Jan. 27, 1778.
Jonathan W. born Jan.   7, 1780.
Mary,   born April 10, 1882.

Thomas Gruman married Deborah Deolf, Aug. 27, 1772.

William,   born Mar. 20, 1774,   ▲
Hannah,   born June   5, 1777.
Sarah,   born May   15, 1780.

Stephen Hanford married to Phebe Fitch, 1771.

Hannah,   born May   26, 1772.
Abijah,   born Aug. 27, 1774.
Enoch,   born Jan. 10, 1777.
Fitch,   born April 8, 1779.
Polly,   born June 20, 1781.
Sally,   born Mar. 12, 1784.
David,   born July 16, 1786.
Phebe,   born Dec. 17, 1788.
Zalmon,   born May   26, 1791.
Eliza,   born Sept. 21, 1796.

\ Abijah Hanford married Hannah Warren, May 19, 1796.

Daniel,   born May   24, 1797.
Stephen,   born Sept. 24, 1799.
William,   born May   27, 1803.
Thomas Cook, born Feb.   24, 1805.
Esther Martha, born Feb. 9, 1807.
Elizabeth May, born Feb. 24, 1809.

Ebenez'r Weed married Sarah Fairweather, Dec. 25, 1769.

Mary,   born July 25, 1770.
Hannah,   born June 22, 1771.
Henry,   born June 14, 1774.
Sarah,   born Mar, 30, 1778.
William H.   born July   4, 1782.
Frederick,   born Sept. 28, 1785.

Jonathan Seymour married to Hannah Betts.

Henry Betts. born May   18, 1787.
Mehitabel,   born Nov. 30, 1789.
John,   born Oct. 14, 1793.
Sarah,   born Aug. 24, 1796.

Matthew Hayt married Mary Lockwood, June 2, 1761.

Noah Morehouse married Hannah Gregory, Mar. 9, 1797.

Joseph Clinton, married Phebe Benedict, Sept. 1, 1757.

Levi,	born Mar. 26, 1758.
Esther,	born June 15, 1760.
Joseph,	born May 28, 1762.
Allen,*	born Mar. 7, 1764.
Salmon,	born July 13, 1776.
Simeon,	born July 3, 1768:
Martha,	born Oct. 15, 1770.
Isaac,	born June 4, 1775.
Phebe,	born Aug. 9, 1777.

Eli Tuttle married to Sarah Smith, Dec. 8. 1765.

Mary.	born May 8, 1766.
Hannah,	born Nov. 25, 1767.
Rhoda,	born Nov. 29, 1770.
Cate,	born Sept, 15, 1772.
Abraham,	born Dec. 27, 1774.
Johnson,	born Oct. 15, 1775.
Sally,	born Oct. 20, 1779.
Phebe,	born Sept. 15, 1782.

Ebenezer Tuttle, married Charity Pennoyer, Feb. 7, 1765.

David,	born Jan. 8, 1766.
Lydia,	born Mar. 10, 1769.
Smith,	born Sept. 21, 1773.
-- Azor,	born July 20, 1775.
Smith,	born June 20, 1778.
Abigail,	born Feb. 25, 1788.

Patty, daughter of Wid. Abigail Tuttle, born June 18, 1776.

Enos,	born Mar. 20, 1779.
Henry,	born April 9, 1781.
Anna,	born June 3, 1783.
Azor,	born Aug. 30, 1785.

Mathew Hayt married Mary Lockwood, Jan. 2, 1761.

Annah,	born July 22, 1761.
Thaddeus,	born Nov. 21, 1763.
Mercy,	born Aug. 17. 1765.
Thankful,	born Mar. 4, 1767.
Mary,	born April 30, 1769.
Phebe,	born Oct. 4, 1773.
Ephraim,	born May 2, 1775,
Phebe,	born Feb. 21, 1777.
Esther,	born Dec. 14, 1778.
Liffe,	born Aug. 15, 1780.
Samuel,	born May 6, 1782.

Mathew Hayt, jr. married Mary Keeler, Nov. 14, 1793.

Chauncey,   born Sept. 17, 1795.
Polly,   born Dec. 16, 1798.

Enoch Scribner married Betty Benedict, March 22, 1781.

Jeremiah,   born Feb. 19, 1782.
William,   born June 14, 1783.
Mary,   born Sept. 15, 1785.
George,   born Mar. 11, 1780.
Sally,   born Sept. 14, 1790.
Charles,   born Mar. 24, 1793.
Joseph,   born Oct. 30, 1796.

Bartlet Hanford, married Hannah Raymond, May 6, 1798,

Hugh Dickson married Mary Stuart, Jan. 3, 1797.

Peter Smith married Esther Green, Aug. 1770.

Henry,   born Dec. 20, 1778.
Sarah,   born Nov. 20, 1784.

Moses Hanford, married Mercy Kellogg, Oct. 1, 1761.

Moses,   born July 1, 1767.
Nathan,   born July 19, 1770.
Thaddeus,   born Nov. 1, 1772.
Martin,   born July 18, 1775.
Mercy,   born Mar. 3, 1778.
Betty,   born Aug. 13, 1780.
Seth,   born Mar. 28, 1783.
David,   born Sept. 2, 1785.

Thaddeus Hanford, married Sally St. John, Oct. 4, 1797.

Sally,   born Nov. 27, 1798.

Sam'l St. John married Hannah B. Richards, Mar. 1, 1798.

Uriah Selleck married Hannah Smith, May 18, 1784.

Zalmon,   born Mar. 31, 1795.
Nancy,   born July 6, 1806.

Aaron St. John, married Mercy St. John, March 23, 1784.

Platt,   born March 2, 1786.
Sarah,   born July 13, 1788.
Cynthia,   born Mar. 8, 1790.
Mehitabel, born Feb. 19, 1792.
Esther,   born Feb. 17, 1794.
Maria,   born Dec. 28, 1795.

Phinehas Keeler married Mary Camp, May 16, 1769.

Luke,	born Feb. 15, 1770.
Anna,	born Oct. 8, 1771.

The said Mary, wife of Phinehas, died May 7, 1774.

The said Phinehas married Rebeckah Mead, July 9, 1775.

Phebe Baxt'r,	born March 9, 1779.
Thaddeus M.	born April 16, 1786.

Luke Keeler married Jemimah Benedict, May 20, 1783.

Lewis,	born June 1, 1794.
Amy,	born May 7, 1797.

Zalmon Morgan, married Mary Rockwell, Dec. 29, 1790.

Sarah,	born April 26, 1791.
Zalmon,	born Oct. 19, 1792.
Thaddeus,	born July 30, 1796.
Curtis,	born July 5, 1798.

Timothy Keeler married Hannah Hickox, April 15, 1757.

Uriah,	born Mar. 19, 1760.
Hannah,	born Feb. 24, 1762.
Sarah,	born Sept. 16, 1765.
Benjamin,	born Aug. 1, 1771.
Stephen,	born June 27, 1776.

Eliud Deforest married Isabel Hayt, April 29, 1791.

Fanny,	born Sept. 12. 1791.
Hiram,	born Jan. 12, 1793.
Sally,	born Nov. 26, 1794.
Charles,	born Nov. 22, 1796.

Nathan Sandford married Abigail Bennett, Sept. 9, 1781.

Polly,	born May, 1792.
Nath'n Platt,	born July 12, 1784.

The said Abigail, wife of Nathan died, Sept. 30, 1788.

The said Nath. Sandford married Eliz. Mead, Jan. 10, 1789.

James,	born May 6, 1792.
Charity,	born April 20, 1795.

Elijah Gregory married Rhuama Gregory, Nov. 175-.

Joseph,	born Feb. 1758.
Jemima,	born April, 1760.
Elizabeth,	born Oct. 1761.

Richard Sherman and Betsey Whitney married Feb. 1, 1793.

Eliza,	born July 17, 1795.
Richard,	born Jan. 25, 1794.

Eliphalet Lockwood married Susannah St. John, Jan. 8, 1766.

William,	born May	12, 1768.
Susanna,	born April	1, 1767.
Susanna 2d,	born May	28, 1771.
Buckingham St. John,	born Dec.	23, 1774.
Abigail,	born July	15, 1776.
Eliphalet,	born Dec.	17, 1778.
Hooker St. John,	born April	8, 1782.

The said Eliphalet Lockwood, Sen., died March 19, 1814.

Buckingham Lockwood and Polly Esther St. John were married February 17, 1805.

Julia Abigail,	born Jan.	18, 1809.
Elizabeth,	born July	28, 1813.
Mary Esther,	born Sept.	25, 1815.
Wm. Buck'm. Eliphalet,	born Dec.	27, 1820.
Wm. Buck'm. Eliphalet 2d	born Dec.	23, 1822.
Frederick St. John.,	born Aug.	23, 1825.

Stephen Buckingham St. John, married Sarah Cannon, daughter of John Cannon, February 14, 1801.

George,	born Aug.	21, 1803.

The said Sarah died April 14th, 1808, and the said Stephen Buckingham married Charlotte Bush, of Greenwich, May 21st. 1811.

Elizabeth, born June 30, 1814.
Frances Bush, born Nov. 16, 1819.—d. April 27, 1844;

The said Stephen Buckingham died August 12, 1831.

George St. Sohn married Susannah Lockwood, daughter of William Lockwood, Feb. 14, 1826.

Susannah L. born Feb. 2, 1827.—d. Aug. 1, 1832.
Charlotte Bradley born Aug, 21, 1828.—d. Aug. 17, 1832.
Geo. Buckingh'm born Sept. 14, 1832.

The said Susannah, wife of George, died Sept. 23, 1832.

The said George married Mary Lockwood DeForest, of Bridgeport, March 6th, 1834.

Sarah Cannon, born Oct. 22, 1836.
Charles, born June 29, 1838.—d. Jan. 23, 1845.
Mary Amelia, born June 25, 1840.
Leonard, born June 28, 1842.
Marcus De F. born May 21, 1845.

William S. Lockwood and Catharine Hawley were married at Ridgefield, October 26, 1831.*

Jane Elizabeth,	born July	20, 1839.
Wm. Augustus,	born Mar.	26, 1841.
Charles Edward,	born Dec.	31, 1842.
Arthur Hawley,	born July	17, 1844.
Hannah Selleck,	born Feb.	9, 1846.

John P. Treadwell and Mary Esther Lockwood were married December 8, 1841.

| ‡ Mary Elizabeth, | born July | 19, 1843. |
| Julia Abigail L., | born Dec. | 6, 1845. |

Nathan Benedict married Susannah Samiss, May 6, 1795.

James,	born Oct.	16, 1797.
William,	born April	23, 1799.
Nathan,	born
Susan,	born

*Peter Betts, (born Oct. 1, 1739), married Sarah White, (born March 19, 1741.)

Hannah,	born Oct.	26, 1761.
John,	born July	22, 1764.
Henry,	born Nov.	23, 1766.
†William,	born May	15, 1769.
‡Peter,	born Jan.	17, 1772.
§Lewis,	born Mar.	17, 1774.
‖James,	born Mar.	31, 1776.
Stephen,	born Mar.	31, 1780.
¶Sarah,	born June	2, 1782.
Polly,	born Mar.	17, 1785.

Henry Betts,	born Nov.	23, 1766. ⎱ Married Febru-
Rebecca F.,	born Jan,	31, 1771. ⎰ ary 12, 1794.
Daniel F.,	born Nov.	7, 1794.
Rebecca,	born Dec. 20, 1796—m. Chs. Isaacs.
Susan,	born Feb. 12, 1799—m. T. Benedict, jr.
Henrietta,	born	—m. Chs. Mallory.
Harriet,	born	—m. T. C. Hanford.

* Died in Franklin, N. Y., August 10, 1807.
† Living in Franklin, N. Y.
‡ Living in Bainbridge village, N. Y.
§ Enlisted in the army, 1813, supposed to have been slain in the battle of Chippewa.
‖ Living in Chemung Co., N. Y.
¶ Mrs. Henry Flint, Deposit village N. Y.

14

Jonathan Fitch (born January 18, 1777,) married Sarah Cannon (born March 9, 1780), March 28, 1802.

Rebecca Fitch,	born April	6, 1803.
Amelia Fitch,	born April	28, 1806.
Sarah Fitch,	born Jan.	2, 1816—d. Sept. 25, 1816.
Jonathan Fitch,	born April	29, 1818—d. May 20, 1818.

The said Jonathan Fitch, died July 27, 1823.

Isaac Hoyt, son of David Hoyt, born December 28, 1737.

Timothy,	born May	29, 1739.
Ruth,	born Feb.	4, 1741.
David,	born April	2, 1744.
Mary,	born May	2, 1748.
Joseph,	born Nov.	3, 1751.
Noah,	born Nov.	3, 1753.
Caleb,	born Nov.	28, 1755.
Ezekiel,	born Dec.	25, 1758.

Family of Timothy Hoyt, and Sarah his wife.

Jachin,	born June	28, 1761.
Ruth,	born Oct.	2, 1762.
Sarah,	born July	28, 1764.
Timothy,	born Feb.	8, 1766.
Simeon,	born July	1, 1767.
Isabel,	born Feb.	2, 1769.
Joel,	born Oct,	29, 1770.
Lois,	born April	5, 1772.
Mary,	born Jan.	27, 1774.
Joseph,	born Sept.	6, 1775.
Deborah,	born April	6, 1777.
John,	born Jan.	3, 1779.
Dinah,	born Sept.	23, 1781.
Hetty,	born Mar.	23, 1783.

Isaac Jennings married Elizabeth Samiss, Feb. 26, 1796.

Almira,	born Nov.	9, 1795.
Eliza,	born Oct.	14, 1797.
Sally Ann,	born June	6, 1799.
Cornelia,	born Feb.	13, 1801.
Antoinette,	born Mar.	18, 1803.
Gould D.,	born Jan.	13, 1805.
William S,	born Mar.	20, 1807.
Magaret,	born Mar.	18, 1809.
Catharine F.	born Jan.	20, 1811.
Joseph H.,	born April	14, 1813.
Edgar A.,	born June	9, 1815.

Samuel Seymour and Anna Whitney married Feb. 7, 1774.

Lewis,	born April	10, 1756.
Thaddeus,	born June	4, 1776.
Polly,	born Feb.	11, 1778.
Betty,	born Mar.	20, 1780.
Samuel,	born July	1, 1784.
Sophia,	born Feb.	25, 1790.
Andrew,	born May	27, 1792.
Hannah,	born Sept.	20, 1794.
Elizabeth,	born Aug.	19, 1797.
Emma L.,	born April	14, 1801.

Lewis Seymour and Hannah North married Oct. 17, 1798.

William N., born July 30, 1802.
Eleanor C., born April 5, 180-.

Isaac Keeler and Deborah Whitney married Sept. 27, 1781.

William,	born Oct.	27, 1782.
David,	born Aug.	9, 1786.
Delancy,	born Oct.	2, 1788.
Harriet,	born June	25, 1792.
Edwin,	born Sept.	22, 1795.
James,	born Dec.	24, 1799.
James,	born July	17, 1801.

Henry Fitch and Abby Whitney married July 19, 1796.

Rebecca,	born March	1, 1798.
Daniel,	born April	2, 1799.
Angeline,	born Mar.	14, 1801.
Edwin,	born Nov.	1, 1802.
Fanny,	born Aug.	6, 1806.
Catherine,	born Jan.	25, 1812.

Isaac St. John,	born April	15, 1739. { Married Jan. 15,
Deborah Guernsey,	born June	26, 1741. } 1761, N. S.
Jonathan,	born Jan.	26, 1762.
Silas,	born Feb.	14, 1763.
Isaac,	born Dec.	1, 1764.
Henry,	born Oct.	26, 1766.
Mary,	born Aug.	21, 1768.
Deborah,	born Aug.	12, 1770.
James,	born Mar.	11, 1772.
Samuel,	born April	7, 1775.

Deborah St. John, died Sept. 14, 1792.

Isaac St. John, Sen., and Eunice Smith married March 13, 1796.

Matilda, born Mar. 12, 1797.

The following was furnished by Bela St. John, Esq. (aged 74), of Wilton.

Matthias St. John died in 1740, aged (about) 80, and was born (about) 1660, a son (probably) of the first Matthias St. John, of Norwalk. His sons were—

John,
Benjamin,
Matthias,
Samuel,

John St. John (son of the above Matthias), married Eunice Hayes.

John,   born April 2, 1735.
Abigail,
Timothy
Rachel,
Eunice,
Sarah,
Hannah,

John St. John (son of the above John), married Martha Northrop.

Eunice,   born Mar. 31, 1763.
John,   born July 15, 1764.
Gamalie   born Sept. 21, 1766.
Joel,   born Oct. 16, 1768.
*Bela,   born Aug. 11, 1773.
Northrop,   born Feb. 11, 1773.
Mary,   born Jan. 15, 1777.
Rachel,   born Nov. 22, 1778.
Timothy,   born Mar. 20, 1784.
Anna,   born June 6, 1786.

* Bela St. John's father used to say that he had been to school down town, when his grandfather, Matthias, was living. Bela also remembers hearing his father and aunt often tell, when he was a boy, that one woman came with the pioneers (in 1650), into cook for them, before their families came on. They pitched near the site of the first meeting-house ; (another tradition says that they spent the winter of 1650-51, in a hollow directly back of the house, now occupied by Rev. Mr. Ellis ; which agrees with the account of Mr. St. John). When the men went down to the meadows to work, the woman refused to stay behind at their quarters unless they would leave the dog with her. She tied the dog that he might not leave her. The Indians came and began to molest her ; she let the dog loose, when he flew at the Indians, and pulled some of their blankets off. They ran into the swamp, (the present hollow near the road on Mr. Clark's lot—the one originally laid out to Nathaniel Eli), and climbed the cedar trees to escape from the dog.

Children of Walter and Grace Hoyt—see p. 250.

Walter B.,	born June	10, 1787.
Ezra,	born July	17, 1789.
Cornelia,	born Nov.	5, 1791.
Nancy,	born July	25, 1794.
Grace,	born June	25, 1797.
Harvey,	borr. Aug.	19, 1799.
Harvey E.,	born June	20, 1801.
Francis,	born Feb.	7, 1804.
Henry N., }	born Aug.	21, 1807.
Hiram H. }	born Aug.	21, 1807.

Isaac Quintard married Elizabeth Picket, Nov. 13, 1791.

Ann Quintard,	born Feb.	25, 1796
Evart,	born ——	
Charles,	born ——	
Henry,	born ——	
Eliza,	born ——	

APPENDIX A., pp. 182, 183.

Descendants of WILLIAM BOUTON and SARAH BENEDICT.

[William Bouton died May 30, 1838, aged 80 years. Sarah, his wife, died August, 26, 1844 aged 94 years. The * refers to those of their descendants who have deceased.]

WILLIAM BOUTON married SARAH BENEDICT, February 15, 1769.

Second Generation.

Isaac.*

Isaac Bouton married *Almira Seymour*

Third Generation.

Lewis.

Charles. married *Polly Nash.*

Henry.
Harriet.
Julia married *Goold Benedict.*
Esther Mary married *Thaddeus B. Guier.*

Fourth Generation.

Adeline.
Amanda.*
Sylvester.
Amanda.
George.
Charles Edwin.
Mary Louisa.

Henry Otis.

Harriet Almira.

William Bouton* married *Hannah Carrington.*

Anson.
Hannah.
William.
Bennett.
Ira.
Orrin.
Mary.
Almira.
Sarah.

Betty Bouton* married *Benjamin Reed.*

Wilbur married * * *

Maria.
Catharine.
Eliza.
William.
Emily.
Susan.
John and 2 more.

Stephen married * * *

Ann.
Eliza.
Fanny.
John.

Benjamin married *Juliet Bouton.*

Julia Ann.
William.*
William.
Benjamin.
Emeline.
Cornelia.
Harriet.
John.

Eliza Weed.
William.
James M.*
James M. married *Cornelia M. Downs.* } James Marion.*

Fifth Generation

Esther Bouton* married *Nathaniel Benedict.*

Seth Williston married *Fanny R. Benedict.*

Louisa married *Legrand Lockwood.*

Le Grand.
Williston Benedict
Roswell Ebenezer.

Charles Williston married *June McAlpin.*
James Hoyt.
Sarah Esther.*
Sarah Francis.
Emma Jane.

Sally Bouton married *Nehemiah Raymond.* *Seth Seymour.*

Emily married *John Hudson.*
Fanny.*
Julia.*

Marg't (see J.Bouton)
Sarah Ann married — *Gillmore.* } Charles.
John.
Julia.
Susan
Banks.
Wilbur.
Mary.
Harvey.
Emily.

The Descendants of William Bouton and Sarah Benedict, continued.

Second Generation.	Third Generation	Fourth Generation.
Clara Bouton* married *Isaac Russ.*	Isaac Edwin. Isaac Edwin. William.* Martha. John.* Susan Ann Harriet.*	4 children.
Seth Bouton* married *Asenath Raymond.*	Raymond.* Mary Esther.	4 children.
Joseph Bouton married *Betty Bixbee.*	Juliet.* Fanny.* Fanny Esther marri'd *Valentine Merrills.* Amanda married *John Dibble.* Joseph married * * * William. Nathaniel	Elizabeth. Joseph. Charles Edgar. Albert Bouton. Emma Louisa. Melissa Amanda. Julia Frances. Homer Arlington.
Susannah Bouton married *Samuel G. Waring.*		
John Bouton married *Hannah Betts.* Betsey Chichester.*	William married *Margaret Hudson.* Mary.* Clarissa married *Nathan Nash.* John. Elizabeth. Sarah Esther. Hannah Harriet.	Emily. Julia. Le Roy John. Clarissa Ann
Mary Bouton married *Henry Banta.* Christopher Gwyer.* Samuel Raymond.*	Susan Banta* married *William Thomas.* Eliza Banta married *Linus Scudder.* John Banta married * * * William Gwyer. Mary Gwyer married *Daniel Townsend.* Ann.*	Josephine. Virginia. Augusta. Emma.* Susan. George Henry. Linus Melville. William Henry. Cornelia. Leonora. Charles
Anna Bouton married *Horatio N. Downs.*	Harriet Newell.* Charles Algernon. Harriet Angenora. Cornelia Marion.* (see Benjamin Reed.	
Nathaniel Bouton married *Harriet Sherman.* Mary Ann P. Bell.* E. A. Cilley.*	Elizabeth Ripley. Nathaniel Sherman. John Bell. Harriet Sherman. Mary Ann Peris. Samuel Fletcher. Christopher. and 3 more.	

APPENDIX B, pp. 184, 5.

GENEALOGY OF THE BENEDICT FAMILY.

[In the year 1755, Dea. JAMES BENEDICT, of Ridgefield, grandson of THOMAS BENEDICT, sen., of Norwalk, wrote a genealogy of the family, from which, and from a manuscript prepared by ERASTUS C. BENEDICT, Esq., of New York, a descendant of James, the leading facts relating to the first six generations have been derived.

Dea. James Benedict learned the particulars he gives of the early history of the family, down to his own memory, from his grandmother, MARY BRIDGUM, the wife of Thomas Benedict, sen., with whom he lived in his youth. In 1768 this record was copied by his grandson, Rev. ABNER BENEDICT, while a member of Yale College, and by him sent to Thomas Benedict, of Norwalk. Other copies have been made for other branches of the family.

The record here given is confined to a *single line*, viz.: 1. The children of THOMAS, sen. 2. The children of JOHN, his 2d son. 3. The children of his grandsons, JOHN and JAMES*. 4. Of his great grandson, NATHANIEL. 5. Of NATHANIEL 2d, his fifth descendant; and 6th, of NATHANIEL 3d, the sixth descendant; which brings it down to the present generation, and to the writer of this introductory note. Were the descendants of *each* of the children and grandchildren to be traced and recorded the list would make a volume of itself. S. W. B.]

FIRST GENERATION.

WILLIAM BENEDICT, is the first of the family of whom any trace has been found. Tradition says that he resided in Nottinghamshire, England, about the year 1500, and that he was the only son of his father. He had also but one son, who was also called William.

SECOND GENERATION.

WILLIAM BENEDICT, who also resided in Nottinghamshire, and had an only son, also called William.

THIRD GENERATION.

WILLIAM BENEDICT, who also resided in Nottinghamshire. He also had an only son, who was named THOMAS.

* See Appendix C., p. 320.

FOURTH GENERATION.

THOMAS BENEDICT and MARY BRIDGUM, his wife.

He was born in England, 1617. He was an only son, and when he left England, tradition says, the name had been confined to *only sons* for more than one hundred years, and that he did not know another person of the name in existence; from which it would seem that his father was then dead. He lost his mother early, and was put apprentice to a weaver during his minority. His father married a second wife, who was a widow, a Mrs. Bridgum, who had a daughter named MARY BRIDGUM. When Thomas became of age (1638), he and Mary Bridgum came to New England in the same vessel, and first settled in " The Massachusetts Bay." Not long after "the said THOMAS BENEDICT was joined in marriage with said MARY BRIDGUM, and from these have arisen a numerous offspring"—the Benedicts in America.

They lived some time in the Massachusetts Bay, and then removed to Southold, Long Island, where their children were born—five sons and four daughters—THOMAS, JOHN, SAMUEL, JAMES, DANIEL, BETTY, MARY, SARAH, REBECCA. From Southold they removed to Huntington, where they resided several years. They were residing there in June, 1656. They removed thence to Jamaica, on the same Island, where Thomas, the eldest son, married Mary Messenger of that place.

The eastern part of Long Island being at that time considered a part of Connecticut was of course principally settled by the English pilgrims, who gradually extended themselves westward, and rather encroached upon their Dutch neighbors of New York, with whom they were not much disposed to coalesce. The Long Island settlements (except the extreme west), were principally English, and when on the 27th August, 1664, the Dutch Governor, Stuyvesant, capitulated to Col. Richard Nichols, the change of government was highly acceptable to the English settlers, and they immediately set about extending their settlements. On the 26th September in the same year, John Bailey, Daniel Denton, and Thomas Benedict, and others, made a written application to Col. Nichols for liberty to settle a plantation upon the river

14*

called Arthur-Cull Bay, in New Jersey. On the 30th of the same month he granted the petition and promised encouragement. That place is now Elizabethtown. The principal petitioners were in Jamaica in 1665. It is therefore to be presumed that they sent out a colony.

Governor Nichols issued " To the magistrates of the several tounes upon Longisland," an order of election, dated James ffort, in New York, 8th February, 1664, reciting that the inhabitants had for a long time groaned under many grievous inconveniences and discouragements occasioned partly from their opposition to a foreign power, in which distracted condition few or no laws could be put in due execution, bounds and titles to lands disputed, civil liberties interrupted, and from this general confusion private dissentions and animosities had too much prevailed against neighborly love and Christian charity, and in discharge of his duty " to settle good and known laws," requiring two deputies to " a general meeting," to be chosen from each town " by the major part of the freemen," and recommending " the choice of the most sober, able and discreet persons, without partiality or faction," to meet " on the last day of February at Hempstead." The delegates from Jamaica were DANIEL DENTON and THOMAS BENE-DICT. This is believed to be the first English legislative body ever convened in New York.

In 1665, he was commissioned by Gov. Nichols as a Lieutenant "of the Foot Company of Jamaica." His commission was dated at " Fort James in New York, the 7th day of April, 1665." Whether he accepted the commission is not known. It is certain, however, that he did not hold it long, as during the same year he removed from the State to Norwalk, in the Colony of Connecticut, with all his family. There they lived together, and thence they scattered abroad in little colonizing parties to let in the light on other parts of the neighboring wilderness, or to swell the numbers of the pioneer bands who had already planted settlements in the vicinity.

In 1666, February 19th, he was chosen town clerk and selectman of Norwalk

In 1669 he was again chosen town clerk, and the list of freemen of Norwalk contains his name as one of 42 of which the list was composed Oct. 13, 1669. In 1672 he was again chosen town clerk, and held the office for many years afterwards. The records, in his own hand writing, are still preserved and are legible, properly attested by his own signature, a *fac simile* of which, as here given, it may also be interesting to preserve.

This primitive pilgrim pair are thus described in the manuscript of Dea. James Benedict already referred to :

"They walked in the midst of their house with a perfect heart. They were strict observers of the Lord's day from even to even. It may be said of them as it was of Zachariah and Elizabeth, that they walked in all the commandments and ordinances of the Lord blameless, and obtained a good report through faith. Their excellent example had a good effect through the blessing of God upon their children. He was made a deacon of the church in Norwalk, and used that office to good satisfaction of that church to his death, which was in the year of our Lord 1690, in the seventy-third year of his age, and was succeeded in his office as deacon by two of his sons, viz. John and Samuel, who used that office until old age and its attendants rendered them unable to serve ; and there are at this time seven of the family and name which use the office of a deacon, and I trust some of them, at least, to good acceptance both to God and man." His wife survived him and lived to the age of one hundred years.

FIFTH GENERATION.

(*The children of Thomas Benedict and Mary Bridgum*)

THOMAS BENEDICT, 2d, was born at Southold, Long Island. From Southold he went with his father to Huntington and thence to Jamaica, where he married MARY MESSENGER of that place. In 1665 he removed with his father to Norwalk, in the Colony of Connecticut. In the Wylys's manuscripts his name is, with that of his father, among the names of the 42 freemen of Norwalk, taken Oct. 13, 1669.

He had six children—Mary, born 1666 ; Thomas, born
1670; Hannah, born Jan. 8, 1676; Esther, born Oct. 5, 1679 ;
Abigail, born 1682 ; Elizabeth, born ——

JOHN BENEDICT was born at Southold, Long Island. He
continued to reside with his parents till they removed to Nor-
walk. He there married Phebe Gregory, daughter of John
Gregory of Norwalk, Nov. 11, 1670. They had nine children.
Sarah, Phebe, born 1673, John, March 3d, 1676, Jonathan,
Benjamin, Joseph, James, born January 5, 1685; Mary or
Mercy, and Thomas.

He succeeded his father as deacon of the church in Norwalk,
and used that office until old age rendered him unable to serve.

SAMUEL BENEDICT was born at Southold, Long Island. He
continued to reside with his father till after his removal to
Norwalk. He married Rebecca Andrews of Fairfield, 7th
July, 1678. They had seven children. Joanna, born 22d Oct.,
1673, Samuel, 5th March, 1675, Thomas, 27th March, 1679,
Rebecca, Esther, Nathaniel, and Abraham born 21st June,
1681.

In the fall of 1684 and spring of 1685, he, with seven other
families, including his brother James and his brother-in-law,
James Beebe, (Dr. Wood, another brother-in-law, soon followed), purchased land of the Indians and made the first settlement at Paquiogue, which they called Danbury. They soon
built a little church only forty feet by thirty. When its frame
was raised every person in the town was present and sat together on the sills. He conveyed his property in Norwalk February
3, 1685, to Samuel Betts. He is described as of Paquiack,
formerly of Norwalk. On Sunday morning, April 27th, 1777,
the British under Governor Tryon, burned Danbury—excepting the houses and the property of the Tories. Nineteen
dwelling-houses, besides other buildings, were consumed with
all their contents. Among the nineteen principal sufferers
were Thaddeus Benedict, Matthew Benedict, Matthew Benedict, junr., Jonah Benedict, and Zadock Benedict.

JAMES BENEDICT was born at Southold, Long Island. He
continued to reside with his parents until after their removal

to Norwalk. He there married SARAH GREGORY, May 10, 1676. They had seven children. Sarah, born 16th June, 1677 ; Rebecca, Phebe, James, John, Thomas, and Elizabeth. He was one of the eight who purchased and settled Danbury. He sold his property in Norwalk, 26th March, 1691, to Samuel Smith.

DANIEL BENEDICT was born at Southold, Long Island. He also removed with his father to Norwalk. He married MARY MARVIN of Norwalk. They had four children. Mary, Daniel, Mercy, and Hannah. He removed to Danbury. He conveyed his land in Norwalk 25th March, 1690.

BETTY BENEDICT was born at Southold. She married JOHN SLAUSON of Stamford. Their children were Mary and Thomas.

MARY BENEDICT was born at Southold. She married JOHN OLMSTEAD, " Lieut. Olmstede" of Norwalk, 11th Nov. 1670. Their children were John, Mary, Jane, Sarah, Rebecca, Elizabeth, Daniel, Richard, Eunice, and Deborah.

SARAH BENEDICT was born at Southold. She married JAMES BEEBE of Stratford, Dec. 19, 1679. Their children were Sarah, born 13th November, 1680, and James, born —— ——. James Beebe was one of the eight who purchased and settled Danbury. He conveyed his property in Norwalk January 2d, 1685, in which he is described as of Paquiack, formerly of Norwalk.

REBECCA BENEDICT was born at Southold. She married Doctor SAMUEL WOOD. He was an able physician, born and educated in England. He was one of the first settlers of Danbury after the first eight families. Dr. John Wood and David Wood are also among the 19 principal sufferers by the British attack in 1777.

SIXTH GENERATION.

(*The children of John Benedict and Phebe Gregory.*)

SARAH BENEDICT.

PHEBE BENEDICT was born at Norwalk, 1673.

JOHN BENEDICT was born at Norwalk, March 2d, 1676.

His children were John, born 1701; Matthew, born 1702;
Caleb, born 1709 ; Nathaniel, born 1717 ; Anna, and Phebe.

He was for many years deacon of the church in Norwalk.
He died there January 16, 1766.   He and his wife were bu-
ried side by side in the grave-yard near Pine Island, Norwalk.
His grave-stone bears this inscription:

TO THE MEMORY OF

Deacon JOHN BENEDICT,

who departed this life
JAN'Y. YE 16, 1766,
in ye 90 year of his age.

And that of his wife this :

HERE LIES THE BODY
of
Mrs. MARY BENEDICT,
wife of
Mr. JOHN BENEDICT,
who died June ye 5, 1749,
AGED 72 YEARS.

JONATHAN BENEDICT.

BENJAMIN BENEDICT was born at Norwalk.   He married
Mary ———.   He removed to Ridgefield, and in 1720 was
selectman of Ridgefield, and was the third deacon of the
church there.   He   died   July 3d,   1773,   at   Stamford,
Conn.   His children were Elizabeth, born 1705 ; Benjamin,
born 1707 ; Timothy, born 1709 ; Mary, born 1711 ; John,
born 1714 ; Daniel, born 1716 ; Samuel, born 1719 ; Rachel,
born 1721 ; Amos, born 1722 ; Thankful, born 1727.

JOSEPH BENEDICT was born at Norwalk.   He married Anne
———, by whom his children were Joseph, Gideon, Anna,
and Pitman.

He removed to Ridgefield, where his wife died, Dec. 9, 1716,
In March 21, 1721, he married his second wife Mary ———
by whom his children were Jonathan, born 1722; Mary, born
1726 ; Ezra, born 1730 ; and John.

JAMES BENEDICT was born at Norwalk, January 15th, 1685. He married Sarah Hyatt, daughter of Thomas Hyatt of Norwalk, in 1709. He settled in Ridgefield. He was one of the original settlers who purchased of the Indians and settled the township of Ridgefield. In 1715 he was chosen one of the fence-viewers of that town. In 1719 he is called Ensign, afterwards Captain, and in 1737, Esquire. He was a justice of the peace and for many years he represented that town in the Connecticut Legislature. He died November 25, 1762. His wife survived him four years. Their children* were Sarah, born 1709; Ruth, born 1711; PETER, born 1714; Hannah, born 1716; Phebe, born 1718; James, born 1720; Martha, born 1722; John and Thomas, twins, born 1726.

He was the first to write the genealogy of the Benedict family. In his youth he lived with his grandmother, MARY BRIDGUM, wife of the first THOMAS BENEDICT, and she delivered to him, from her own mouth, the genealogy down to his own memory, and he reduced it to writing. His "Genealogy of the family of the Benedict's," dated March 14, 1755, has been the foundation of all the subsequent ones. His grandson, ABNER BENEDICT, a member of the Junior Class in Yale College, made an exact copy of it June 23d, 1768. He was the second deacon of the church in Ridgefield, till old age and its attendants rendered him unable to serve. He sustained the character of a pious and exemplary Christian.

The following inscription is on his grave-stone in Ridgefield:

HERE LIES INTERRED
the body of
JAMES BENEDICT, Esq.,
Deacon of the first Church of Christ in this town;
TOGETHER WITH
SARAH, HIS WIFE,
who, after having served their generation
according to the will of God,
fell asleep and were gathered to their fathers,
the first on Nov. 25, 1762,
in the 77th year of his age; the other February
ye 9th, 1767, in the 61st year of her age.

* See Appendix C.

MARY or MERCY BENEDICT.

THOMAS BENEDICT was born in Norwalk. His children were Ebenezer ? Thomas, John, David, Betty, Seth, and Moses ? He was known as "Capt. Thomas Benedict," see page 212. He was remarkable for the loudness of his voice—could be distinctly heard and understood at the distance of more than a mile. He was a great singer, and the leader of the choir of singers at Norwalk.

SEVENTH GENERATION.

The Children of John and Mary Benedict, (p. 310.)

JOHN BENEDICT —born 1701—married DINAH BOUTON—was Deacon of the Church in New Canaan ; and died February 7, 1770, aged 69 years.

MATTHEW BENEDICT.

CALEB BENEDICT—born 1709—married MEHITABLE HOYT. He was known as "Ensign Benedict." He lived on Brushy Ridge, and died May 19, 1761. His children were—

    (1) *Ruth*—married David St. John.
    (2) *Caleb*—married Deborah St. John.
    (3) *James*—born Dec. 25, 1713—married Thankful Lockwood.
    (4) *Ezra*—married Molly Benedict.
    (5, 6) *Aner* and *Anah*, twins, born 1751. Aner married Joseph Stevens, and removed to Danbury. Anah married Eliasaph Kellogg.
    (7) *Benjamin*—married Elizabeth Gilbert.
    (8) *Mehitable*—married Jonathan Stevens.

NATHANIEL BENEDICT—born 1786—married Mary Lockwood, daughter of Deacon Lockwood. She died January 12, 1763, aged 42 years. He afterwards married Hannah Hawley, daughter of Rev. Thomas Hawley, who died January 31, 1795, aged 67. He died April 2, 1806, in his 90th year. In a manuscript of that date, we have the following notice :

"He died in Norwalk on the morning of the 2d of April, 1806, after a shock of the palsy, with which he lingered about twelve days, in the 90th year of his age. On the 3d his remains were followed to the grave by a large concourse of friends and relatives, among whom were his twelve surviving children, and many of his more remote posterity. He has left ninety-one grand-children, and eighty-eight great-grand-children, the whole number of his descendants, now living, being 191.

" For about thirty-two years he sustained the office of Deacon of the First Congregational Church in that town. Dea. Benedict was one of those venerable personages by whom what remains of the pious habits of our forefathers, have been transmitted to the present generation. His long life has been eminently exemplary, and years to come will feel its happy influence. Every morning and evening witnessed his devotion. His Sabbaths were faithfully appropriated to public worship, and religious family instructions. An amiable, cheerful disposition, a sound mind, improved by a good degree of reading and much reflection, and adorned with a bright constellation of Christian graces, comprised his character. At his funeral an appropriate Sermon was delivered by the Rev. Dr. 'Burnett, from Prov. xiv. 32d. ' The wicked is driven away in his wickedness; *but the righteous hath hope in his death.*' "

HANNAH BENEDICT—married Matthew Gregory, and removed to Danbury.

PHEBE BENEDICT—married Ezra Hoyt.

EIGHTH GENERATION.

Children of Nathaniel Benedict and Mary Lockwood (p. 313.)

ANER—born 1740—married Seth Seymour.

MOLLY—born 1741—married Deliverance Bennett, removed to Saugatuck.

NATHANIEL—born March 26, 1744—married Anah Raymond, June 6, 1758—died February 24, 1833 —aged 88.

JOSEPH—born 1746—married Hannah, removed to Danbury —died December, 1835—aged 89.

ISAAC—born 1751—married Jane Raymond, daughter of Samuel Raymond, October 13, 1773, and removed to New Canaan, where, for many years, he was Deacon of that Church. For the record of his children, see page 290.

WILLIAM—born 1753—married Nancy Fitch, February 20. 1782—died September 2, 1821—aged 68. For the record of his children, see page 248.

SALLY—born 1756—married Nathan Hoyt,'removed to New Milford.

BETTY—born 1761—married Enoch Scribner, March 22, 1781—died 1835. For the record of her children, see page 298.

Children of Nathaniel Benedict, by his 2d wife, Hannah Hawley.

NATHAN—born 1766—married Susannah Samiss—died Feb. 3, 1832, aged 69. Susannah, his wife, died April 13, 1836, aged 71. For record of his children see p. 301.

HANNAH—born 1767—married Dea. Stephen Wood, April 3, 1782. For record of her children, see p. 289.

LYDIA—born 1768—married Captain Lemuel Brooks.

JOHN—born 1770—married Jane Raymond. For the record of their children, see page 253.

NINTH GENERATION.

Children of Nathaniel Benedict 2d, and Anah Raymond—p. 314.

MARY—born March 23, 1770—married John Eversley. For her children see p. 283.

ANDREW—born June 21, 1772—married Sally Brown—removed to Cayuga Co., N. Y., where he now resides.

NATHANIEL—born July 17, 1774—married Esther Bouton, daughter of William Bouton, January 18, 1797—died May 20, 1834, in his 60th year. Esther, his wife, died May 22, 1843, aged 64.

SIMEON—born September 12, 1776—resides at Brockport.

RAYMOND—born April 2, 1779—married Mary Seymour. His children are Stephen, Ann, Mary, and Gould. His wife died Nov. 2, 1819, aged 30. He afterwards married Nancy Smith.

ASA—born July 7, 1781—married Hannah Reed. His children were Frederick, George, Alfred, Harriet, William Henry, and Charles. Hannah, his wife, died Nov. 11, 1830, aged 46 years; and he afterwards married Ruth Hanford. He now resides in Brockport, N. Y

URIAH—born September 7, 1782—married Sally North—removed to Cayuga Co, N. Y., where he now resides.

ANAH—born July 4, 1789—married Levi Scribner, and removed to Wilton, Conn.

HANNAH—married Nathaniel Furnald, of New York—died—

ALFRED—born May 7, 1791—died —.

ANAH, the wife of said Nathaniel Benedict 2d, died February 26, 1792, aged 42; and on the 2d April, 1794, he married Hannah Selleck, who died Sept. 1800, aged 45. He died on the 24th February, 1833, aged 88.

TENTH GENERATION.

SETH WILLISTON BENEDICT, only child of Nathaniel Benedict, 3d, and Esther Bouton, was born at Norwalk, November 16, 1803, and according to the Family Record was " baptized by Rev. Dr. Matthias Burnett, January 5, 1804." He was named after the pioneer missionary of Western New York, the Rev. SETH WILLISTON, now of Durham, N. Y. At the commencement of the tide of emigration to what was then called "*the west*," his father and Andrew, an older brother, settled near the banks of the Chenango River, where they resided for some time, but not liking the location, they relinquished their settlements, Andrew going farther west, and his father returning to his native town. It was there the family enjoyed the labors of that indefatigable missionary, whom his mother regarded as her spiritual father, and whose name she gave to her first and only child.

At the age of fifteen, he entered the office of the Norwalk Gazette, then just established in his native town, to learn the art and mystery of printing. Four years after he purchased the paper and continued to publish it until January 1, 1833, when becoming interested in the New York Evangelist, he removed to New York, and published that paper till September, 1837. Since that time he has devoted himself mainly to his profession as a printer.

APPENDIX C.

The descendants of Dea. JAMES BENEDICT, of Ridgefield, form a distinct branch, which it does not come within the design of this work to give at length. He was the father of PETER BENEDICT, of North Salem, who was Deacon of the Church there for many years; also of JOHN BENEDICT, of Ridgefield, the fifth Deacon of that Church.

His son PETER was the father of Rev. ABNER BENEDICT, who graduated at Yale College in 1769, and was settled in the ministry at Middletown (Middlefield Parish), for fourteen years, during which time, by his address and efforts he procured the emancipation of all the slaves held by his people. He died at Roxbury, November 19, 1818. He was also father of Rev. JOEL BENEDICT, D. D., who graduated at Princeton, 1765, and was settled in the ministry at Lisbon, Conn., eleven years, and afterwards at Plainfield, Conn., where he died February 13, 1816 : also father of Lieut. PETER BENEDICT, an officer under Gen. Washington in the Revolutionary war.

Rev. ABNER BENEDICT (grandson of James), was the father of Rev. JOEL T. BENEDICT, who was born September 6, 1772, and admitted to the bar in Fairfield Co., in 1794. After six years practice he changed his profession, and was settled in the ministry in Bethlehem, N. Y., and afterwards in Franklin, from whence he removed to Philadelphia, to take charge of the operations of the Pennsylvania Branch of the American Tract Society, where he died in October, 1833. [He was also the grandfather of Rev. JOEL TYLER HEADLEY, author of several of our recent popular works.

Rev. JOEL TYLER BENEDICT was the father of Prof. GEORGE WYLLIS BENEDICT, of the University of Vermont, and of ERASTUS C. BENEDICT, Esq., and of ABNER BENEDICT, Esq., both members of the present bar of the City of New York, and of ADIN W. BENEDICT, Esq., of Huntingdon, Pa.

www.ingramcontent.com/pod-product-compliance
Lightning Source LLC
Chambersburg PA
CBHW021124270326
41929CB00009B/1040